John Wilcockson

A graduate of the University of London, John Wilcockson was the first-ever cycling correspondent of *The Times*, and has reported for that and the *Sunday Times* for many years. Since 1968 he has been the editor of five different cycling magazines, and is currently the editorial director of the world's leading competitive cycling magazine, *VeloNews*. For his journalistic services to the Tour de France, Wilcockson was presented with the Medaille de la Reconnaissance and the Plaque de la Reconnaissance du Tour by the race organisers. In 2004 he reported on the Tour for the 36th time. He has written a dozen books and now lives in Boulder, Colorado.

D1101029

23 DAYS IN JULY

INSIDE LANCE ARMSTRONG'S RECORD-BREAKING VICTORY IN THE TOUR DE FRANCE

John Wilcockson

PHOTOGRAPHS BY GRAHAM WATSON

JOHN MURRAY

To my mother, Dorothy,
for all the years of putting up with my cycling addiction,

and to my wife, Rivvy,
for her unwavering love and encouragement

Copyright © John Wilcockson 2004

Photographs © Graham Watson 2004

First published by Da Capo in the United States of America

First published in Great Britain in 2004 by John Murray (Publishers)
A division of Hodder Headline

Paperback edition 2005

The right of John Wilcockson to be identified as the Author of the Work
has been asserted by him in accordance with the Copyright, Designs and
Patents Act 1988.

1

A CIP catalogue record for this title is available from the British Library

ISBN 0 7195 6717 3

Printed and bound by Clays Ltd, St Ives

Hodder Headline policy is to use papers that are natural, renewable and
recyclable products and maed from wood grown in sustainable forests.
The logging and manufacturing processes are expected to conform to the
environmental regulations of the country of origin

John Murray (Publishers)
338 Euston Road
London NW1 3BN

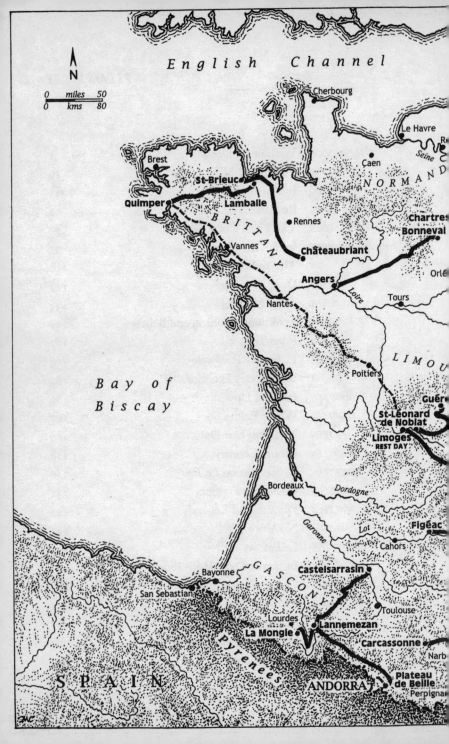

Ghent
BELGIUM
Wasquehal
Lille
Brussels
Waterloo
START
Liège
Arras
Charleroi
iens
PICARDY
Cambrai
Namur
LUX.
Luxembourg
GERMANY
Rhine
REICH
Reims
FINISH
Paris
Marne
Mosel
Montereau
Nancy
Oise
CHAMPAGNE
Strasbourg
Troyes
LORRAINE
FRANCE
Loire
Dijon
BURGUNDY
Besançon
Basel
Rhine
Lons
le-Saunier
Bern
Lake Geneva
SWITZERLAND
rmont-Ferrand
Geneva
Annemasse
Massif
Lyon
Le Grand Bornand
Central
Aix-les-Bains
Alps
St-Flour
Grenoble
L'Alpe d'Huez
Villard-de-Lans
Bourg-
d'Oisans
Turin
Gap
Rhône
ITALY
Valréas
Nîmes
REST DAY
PROVENCE
Nice
Marseille

Mediterranean   Sea

I asked Eddy Merckx, the greatest cyclist of all time, if the Tour de France is the hardest race to win. "No," he said, "it's the easiest race to win. When you are the strongest, the Tour is the easiest race to win because it is the hardest race of all."

> "I told you it wasn't even going to be close. You gotta know the intensity of this guy. Nobody has got his intensity. Nobody."
>
> —*Chris Carmichael*, *Lance Armstrong's personal coach*

Waiting for Destiny

DECEMBER 18, 2003: *Austin, Texas.*

Taped across the doorbell is a note, neatly written, all caps: "PLEASE DO NOT RING. CHILDREN SLEEPING." A petite woman with ash-blonde hair answers my knock on the heavy oak door. She's wearing an apron. Her only son, wearing navy sweats, stands barefoot behind her on the dark parquet floor. "I just got up," explains five-time Tour de France champion Lance Armstrong. He'd been napping after a morning training ride, still jet-lagged from a weeklong trip to Europe. He was there with his girlfriend, the singer Sheryl Crow, attending her concerts in Paris, Brussels, and London, and fitting in his daily workouts while she rehearsed. On the way home he stopped in Washington, D.C., to speak about cancer survival at a National Press Club luncheon. And tomorrow he's off to Seattle for some testing in a wind tunnel at the University of Washington. But today, right now, he's made time to talk.

As we walk quietly into an open living area, Armstrong says that his two-year-old twin daughters, Grace and Isabelle, are asleep upstairs. His four-year-old son Luke sits on his nanny's lap in a deep armchair, reading a storybook. And Lance's mother, Linda, is back in the kitchen. "I'm cooking chicken enchiladas," she calls out. "The Texas thing." It's a thoroughly domestic, simple scene, in no way revealing that the man at the center of it all is one of the world's greatest athletes.

Armstrong guides us into a narrow, high-ceilinged dining room that's also used as a den. He settles into a straight-backed leather chair and props his feet up on the table, stretching out his solid five-foot-ten-inch frame until it appears much longer. He's relaxed and talkative, and when the questions begin, his answers flow freely. But when I ask him how important it is for him to win another Tour de France—a record-breaking sixth—he suddenly becomes silent.

After a long pause, Armstrong's square jaw loosens, and his thin upper lip hints at a proud grin. He then turns his head to the left and points out, with a sweep of his arm, four massive picture frames hanging along the far wall. A fifth one hangs next to the open doorway leading from the kitchen. Vacuum-sealed in each of the five bulky frames is a cyclist's racing jersey—the special, shiny golden-yellow kind that's awarded to winners of the Tour de France. Each of his hanging jerseys remains unwashed, with the race numbers still attached, from the day he wore it into Paris at the end of a victorious Tour.

Armstrong remains silent, my question unanswered. That's unusual, since he's rarely at a loss for words. In one of the first magazine interviews he ever gave as a young cyclist, he told me, "I like the question-and-answer format the best. I like to see what people *say*." He was intimating that he doesn't have the patience to read all those words a writer puts between the quotes, words that might attempt to give some insight into a personality. Armstrong wants to figure that out himself, not from what the writer writes, but from what the person says. After all, he expects others to judge him by what *he* says. And he loves to talk.

Eventually, while staring at his five framed jerseys crowding the walls, Armstrong responds, talking so softly it's as if he's whispering to himself. "Can't place them much longer . . . no more room . . . maybe one or two can keep going around." He seems wistful, pensive, perhaps realizing that just as space on his den wall is running out, so too is his time as a potential Tour champion. He'll be 32 when he starts the 2004 race. By that age, the four other legendary racers who won five Tours had either retired from cycling or failed in their attempt to win a sixth. That thought doesn't deter Armstrong. He's confident that he can become the Tour's first six-time champion.

But just *how* important for him is it, making history by winning a sixth Tour de France, his sixth in a row? Can he possibly have the same hunger he had back in 1999, when he won his first?

"It's *very* important," Armstrong replies, his voice louder, hitting his stride. "Just as important as all the other ones. I have no real personal pressure to try and win because it's never been done before, or for any reason like that. It's just important because on a basic level, it's all that matters. . . ."

All that matters. Perhaps only a man as single-mindedly focused as Armstrong, a man who rose Lazarus-like from a cancer bed, a man whose friends say has more drive than anyone they know, would make such a statement. As if to justify his sweeping words, Armstrong adds that the Tour de France is the biggest bike race in the world, that it means everything to his team sponsor, the U.S. Postal Service, and that it's the only bike race of which the American public is aware. "So it's *huge*," he says reverentially, adding that he has to be prepared, before concluding more urgently, *"It's important."*

More important than all of the other things in his life? More important than staying close to his three children, developing a new love relationship, keeping on top of his cancer foundation work, fulfilling the media and commercial obligations of a national sports icon? "I think I can juggle them all," he replies, looking as if he suddenly realizes the enormity of what he has to accomplish in the next six months before starting the Tour de France. "It's hard. But if I lose the Tour because I'm trying to manage my life—spending time in Europe and spending time here and seeing my kids—if I lose because of that, then you know what? It was worth it." He pauses to let that sink in, as much for his own benefit as for mine. "But I think I can do it. It's a big challenge—and I *always* like challenges."

More than anyone else, Armstrong understands the difficulty of that challenge: winning the Tour de France. He knows that both he and his team will have to be at the very top of their game to defend his title in July.

Winning the Tour is one of the supreme accomplishments in modern sports, and yet Armstrong's repeated victories and down-home demeanor have tended to trivialize an event that is so physically, emotionally, and mentally demanding that it borders on sadism. If a three-week bike race of this intensity—circumnavigating a whole country—were proposed today, its advocates would probably be ridiculed. But the Tour was invented in flamboyant times, when bold projects were encouraged. After the first Tour was announced in January 1903, it was hailed as "a colossal event" by the French daily *Le Figaro*. And why not? It was as outrageous as the French capital's daring, 1,000-foot-high Eiffel Tower that remained the world's tallest structure until 1930.

That first Tour de France was "only" 1,508 miles long, divided into six separate marathon "stages," with rest days in between, and lasting almost three weeks. Only twenty-one of the sixty starters completed the full distance. They raced on dusty, unpaved roads and cobblestone streets. Their all-steel bikes weighed twice as much as today's carbon-fiber, aluminum, and titanium creations, and they had only one gear, not twenty. The overall winner, Frenchman Maurice Garin, was a chimney sweep before becoming a professional cyclist. He rode for an accumulative 94 hours over the six stages at just over 16 miles per hour. One hundred years later, Armstrong set the event record average speed of 25.4 miles per hour, and that included climbing more than twenty mountain passes—they climbed none in 1903.

Over time, the organizers added more and more daily stages to generate greater interest from the public and increase the circulation of *L'Auto*, the sports newspaper that promoted the race. Many of the new stages ventured over the mountains on crude dirt roads that were otherwise used for herding cattle and goats. By 1926, the race lasted four weeks, and measured a gargantuan 3,570 miles; it took the Belgian winner, Lucien Buysse, more than 238 hours to complete. That truly *was* sadistic, so the distance and number of days were gradually reduced until 1989, when the length of the race was standardized at three weeks and two days. The twenty-three days of the 2004 Tour cover a total distance of 2,107 miles with the winner's time likely to be about 84 hours.

At a hundred years and counting, the Tour is not as old as the Kentucky Derby (established in 1875), British Open (1860), or Wimbledon (1877), yet it's more universally popular than all three of those events. One reason is that virtually all of us on this planet ride a bicycle at some point in our lives, whereas a relatively privileged few saddle up a horse, pick up a golf club, or swing a tennis racket. As for the top annual sports events in North America, neither the World Series (founded in 1903) nor the Super Bowl (1967) has made much impact beyond American shores. Similarly, auto racing's Formula One Grand Prix circuit (started in 1950) and soccer's European Champions League (1955) have a tiny following in the United States. Only the

Tour—Europe's most popular annual sports event—has recently gained crossover power, largely because an American cancer survivor is beating Europe at its own game.

But what most dramatically sets the Tour apart is its setting and duration. In vivid contrast to most American sports events, which are confined to stadiums, ballparks, or familiar courts and fields, with none lasting longer than the best-of-seven World Series . . . you have, *mesdames et messieurs, le Tour de France!* What can compare to a two-thousand-mile course that encompasses everything from teeming cities to medieval villages, sprawling pasturelands to rolling vineyards, ocean-swept coasts to remote mountain peaks?

On some of the Tour's race days, millions of people from dozens of countries show up. They come to watch the 180-plus competitors whoosh by at speeds that can top 70 miles per hour, or gasp and strain as they pedal up dramatically steep ascents heading toward a distant summit that's more than a mile high. And as the fans watch from their roadside perches and picnic tables, they become part of the event, with their irreverent humor and roaring cheers, ringing cowbells, and fluttering flags and signs.

Hundreds of millions of others watch the race on television in some 170 countries, all of them awed by the stamina and bravery of the cyclists, who in burning heat or chilling wind and rain have to conquer an array of difficulties, crowned by the fierce mountain ascents and crash-ridden descents in the French Alps and Pyrenees.

From its beginning, the Tour has been compared to other epic challenges. French author François Cavanna proclaimed, "The Tour de France, that's our *Iliad*, our *Odyssey*, our *Song of Roland*." After seeing the Tour one day in 1912, the Parisian novelist Colette said about the racers: "Their faces are obscured, their moustaches matted by a paste of sweat and dust; their hollow eyes, between caked lashes, make them look like rescued well-diggers." In the 1930s, when he lived in Paris, Ernest Hemingway loved to watch the Tour. He wrote stories about bike racing but reportedly never tried to publish them because "French is the only language it has ever been written in properly and the terms are all French and that is what makes it hard to write." Three decades later, America's most widely read sports columnist, Red Smith of the *New York Herald Tribune*, had no trouble reporting the Tour when he took in a few days of the 1960 edition. "There is nothing in America even remotely comparable with it," wrote Smith, who marveled at the crowds on the stage into Gap when he stood atop a hill "not close to anything or anybody, yet it looked like the bleachers in Yankee Stadium on a good day with the White Sox."

The Tour has always fascinated writers, especially those who were the event's only true witnesses in the six decades before television began to have a presence. Henri Desgrange, the autocratic Parisian newspaper editor who founded the Tour and shepherded it through its first thirty-three years, cryptically claimed, "Suffering on a bicycle is noble since it equates to the full evolution of the will." His successor as race director, the gentlemanly Jacques Goddet, was also a writer and editor. He captured the complexities of the event when he noted: "The Tour de France is a world on the move, with the astonishing entanglement of all its diverse components, its dramas and its laughter, its triumphs and its catastrophes, its heroes and its anonymous servants." The Tour's current director, former sportswriter Jean-Marie Leblanc, has championed the event's social and economic clout. "The Tour de France contributes in its fashion to the well-being of the land," he proclaims, "but it's also a marvelous exportable product."

———

The Tour de France didn't really become a "marvelous exportable product" to America until Lance Armstrong won the 1999 edition, just two years after he recovered from a near-fatal cancer. That's not to say that he was the first American to defeat the Europeans at the pinnacle of their sport. That honor went to Greg LeMond, a bright-eyed blond Californian who won the Tour in 1986, just five years after Jonathan Boyer became the first American ever to compete at the event.

But general U.S. awareness of the Tour didn't perk up until 1989, when LeMond won the event a second time, in dramatic fashion, coming from behind to defeat Frenchman Laurent Fignon by the smallest margin in race history: a mere eight seconds. LeMond was named *Sports Illustrated*'s Sportsman of the Year, partly because he achieved his stirring victory with a body still laced with buckshot from a 1987 hunting accident in which he almost bled to death. Few Americans remember that LeMond won a third Tour in 1990, but most know that Armstrong won his fifth in a row in 2003. In fact, because of his dominance, many assume that Armstrong has won every Tour he started.

Winning the Tour is not that simple though. Road cycling is one of the few sports that is contested by teams and yet results in an individual winner. That winner has to be physically gifted and mentally strong, and he has to train his body to race a bike for up to eight straight hours, day after day after day. He needs a high power-to-weight ratio, a strong heart, and fine pedaling skills to conquer the mountain climbs; and he has to lift weights and ride his bike in high-speed motor-paced sessions, so that he can race at an *average* speed of 35 miles per hour in the Tour's time trials—individual races against the clock. But to win the Tour, he also needs eight strong teammates.

These dedicated teammates (called *domestiques*) must forego their individual ambitions and become strong and strategically unified enough to do all it takes to make their leader win. They must protect him from crashes and from the wind on the flats; and they will race for hours at the front of the pack (the largest mass of riders, also called the *peloton*) to discourage his rivals from breaking away ("attacking") and gaining time. Should such breakaways succeed in getting clear of the pack, then the domestiques will be the ones to lead the chase after them. And, finally, they need to pace their leader partway up the critical mountain climbs where *he* has to attack and gain the time he needs to defeat the opposition.

A team's support riders have to work as hard as the leader to be ready for the Tour. Most have their own coaches who set their training schedules and help prepare them for the dozens of springtime races that are needed to bring them to their physical peak in July. Each of the twenty or so teams invited to the Tour can contract up to twenty-eight riders a year, but the race is contested by nine-man teams, so only the strongest ones with the best form are selected for the Tour. There, they will be devoted to making their leader the winner, to giving their sponsors the name recognition they're counting on, and to showing the world that they are the best team at the Tour.

Finally, without the optimum combination of teammates, knowledgeable coaches to train them, experienced team directors to set strategies, highly skilled engineers to build their bikes, and a well-orchestrated backup crew of masseurs, mechanics, doctors, and dieticians, not even an Armstrong could win the Tour. He *did* win the first five Tours he started after surviving the cancer that threatened his life in late 1996, but before that the Texan rode the Tour de France four times and finished only once, taking 36th place in 1995. Losing the Tour was an important step toward learning how to win it.

———

Armstrong's early Tours taught him the event's complexities, its harshness, and some of its joys. He was only 21 and in his first year as a professional cyclist when he debuted at the 1993 edition. It was an absurdly young age to tackle what is arguably the toughest sports event in the world. Even the prodigious Belgian cyclist Eddy Merckx, who in the late 1960s and early 1970s won more professional races than anyone in history, didn't start his first Tour until his fifth year of racing, when he was 23. And even that was considered too young by Europe's cycling insiders, who know that a racer rarely reaches maturity until his late twenties.

But the young Armstrong knew nothing about protocol. His drive, even then, was exceptional. The product of a childhood troubled by broken marriages and an adolescence in which his talent as an endurance athlete was looked down upon by his football-playing peers, he relished big challenges. "He wanted to race with the big guys," remembers Jim Ochowicz, his first professional cycling team manager, "but we didn't want to put him in a race that was over his head. So the deal we made was that he could take the Tour start, but we wouldn't let him ride more than ten, twelve days, fourteen maximum." Despite that restriction, Armstrong became the youngest rider in more than fifty years to win one of the Tour's daily stages. "The stage into Verdun was not an easy stage to win," says Ochowicz, "but he won a field sprint with six guys, and I thought it brought out all the good things in Lance, all in one day." That small taste of glory was somewhat mitigated by two days of struggling up the mountain passes in the Alps, where Armstrong conceded almost an hour to the race leaders before making his programmed exit from the Tour at the halfway point.

Finishing so far behind on the climbs hurt Armstrong's pride, but he would receive a greater lesson in humility at the 1994 Tour. On a blisteringly hot afternoon in the Dordogne hills, between the weathered-brick towns of Périgueux and Bergerac, Armstrong had ambitions of putting in a great performance at that day's time trial. This is a stage in which each man starts at set intervals, usually two minutes apart, and rides completely alone and against the clock on a short but demanding course. It's cycling's equivalent of hand-to-hand combat, and a discipline that has to be mastered by any potential Tour winner. Armstrong was already somewhat proficient, but only 10 miles into the 40-mile test, that year's defending Tour champion, Miguel Induráin of Spain, who started the stage two minutes behind the young American, came roaring past him. Armstrong tried to keep Induráin in sight to learn more about the champion's renowned time-trial skills, but he eventually cracked and lost more than four minutes to the Spanish star.

One year later, Induráin would win *his* fifth consecutive Tour, while the still-youthful Armstrong was forced to confront a tragedy that made him face mortality for the first time in his life. On the fifteenth stage, the Texan's teammate Fabio Casartelli, only 24, was killed. The young Italian lost control of his bicycle coming down a frighteningly steep mountain road in the Pyrenees and cracked his head open on a concrete post.

Casartelli was neither the first nor the last Tour athlete to have his life or career ended by a high-speed crash, exhaustion, or misguided use of drugs. These are risks that all of the racers are aware of when they line up at the Tour.

The day after Casartelli died, the riders agreed to honor him by riding the marathon stage through the mountains at a pace that would allow everyone to finish together. Looking back at that somber day, when the field rode as one over long mountain passes under a burning sun, Armstrong said, "Even though they were going easy, it was hot, and physically it was damn hard. Mentally, I was so far away. . . . I don't want ever to have a day like that again. That was the hardest day of the Tour de France."

Before Casartelli's fatal crash, Armstrong was a brash 23-year-old Texan who didn't have a great deal of respect for European professional cyclists. His feelings changed radically by the end of that grueling day, after the other riders in the pack allowed him and his teammates to move ahead and cross the finish line with heads bowed. "For everybody to sit up and say this is not a day to race, this is a day to mourn . . . that says a lot," Armstrong said. "Certainly my attitude toward the peloton completely changed that day. I was impressed by their class."

———————

Eerily, Armstrong would have to face his own mortality the following year. On October 2, 1996, he was diagnosed with stage three testicular cancer that had spread to his abdomen, lungs, and brain, and he was given less than a 50 percent chance of living. Looking back, he now knows that his body was already diseased when he took part in his fourth Tour de France, three months earlier. It was a Tour that didn't last very long for Armstrong. After a week of racing in persistently cold, wet weather across the Netherlands, Belgium, and northern France, he was having respiratory problems. The weather worsened on the seventh day, when the rain fell with Niagara-like force on the dolomitic peaks of the Jura mountains. Normally, Armstrong excelled in such conditions, but this time he couldn't keep up with even the slowest riders. Halfway up a long climb, his body shivering beneath a plastic rain jacket, the American coasted to a halt and dropped out of the race. After being driven to his team's hotel and taking a shower, he told me, "I'm bummed . . . I had no power . . . couldn't breathe . . . I had an infection set in last night. I didn't expect to come here and get sick. I never get sick. But I am, so what can I say?"

Despite that disturbing experience, Armstrong raced at the Olympic Games in Atlanta that August. Other than the Tour setback, he had won eight times in what had been the best year of his career. He came to Atlanta expecting to medal, so he couldn't understand it when he finished only twelfth in the Olympic road race and sixth in the time-trial event. Undaunted, the American returned to Europe, placed second at the Tour of the Netherlands, and was the runner-up at a time trial in Brussels. In retrospect, such high-class performances—only weeks before his widespread cancer was discovered—appear superhuman.

At the end of that September, I interviewed Armstrong at a cycling event in Bend, Oregon, and asked about the French team, Cofidis, he was going to race with the following year, and the expectations of its French sports director, Cyrille Guimard. "He doesn't expect me to win this year's Tour. But he thinks that I could win it someday," Armstrong said. "I don't even know if *I* think that. It's not even easy to be *top ten* in the Tour de France."

Just three days after that interview, Armstrong was on an operating table having a cancerous testicle removed. Instead of starting intensive training to contest the 1997 Tour, he was fighting for his life with the first of several rounds of aggressive chemotherapy. The chemo was more excruciatingly painful than it needed to be, since he chose drugs that wouldn't affect his lungs, wouldn't harm his racing potential. He knew he wanted to race again, and in late 1997—around the time he became engaged to Kristin Richard after a short courtship— he restarted serious training. He didn't know if he'd ever be able to race like he did before, or whether the cancer would reappear.

The French team, Cofidis, sponsored by a telephone credit company, treated Armstrong badly. Not believing he'd ever return to cycling, it pulled out of its two-year, $2.5 million contract, and offered a much-reduced, incentive-based deal should he come back. Armstrong and his lawyer/agent, Bill Stapleton, were furious, especially when other big-league, European-based teams either refused to sign the Texan or offered him a derisory salary. He eventually accepted a better incentive-based deal with an American team, sponsored by the U.S. Postal Service, which was then just establishing a foothold at the elite level. The Postal deal allowed Armstrong to start racing in Europe again in February 1998. But on the second day of a weeklong race in March, after riding in cold, slashing rain, Armstrong pulled to the roadside and quit. He realized he wasn't mentally ready for a return to the harsh conditions of continental racing. Demoralized, he said he'd never race again, packed his bike away, and didn't touch it for weeks. To fill the sudden vacuum, Armstrong found a series of diversions. As he wrote in his book *It's Not About the Bike*: "I played golf every day, I

water-skied, I drank beer, and I lay on the sofa and channel-surfed."
But he had an obligation to compete at a race, a very special race, in
Austin on May 22 to kick off a fundraising weekend for his newly
formed cancer foundation.

So after being goaded by his friends, Armstrong accepted the challenge of his coach Chris Carmichael to train for a week in the hills of
North Carolina with a former Motorola teammate, Bob Roll. Despite
having to ride their bikes for several hours a day in torrential rain, it
was there that Armstrong rediscovered his love of cycling. At the end
of the week he competed at a race in Atlanta and finished 52nd. He
took his bike with him to Santa Barbara, California, where he married
Kristin Richard on May 4. Two weeks later, he won the short Austin
race before his hometown fans, and then rode strongly at America's
largest bike race, the 156-mile USPRO Championship in Philadel-
phia. He was ready for Europe. Incredibly, he immediately won the
four-day Tour of Luxembourg. He wasn't yet ready to race the following month's Tour de France; but when he placed fourth in the
September 1998 Tour of Spain, a three-week race where he displayed
new climbing skills in the high mountains, people began speculating
just how far this American athlete's metamorphosis might take him—
particularly at the Tour.

Johan Bruyneel, the new Belgian sports director at the U.S. Postal
Service team, later convinced the now 27-year-old Armstrong that he
could indeed do well at the Tour—that he could even win it!

Armstrong *did* win the Tour in 1999, and went on to take the next
four editions as well. But it was after his first Tour victory that he
emotionally said those words that help explain him: *"I want to be re-
membered as the first cancer survivor to win the Tour."* That legacy grows
more important to him each year. It's one of the things that drives
him and sets him apart from every other competitor. And there's
something else he has gained as a cancer survivor—an aura of invinci-
bility and fearlessness. So what if no one else has ever won six Tours.

So what if he's now 32, an age at which most professional cyclists have already retired. And so what if he's facing formidable challengers—men like Jan Ullrich, the German who won the Tour in 1997 as a precocious 23-year-old, has since been the runner-up five times, lost by mere seconds to Armstrong in 2003, and wants nothing more than to topple his American rival. Or Tyler Hamilton, the feisty American who once rode on Armstrong's team and helped him win three Tours, but now races on a rival team and proved his own superhuman ambition by finishing fourth at the 2003 Tour—despite riding for three weeks with a broken collarbone suffered in a crash on the event's second day. Or Ivan Basso, the rising Italian star, who looked as if he were ready to make a breakthrough.

Armstrong would also be facing powerful contenders from countries like Spain, Italy, and Russia, men who'd been training half their lives for this unique chance at sporting glory, and whose teams would battle Armstrong's every day, fighting to give their leader a chance at victory. Like Armstrong, they'd be playing with fate, not knowing how their bodies would react to the extreme conditions, the Olympian test of endurance, or if they would succumb to the sickness, injuries, and crashes that take out forty or fifty men each year.

———

Sitting in his den that December afternoon, Armstrong gestures to an empty space on the wall, where there's room for a sixth yellow jersey. *"It's all that matters,"* he says, as if that settles it. And to make that happen, he's about to undergo months of conditioning, ride thousands of miles, and train as intensively and far as a human body can go, before lining up to face his opponents in a race that lasts 23 days in July.

Only 2,107 Miles to Go

JULY 3: *A flat 3.8-mile time trial, called the prologue, around the streets of downtown Liège, a Belgian steel town that's shaking off the grimy remnants of its industrial past. The course favors short-distance specialists who have the power to accelerate out of the sharp turns and maintain a high speed on the straights.*

It's just after 7 p.m. on a breezy, springlike evening in the heart of Liège. Down on Avenue Rogier, a handsome boulevard now flanked by thousands of rowdy spectators, Lance Armstrong guides his bike up a long ramp to the five-foot-high platform. From here, he'll start his opening time trial—and his tenth Tour de France. A remote-control TV camera swings down from a gantry and zooms in on Armstrong's tan, gaunt face. His closely cropped hair lies flat beneath the bright blue, streamlined helmet that has a white lone star of Texas fused to its shiny plastic coating. He felt good during his intense, just-completed warm-up on a stationary bike, when he listened to rock music on his iPod, wiped sweat from his face with clean white towels, and only stopped pedaling now and again to stretch each leg backward until the heel touched his back.

A few drops of sweat most likely remain in the recess of his neck, beneath the slightly opened white nylon zipper of his blue U.S. Postal Service team uniform. The aerodynamic skinsuit is designed to hug his ripped body like a second skin. It uniquely combines panels of slick material to enhance the flow of air at the front, fuzzy panels to break up vortexes at the rear, and stitches that follow the direction of the airflow. Perhaps all that will help him race a second or two faster in this 3.8-mile individual time trial, the prologue of the 91st Tour.

Over the past three hours, launched at one-minute intervals, the Tour's other 187 racers have sped around this completely flat course with all the power their fine-tuned bodies can muster. Dashing through the streets like space-age centaurs, their 35-mile-per-hour progress is followed by a flowing roar of cheers, shouts, catcalls, and clapping from a quarter-million energized fans. Their ears are further assaulted by the amplified commentary of the French race announcers and the throbbing blades of helicopters filming the race.

The man who clocks the fastest time in this opening stage will be awarded the Tour's symbolic yellow jersey, his to wear until a new race leader emerges. The Tour organizers like dramatic endings, so they seed the riders according to the previous year's results, making the top men the last to go. Lance Armstrong, as the five-time defending champion, is the final starter.

Some raucous German fans have just given their countryman, 2003 runner-up Jan Ullrich, a rousing send-off. They have a different greeting for Armstrong: a loud chorus of boos. The American takes no notice, and stares straight ahead as he waits for the starter's countdown.

Thirty seconds to go . . .

Behind the contoured acrylic lenses of his bronze-tinted Oakley shades, Armstrong's intense blue eyes are focused on the road before him as he ignores the catcalls. He sits on a narrow racing saddle astride a low-slung, carbon-fiber bicycle that weighs just above the minimum weight allowed, 14.9 pounds, and that took months to fine-tune to his liking. His fingers tighten inside black padded leather gloves, gripping his straight carbon-fiber handlebar. His left leg is poised, the foot tensed inside a handmade artificial leather race shoe.

Twenty seconds to go . . .

Armstrong gets ready to make a first thrust on his shoe's rigid sole that contacts with an aluminum pedal via a metal cleat. The pressure will begin to turn the 175-millimeter-long crank arm that's attached to a 55-tooth chainring. That will set in motion a titanium bicycle chain, which pulls one of ten rear cogs and starts to rotate the carbon-fiber rear disc wheel. Man and machine will then be in motion.

Fifteen seconds . . .

The Texan looks calm, but inside he is anxious. He knows that he has to gain a psychological advantage this evening, to show his opponents that he has overcome his loss at the pre-Tour Dauphiné Libéré race, and that he's ready for any challenge they can throw at him in the next three weeks. One year ago, when the centennial Tour de France started in front of the Eiffel Tower, Armstrong finished only seventh in the prologue—and it took him sixteen of the twenty-three days to gain the upper hand on his opposition. He has to do better tonight.

Ten seconds . . .

To race a good time trial, a rider has to exclude unnecessary thoughts before he starts. One of Armstrong's chief rivals, Tyler Hamilton, put it this way: "I don't meditate, but I do special things just to try to relax, like taking deep breaths. A time trial is a very big effort for which your body should be as relaxed as possible. If you're all pent up, the body is not going to be very efficient. You're not going to be at your best."

When I asked Armstrong if he ever meditated, he derisively exclaimed: "Nooooh! Christ!" Why would he, since many claim that it's his pent-up fury that makes the Texan such a formidable competitor. Now he's ready to channel that energy into seven minutes of supreme effort. He can't wait to be under way. In his fastidious manner, he goes through a mental checklist of things like: Is the chain on the right cog? Is the strap on this new helmet tight enough? Are my aerodynamic shoe covers on straight?

Five seconds . . .

The French timekeeper begins his countdown. *"Cinq."* Five long, slim fingers appear in front of Armstrong's face. They belong to Jérôme Lappartient, a French race official who is timing the Tour for the first time. *"Quatre."* Four fingers. Armstrong stares ahead. The fingers are in sync with the piercing digital beeps of the 12-inch-diameter Festina timing clock facing Armstrong, its long, sweeping second hand heading for the top of the dial. *"Trois."* Three fingers. Armstrong tenses the fibers of his powerful thigh muscles. *"Deux."* Two fingers. He grips the handlebars even tighter. *"Un."* One finger. His mind suddenly clears. This is it!

"Partez!"

It's 7:08 p.m. Armstrong launches the combined 170 pounds of his bike and body down the rubber-surfaced four-foot-wide ramp onto the smooth blacktop of Avenue Rogier. He stands on the pedals to accelerate to top speed, moves his hands onto the forward-pointing parts of his bars, and drops into an aerodynamic tuck position.

Only two thousand one hundred seven miles to go!

Each year, the Tour de France follows a different route, proudly showcasing different parts of the country, but always ending on the Champs-Élysées. Opening stages of the event are often held in neighboring countries—whichever bids the most for that privilege. This year, the honor goes to the Wallonia region of Belgium, which paid the organizers $2 million for the rights. Well worth it, locals say. They're delighted that overhead television shots, beamed to an estimated 120 million people around the globe, ignore the rusted steel mills and smoke-stained row houses that surround the city's core, to focus instead on the sweeping curves of the Meuse River, the historic downtown's cobblestone streets, and the Gothic glory of Liège's ancient churches and statues.

One mile down the prologue course, just where the Boulevard de la Sauvenière emerges into the Place de l'Opéra, one of the city's main squares, spectators lean forward over the metal crowd barriers in front of the regal Hellenic-style opera house. Across the street, patrons at the sidewalk tables of the Café du Point de Vue crane their necks to glimpse the racers and their support vehicles as they flash past. This is where Adrie Houterman, a Dutch bank manager, is waiting with some friends to see Armstrong go by. "I brought fifty-five clients by bus to see the race today," he tells me. They are just a sampling of the tens of thousands of visitors who have poured into Liège for the Tour's *grand départ*. These are the biggest crowds Liège has seen since a quarter-million citizens celebrated the end of World War II six decades ago.

Much has changed, but not the sweet-smelling onions and sausages of the hotdog stands, or the *frites* smothered in mayonnaise and washed down with a glass of Jupiler beer. The city's pubs and bistros are packed, particularly the Point de Vue, which besides being on the prologue course is only a short walk from the Place Lambert, a recently renovated downtown gathering area that artfully integrates paved pedestrian promenades and wide stone stairways. The night before the race, this square was filled with crowds attending the Tour's opening festivities: rock bands galore, the presentation of the twenty-one teams, and an outdoor concert given by hometown crooner Frédéric François, who regularly plays to packed houses at the Olympia in Paris. One young woman wasn't too impressed. "He's for the grandmothers," said Laurie Di Stefano, suggesting that the promoters were expecting an older crowd.

Typical of the audience were American ex-pat Elise Edwards and Welshman Nick Corfield, both in their forties. "I come every year and meet great people," said Edwards, who met Corfield at the Tour a couple of years ago. Corfield was wearing the distinctive orange cycling jersey and cap of the Basque team, Euskaltel, because the Basques and the Welsh are both indigenous peoples. "I love the Basques, and I love Mayo," he said, referring to Euskaltel's team leader and one of the race favorites, Iban Mayo. "I was amazed when he gave me a wave from the stage." Edwards, an Armstrong fan, had on a U.S. Postal team baseball cap. She was one of the few people waving an American flag. "I think Americans are quite afraid to show their stars-and-stripes because of a huge anti-American feeling in Europe," she said. "But I'm not afraid of cycling fans."

After the eve-of-the-race ceremonies, some of those fans moved on to the Point de Vue café. This ancient tavern, which has been serving customers since 1652, has stone, brick, and timber walls and a steeply pitched, black-slate roof. Its main deference to modernity, a 20-inch television, is never turned on, but hangs from the ceiling, collecting dust.

No television is needed today though, when the racers whiz past the front door of the café. Most of the patrons are outside, some standing on cane chairs and tables for a better view. One of them is the bank manager from the Netherlands, who stands on a table with a Belgian friend. "Who do you think will win the Tour?" I shout, trying to be heard above the thundering reverberations of rock and rap emerging from the packed bars and street parties. "Armstrong," they both say. "He is superb."

"And who will be his main challenger?" "Ullrich," they agree.

"The Spanish riders, Roberto Heras and Mayo. And then there's Tyler Hamilton. The Americans are *good*."

7:09 p.m. Armstrong sweeps between the Point de Vue café and the Royal Walloon Opera House. The fans shout with excitement, happy that Armstrong is racing with his usual fire. Their cheers are muffled by the revving engines of motorcycles and race cars pursuing the Texan. His Belgian team director Johan Bruyneel, driving one of the Postal team's Subaru station wagons 20 feet behind him, can see the speedometer touching 60 kilometers per hour—nearly 40 miles per hour. Bruyneel is trying to talk Armstrong through the course's upcoming turns, the way a navigator calls out road directions to the race driver in a car rally on their wireless radio setup. "Lance didn't hear much as the transmitter was in and out," backseat passenger Jim Ochowicz later reveals.

Armstrong hasn't needed much assistance so far because he has had a straight shot along wide, newly paved streets sheltered by six-story office and apartment buildings. And he knows from scouting the course earlier that he has to be careful across the bumpy cobblestones next to the opera house, before he heads along a narrow street that leads to a sharp left turn just past the main building of the University of Liège, where he halves his speed and then accelerates smoothly onto a divided highway alongside the Meuse River. Once there, Armstrong shifts into his highest gear to take advantage of the blustery southwest wind blowing him along.

In Europe, the Texan is not the most popular of race champions. That was clear when he was booed at the start. He's considered too distant and cocky, and is more respected than liked. Jean-Marie Leblanc, the Tour de France race director for the past fifteen years, offered some insight into this when he compared Armstrong with the other four men who won five Tours: the Frenchmen Jacques Anquetil (whose wins came between 1957 and 1964) and Bernard Hinault (1978 to 1985), the Belgian Eddy Merckx (1969 to 1974), and the Spaniard Miguel Induráin (1991 to 1995). According to Leblanc, "Lance is more of a winner than Anquetil, who didn't always have the ambition to win. He was a great champion, but 'cool.' Induráin the same. Hinault was more combative. Merckx wanted to win every race he entered, but Lance wants to win the Tour, only the Tour. The rest mean nothing to him."

As for their popularity, Leblanc said, "Armstrong is a little less liked than the other four. The public knew them better than they do Armstrong. He has remained a little mysterious. When he came back from cancer, people couldn't believe that a guy who had almost died had become an immense champion. The public hardly saw him until—*hop!*—he wins the Tour. So there's some admiration, but he is not as warmly liked as the others. That's not my judgment. It's a fact. *Voilà!*"

That fact was evident when Armstrong and his U.S. Postal teammates were introduced at the 2001 Tour start in Dunkirk, France, and were greeted with a mixture of boos and catcalls amid the applause. But Armstrong is more well-liked and appreciated by the Belgians. At the Place Lambert opening presentations, they gave him a warm reception, as they did to all of the main contenders: the German Ullrich, the Americans Hamilton and Levi Leipheimer, the Spanish riders Mayo, Heras, Haimar Zubeldia, and Carlos Sastre, the Italians Ivan Basso and Gilberto Simoni, and the Russian Denis Menchov.

7:11 p.m. With 1.8 miles covered, Armstrong is *flying*, his stretched-out position helping him cut smoothly through the gusting air. His streamlined helmet was the last of a string of equipment modifications begun in the fall, designed to improve his time-trial performance by perhaps one percentage point. In tonight's time trial, that seemingly small improvement could cut four or five seconds from Armstrong's time, and prologues are rarely won by more than that.

Armstrong had talked about the changes back in December, the day before he flew from Austin to Seattle for wind-tunnel testing at the University of Washington. "Bart Knaggs, an old friend of mine, just made it his personal mission to create this whole aero plan. We brought everybody together, all the people that are working on that bike, and on me . . . just a complete package." Dubbed F-One, the project produced a narrower bike, a cleaner, lower frontal body position, and a more aerodynamic racing suit and helmet. The details even included angling the brake levers more horizontally and positioning the aerobars with a less upward rake, to improve airflow around the bike.

Armstrong, though, will never have as perfect an aero position as the expert British time trialist Chris Boardman, who in the mid-1990s rode the fastest prologue in Tour history, averaging 34.270 mph over a 4.5-mile course in Lille, France, which was similar to Liège's but had far more turns. "Everyone's body type is different," Armstrong said, "and that really determines your position. Boardman could ride crazy low, uncomfortable positions. His body will do that. Mine never will."

Armstrong's body can't do that because of the way his back automatically humps whenever he leans forward to race. Over the years, this hump's retarding effect has been virtually eliminated by the way his mechanics have built his bike around him. Today, given his morphology, Armstrong has as streamlined a position as he'll ever get. Any slight reduction in the air resistance his body creates when racing at 40 miles per hour can make a big difference. That's because, even in still conditions, the air resistance produced by a cyclist riding this fast makes it feel as if he's heading into a howling gale. So yes, the winter wind-tunnel sessions, springtime road tests, and constant tinkering are worth the effort. But will all the changes produce the cumulative effect that Armstrong's looking for?

The defending champion gets a first indication two miles into his time trial, when he slows his pace to make a U-turn around a small traffic circle at the far end of the Liège prologue course. The official time split shows that he is only two seconds behind Fabian Cancellara, the fastest man to this halfway point. The 23-year-old Swiss has awed the crowds with his final time of 6 minutes, 50 seconds— giving him an average speed of 33.282 miles per hour, and getting folks talking about "the new prologue specialist."

Bruyneel relays the information to his rider, who now knows he has about three more minutes of effort to make up those two seconds on Cancellara.

7:12 p.m. Of Armstrong's main rivals, the ones with the best final times so far tonight are Zubeldia (27 seconds slower than current leader Cancellara) and Sastre (15 seconds slower). The other credible challengers are still out on the course, immediately ahead of the champion. Right now, Ullrich and Hamilton are both 10 seconds slower than Cancellara, Mayo and Basso are 13 seconds back, while Leipheimer is the best at only eight seconds.

"Which of these challengers do you think about the most," I had asked Armstrong. "Only Ullrich," he said. "Ullrich's far and away the biggest rival. He's the only one we really pay attention to what he's doing . . . what he's racing, his race results, what he's saying."

Like Armstrong, Ullrich emerged as a prodigy. While the American won the world championship (a single-day 160-mile road race) at age 21 in his first year as a professional cyclist, the German entered his first Tour de France at age 22 and finished second, in 1996. Significantly, Ullrich won that Tour's final time trial by defeating five-time champion Induráin and almost dispossessing his own team leader, Bjarne Riis, of the race leader's yellow jersey.

When he won the Tour the following year, Ullrich was hailed by the authoritative French sports newspaper *L'Équipe* as a rider who would probably win the Tour six or seven times. Now, after four second places in his past four appearances, he's desperate to win it at least one more time—especially if he can defeat Armstrong. "To have a victory in the Tour de France *without* Lance Armstrong would have way less value," he claimed.

By the age at which Armstrong and Ullrich were battling for glory in the Tour de France, New Englander Tyler Hamilton was only just discovering the sport of cycling at the collegiate level. His late start means that although he is six months older than Armstrong, he is less burned out, and probably has several more years of cycling ahead of him than the Texan. Furthermore, Hamilton didn't become a team leader—the man whom all his teammates help and protect—until 2002, eight years after Armstrong.

As a result, Hamilton didn't gain wide recognition until the 2003 Tour, when besides racing with a broken collarbone and *still* finishing fourth, he also won a famous stage victory in the Pyrenees. That day, on a course that featured a half-dozen mountain passes, the slightly built Hamilton broke clear on the steepest climb of the Tour and raced the final 55 rolling miles on his own in less than two hours. An extraordinary performance at the end of a long day in the mountains, even *without* a broken shoulder. Armstrong called it "the most outstanding athletic feat of the Tour."

Hamilton is now a true contender, not just for a stage win, but for the whole enchilada. Does he think he can win the 2004 Tour? "I'm gonna try," Hamilton told me. "I have to think like I can, and train and focus and believe that. If you arrive at the start line of the Tour de France and think, oh, I'm only racing for a top ten or a top five, you're already a few steps behind."

It was at the 2003 Tour that another man became a familiar name in Europe: Basque rider Iban Mayo. He did it in spectacular fashion in the French Alps. On the climb to L'Alpe d'Huez, where Armstrong had been expected to repeat his emphatic stage win of 2001, it was Mayo who attacked and scored a solo victory more than two minutes ahead of the defending champion. The crowds loved the panache with which Mayo won, the vigor of his climbing style, and his sultry, movie-star looks.

7:13 p.m. After completing the U-turn at the traffic circle, Armstrong accelerates away and is soon back into his aerodynamic tuck, racing along La Batte, the riverside esplanade that's the site of a huge morning flea market every Sunday. The locals that mob the market are probably all watching Armstrong right now, staring at a man in a blue skinsuit cycling at a speed that would get them a ticket on a normal Saturday night.

Armstrong now faces the course's trickiest mile, where skilled bike handling will be as important as pure speed. After veering away from the river past the Chez Sam café, a sharp right turn takes him onto the bumpy Rue Léopold that heads into the Place Lambert. Here, he climbs a slight rise on smooth cobblestones, curves left past the grand sixteenth-century Palais des Princes-Évêques, and then swings sharper left down a short hill. The two fast right turns that follow bring him back past the Point de Vue café, with just one mile of flat-out racing to the finish. The crowds urge him on, shouting "Go, Lance, go!" in English, French, and Dutch.

———————

Race director Leblanc is confident that this is going to be a great Tour de France. "If Lance wins his sixth Tour, he's the greatest, the first one. *Formidable!* There will be lots of publicity, lots of enthusiasm. . . . If Lance is beaten by someone, Ullrich or someone else, the one who beats Lance will become a hero, because he will have pulled down the favorite. So, in one case or the other, it will be a Tour that's well received."

But Leblanc doesn't expect this alternative outcome. "I remember a visit with Lance a month before the Tour in 2002, a fifteen-minute visit in his room, at a time when he had already won the Tour three times," says the balding, avuncular Frenchman. "I understood in his eyes that he wanted to win four, he wanted to win five, he wanted to win six. I understood that. I was certain."

———————

7:15 p.m. Armstrong is straining his whole body as he tears along the Boulevard d'Avroy and makes the final thrust of the evening. Two digital times flash from the gantry above the finish line. On the left is the fastest time so far, still Cancellara's scintillating 6:50. On the right is Armstrong's time that is still clicking up by hundredths of a second at a time. With 200 meters left, it looks as though he will match the best time. Armstrong is a blur of blue, urged on by the screaming crowd, as he races past the bleachers and sprints across the finish line.

The official voice of the Tour, French race announcer Daniel Mangeas, immediately gives the result: "The time of Lance Armstrong is 6:52, second best!" he shouts in the country dialect of his native Normandy. Second best. That's a phrase the German contingent, the ones that booed Armstrong at the start, probably latches onto. It's about all they can take hope in because their man, Ullrich, was a full quarter-minute slower than the Yank they hold in such contempt.

———————

Armstrong may have lost the prologue, but he couldn't have a better position: He has beaten time-trial pro Ullrich by a surprising 15 seconds, Hamilton by 16, Mayo by 19, and Basso by 27 seconds. It's a psychological victory for the Texan, as the gaps are bigger than expected, a reflection on the excellence of Armstrong's performance rather than any weakness shown by his main challengers. "I'm surprised that Jan was that far back," Armstrong says after finishing. "Maybe he wasn't on a good day."

Not so, Ullrich says. "I decided not to take any unnecessary risks, I didn't want my Tour to end in Liège." Hamilton *did* take a risk. He says he made a gamble in using longer cranks than usual, hoping that the extra leverage would "help me go faster on the long straightaways. But in retrospect they may have cost me too much time in the turns." Mayo points out that he was only two seconds behind Hamilton, while Basso never expected to rival Armstrong in the prologue. And all of these challengers have said several times in the lead-up to the Tour that they were planning to start at around 90 percent of their best form, in order to be at 100 percent in the vital final week—"the week from hell," as Armstrong has dubbed it. Yes, the organizers like dramatic endings, and this year they've mapped out a final week that guarantees it, with challenging mountain courses and time trials that could change the outcome of the race until the penultimate day.

But for now, a young Swiss racer from the Italian-based team Fassa Bortolo is on top of the 2004 Tour de France. True, prologue winners rarely end up as the overall race champion, as they are generally big men like Cancellara, who lack the climbing and endurance skills to match the sheer speed they can call upon in a short, flat time trial.

Still, there's glory enough for Cancellara tonight. Standing atop the podium, with the stirring Tour anthem blaring from the loudspeakers, he's honored four separate times: He gets a Val Saint-Lambert crystal glass trophy for winning the stage, the yellow jersey for leading the race, green jersey for leading on points, and white jersey for best young rider. Each time, Cancellara gives a warm smile and poses for the photographers with a different pair of beautiful women, who give him flowers and sweet kisses. Television and radio reporters then surround him like hounds, eager to find out who this young man is, what he has done, what he can do.

At his press conference in the mobile interview room, Cancellara reveals that he started cycling when he found a racing bike in his father's garage at age 15, and that "cycling became my new passion." At 17, he won the world junior time-trial championship, a feat he repeated the following year. As a professional, he has won prologues at several races, including the Tour of Switzerland. And now, on his first appearance at the Tour de France, Cancellara has become the leader of the world's biggest bike race—at least for a day.

There are three more time trials (one for teams, two for individuals), seventeen road stages, and two rest days in this Tour. The final winner, who will stand atop the podium on the Champs-Élysées, will be the man who completes the twenty-three days in the least amount of accumulated time, the man who is first in the overall standings, or General Classification. So theoretically, the overall champion doesn't have to win *any* of the stages, as long as he places well in the time trials and on the tougher road stages. In fact, at the 2000 Tour, with only three days left, Lance Armstrong hadn't won a single stage, yet was leading the race on overall time by six minutes. He went on to win the final time trial, more for prestige than necessity.

Cancellara's best hope for this Tour is to hang on to the yellow jersey for a day or two. He's already had his fifteen minutes of fame, and he's making the most of it. The tall Swiss, with his wavy, light-brown hair and youthful, unshaven chin, is reluctant to leave his press conference. "The time trial is my event," he says. "This is my specialty. But I'm not just a prologue specialist. I'm young, I'm fast, I'm explosive, and I'm thrilled to have beaten Armstrong! I saw that he was very fast today. But it's been a long day, very emotional."

The Tour de France, like a good French movie, is high on emotion. For the next three weeks it promises celebrations and despair, nasty crashes and thrilling feats of athleticism, anxiety and heartbreak, ecstasy and pain. Each stage will present a separate drama, and each night will hold the promise of new fortune for the next day.

On this opening Saturday night in Liège, where the restaurants, bars, and discos will stay open until early morning, the Dutch bank manager and his customers are already back in their bus, headed for home; thousands of fans are driving out to the hills south of town to pick out a spot to watch Sunday's opening road stage; the journalists are wrapping up their stories at the pressroom that's been their home for the last few days; and at the Post Hotel, where Armstrong's and Hamilton's teams are both staying, the mechanics have packed away the time-trial bikes for a few days and prepared the riders' road bikes, the ones they will be using for most of the next twenty-two days.

Looking out from the restaurant of their hilltop hotel, Armstrong and Hamilton can see a brilliant rainbow form as shafts of the setting sun hit the raindrops of a sudden shower. More rain is forecast for tomorrow, the Fourth of July. There'll be celebrations back home, but here in Belgium, the two American contenders will be focused on a more distant celebration, one that's still more than two thousand one hundred miles away.

STAGE RESULT: 1. Fabian Cancellara (Switzerland), 6:50; 2. Lance Armstrong (USA), 6:52; 3. José Ivan Gutierrez (Spain), 6:58; 4. Brad McGee (Australia), 6:59; 5. Thor Hushovd (Norway), 7:00.

*OVERALL STANDINGS: 1. Cancellara; 2. Armstrong, at 0:02;
13. Levi Leipheimer (USA), at 0:15; 14. Carlos Sastre (Spain), same
time; 16. Jan Ullrich (Germany), at 0:17; 18. Tyler Hamilton (USA), at
0:18; 70. Ivan Basso (Italy), at 0:29.*

Independence Day

JULY 4: *The first half of the 126-mile course from Liège to the industrial city of Charleroi features five short climbs in the wooded hills of the Ardennes, while the second half is on rolling roads through open countryside in the Meuse River valley. The stage favors the fast sprinters who have a mile-long finishing straight on which to contest the stage win.*

There's a fluid, almost unruly feel to the crowds that gather to watch the Tour de France. With the roads closed to regular traffic three or more hours before the race comes through, the fans arrive early, many in camper vans and RVs, to stake out their viewing area with giant national or team flags. Some have painted their faces in their country's colors, others dress in outrageous costumes—today's Belgians favor tall velvet jester hats in their national colors of black, gold, and red. Large families bustle about, setting up picnic tables, coolers, portable TVs, and grills. The more energetic paint cardboard signs with words of encouragement for the riders—"Jan Ullrich. Hopp! Hopp!"—or chalk the names of their favorites on the road. And as they wait, everyone socializes with their temporary neighbors. It's a giant tailgate party snaking from one city to the next.

Today they have gathered to watch the Tour's first "road stage"— a race lasting several hours in which all the riders start together and rely on team tactics, instead of racing alone at one-minute intervals on a short course, as they did in the prologue time trial. The thickest crowds usually congregate on the hills, where the peloton stretches out and moves at a slower pace, giving the fans a better chance of spotting individual riders. At times, the density of spectators is so great that they spill across the road from curb to curb. It's up to the motorcycle-mounted gendarmes who precede the race—their blue lights flashing and sirens wailing—to clear a path between them so the riders can come through. But the people surge forward again and only pull back in the seconds before the racers shoot past. "Sometimes we ride over people's toes, they're so close," says Christian Vande Velde, a Chicago-born rider on the Liberty team.

Vande Velde is at the Tour to help his team leader, Roberto Heras, not to seek personal glory. "I don't know where I placed in the prologue," he tells me before today's start. "I didn't even see the results. But I did see four people from Boulder," his adopted hometown in Colorado. "There are *so* many Americans here."

An abundance of stars-and-stripes flags do seem to be waving along the course, although many of them are in the hands of Belgian and French spectators. "We're all Armstrong fans," a middle-aged Belgian explains.

Partway up the Côte de Borlon, the fourth of five climbs on this 126-mile road stage, I spot a U.S. flag that belongs to an American couple, James and Lisa Alexander. They are far from their own backyard in Warrenton, Virginia, but on this Fourth of July by the roadside in the Belgian Ardennes, they are having a grand time, ready to cheer on Armstrong, Hamilton, and the other five Americans racing this Tour. Their only concern is the weather. Holding a small umbrella against a fine drizzle, Lisa asks, "Do you think it's going to rain all day?" I tell her that's not in the forecast, but this *is* Belgium, where it rains more often than not. And when we top the Borlon hill between a small wheatfield and a meadow of lounging white cows, we can see the sky darkening over the distant, rolling woodlands.

When the race reaches this climb, halfway though the stage, five men have stolen clear of the pack and have racked up a three-minute lead. It's a cosmopolitan group, composed of riders from Austria, Estonia, France, Germany, and Italy, and representing five different teams. None of Armstrong's teammates are among them, mainly because their strategy for the day is not to win the stage, but rather to protect Armstrong from the wind and allow him to conserve his energy for more challenging stages ahead, while always keeping an eye on their leader's major rivals.

"Postal has won the Tour the last five years, but it hasn't had one rider other than Lance win a stage," Hamilton points out. "That's incredible! Postal puts all its eggs in one basket.

Hamilton's right: While most teams urge their riders to get into breaks in an attempt to win the stage—a coveted prize that brings a rider and his team considerable kudos—Postal always keeps its eyes on the *big* prize. And on this opening road stage, Armstrong wants as many teammates around him as possible, not only to carry out daily tasks like fetching water bottles from the team car, but also to ride in front of and behind him to lessen the chances of his crashing. Crashing is a very real danger today because of the frequent, twisting descents and roads made greasy by the light rain.

Postal's policy of "everything for Lance" has paid off handsomely. And while Armstrong's teammates have to suppress their own ambitions, they are paid handsomely as well. Like all Tour winners, Armstrong gives the half-million-dollar first prize to his teammates and staff to divide among them, for his potential earnings as the winner are far greater, especially from commercial endorsements like the $12 million multi-year contract he has with Subaru. This year, he is hoping that his team's strategy will again be successful. Winning a record-breaking sixth Tour would be to everyone's advantage and his teammates accept their roles with equanimity.

———————

There is a mythic aura around winning six Tours de France. It's equivalent to Jack Nicklaus attempting to snag a seventh Masters, Martina Navratilova trying to win her tenth Wimbledon, the Red Sox breaking the curse of the Bambino—feats that have never been accomplished.

Of the four cyclists who failed in their attempts to win the Tour de France a sixth time, not one gave the event the singular focus that Armstrong gives it. The Texan is careful to race only enough events to be well prepared, yet not too tired, for the Tour. In contrast, legendary Belgian Eddy Merckx, the man who came closest to winning six Tours, would enter three times as many races as Armstrong competes in each year.

"I never based my season around the Tour de France," says Merckx, who, in the sixties and seventies, won more bike races than anyone in history, and might have won the Tour six or seven times if he had contested it more often. "In 1968, I did the Tour of Italy instead, because I raced for an Italian team. I believe if I'd done the Tour I could have won it. Again in '73, if I'd competed, I'd have won," he says, with the natural confidence that comes from being acknowledged by everyone—including Armstrong—as the greatest bike racer to ever live.

As for the five Tours de France Merckx *did* enter between 1969 and 1974, he won them all. He was favored to win again in 1975, and after the first two weeks of that Tour he was already leading the race by a minute and a half over his major challenger, Frenchman Bernard Thévenet. Then, on the fourteenth stage, which finished on top of the Puy-de-Dôme mountain in central France, a crazed man lurched forward from the crowd lining the steep, narrow road. "I was riding flat out 300 meters from the finish line when I got punched in the kidneys by this spectator," Merckx tells me. "To take a punch like that in full effort was hard to take."

Merckx, now 59, is chatting after taking part in a short charity bike race in Liège, a couple of months before the start of the 2004 Tour. Sweat glistens on his broad, ruddy face, and he gratefully sips from a bottle of Stella Artois as we sit down on the dark stone steps of Liège's historic Princes-Évêques palace. Merckx is a big man, just over six feet. He has put on weight in recent years, and the fibers of his spandex cycling team uniform are stretched to their limit.

Despite that kidney punch back in 1975, Merckx lost only half a minute to Thévenet on the Puy-de-Dôme; but that wasn't the end of his setbacks. "The doctor gave me some medicine for the blow, some enzymes, for reducing the swelling in my kidneys. And I think it was that . . . ," he says. "I think it was the medicine that caused my problems on the next stage."

That next stage was a near-eight-hour day of climbing through the southern Alps. Thévenet attacked repeatedly in an attempt to wrest the leader's yellow jersey from Merckx. But the five-time champion defended every time. Then, over the top of the stage's penultimate climb, Merckx surprised his French rival with an attack of his own. The Belgian was an adept bike handler and he hurtled down the twisting mountain road. "I've never descended as fast as I did there," says Merckx with a glint in his eyes, still remembering the thrill of his solo escape almost thirty years ago. Such was his speed that a team car trying to keep up skidded off the road, and only the trees stopped the vehicle from crashing into a deep ravine.

Merckx's bravado earned him a minute's advantage on reaching the start of the day's final climb to a summit finish at Pra-Loup. It looked as though he was on his way to clinching a sixth Tour victory. Then, partway up the hill, Merckx suddenly slowed. He was running on empty, as if he had the symptoms of what cyclists call "the bonk" or hunger knock, and the French call *fringale*.

"No, it wasn't the *fringale*," Merckx claims. "I say it was purely caused by the blood-thinning medicine the doctor gave me." Thévenet came from a minute back to finish almost two minutes ahead of Merckx and strip him of the yellow jersey. And two days later, Merckx recalls, "I was knocked off my bike by [the Danish rider] Ole Ritter and I suffered a double fracture of the jaw. I should have stopped." Instead, the still-optimistic Merckx, whose injury prevented him from eating solid foods, pushed on. He heroically finished the Tour in second place to Thévenet, and missed taking a record sixth Tour by a scant 2 minutes, 47 seconds.

———————

It's possible that Armstrong, in his quest for a sixth win, could experience the same kinds of problems that Merckx did in 1975. The spectators still stand only inches away from the racers on the climbs, and crashes are an ever-present danger—as Armstrong discovered for himself in the 2003 race. When he cut a corner racing up the mountain road to Luz-Ardiden in the Pyrenees, Armstrong was jerked from his bike by the strap of a fan's plastic shoulder bag that snagged his brake levers. Spanish rider Iban Mayo couldn't avoid crashing into the American, while Armstrong's biggest rival, Jan Ullrich, swerved around them. Armstrong picked himself up and then almost fell again when his chain jumped between the rear sprockets. While Armstrong was desperately chasing back, his former teammate-turned-rival Tyler Hamilton displayed great sportsmanship by racing up to the head of the small group of leaders to tell Ullrich and the others to slow down, and not to race until Armstrong was back with them. But as soon as the injured Armstrong rejoined the group, he followed a new attack by Mayo, and the American then counterattacked, and not even Ullrich or Mayo could follow.

Armstrong's personal coach, Chris Carmichael, says that the Texan's dramatic crash and almost demented rage to come back and win the stage on Luz-Ardiden was typical Armstrong. "He realizes you've just got to go for it, take big risks. You've got to seize it, and that's the way Lance is wired."

Almost everyone I speak with offers some idea about how Lance is wired, what drives him to win. Andy Horning, a psychotherapist and bike enthusiast in Boulder, Colorado, believes that Armstrong is fueled by anger. Horning was fascinated by Armstrong's first autobiographical book, *It's Not About the Bike*. "So much anger comes through in that book, throughout his life," Horning says, referring to Armstrong's account of his troubled childhood and adolescence. "If Lance ever had therapy, he'd lose that anger—and he'd never win another Tour de France!"

Writer Willie Wilson believes that Armstrong's destiny was written in his name. "The name Lance conjures up images of chivalry, the Round Table and shining armor," Wilson says. "Combine that with the name Armstrong and you have the perfect moniker for an American Knight." After all, Wilson reminds us, America once defined heroic in the fictional hero Jack Armstrong, The All American Boy, in a radio series that ran from 1933 to 1951. "To have overcome cancer and the agony of chemotherapy and then gone on to achieve the pinnacle of his sport is inspirational beyond the hard work it has taken," Wilson concludes. "It fulfills the strong and heroic destiny that the name Lance Armstrong evokes."

Tyler Hamilton sees his friend and rival as someone who is extraordinarily confident, determined, and driven by a fighting spirit. "This guy, man, he *always* thinks he can win. I think before Luz-Ardiden 90 percent of the people thought it looked like Ullrich was going to win the Tour. You could feel the Tour slipping away from him. . . ."

After his dramatic Tour-clinching performance at Luz-Ardiden, Armstrong said, "Sometimes you have to survive in order to win." And he knows plenty about survival. That's why Merckx was confident that his friend had everything it takes to win a sixth time.

"This is not Lance's first Tour de France," Merckx said, a few weeks before the 2004 Tour. "It's his *tenth* Tour, so he has the experience, he has the knowledge, he has nothing more to learn, huh? Everything being equal, no sickness or crashes, there's nobody who can beat Armstrong at the Tour de France."

Merckx has been one of Armstrong's best friends since they met at the Barcelona Olympics in 1992. When the Texan is in Brussels, they go riding together and usually end up at Merckx's favorite Italian restaurant. And although they're from different generations, there's a mutual respect between them. Armstrong sees Merckx as "the greatest cyclist in the world," along with being "a normal, humble good guy who I love being around." Merckx, who remained close to Armstrong when he was fighting cancer, says admiringly, "He suffered a lot, he worked hard to return, and he became an even stronger rider."

After Armstrong underwent heavy chemotherapy and surgery to remove lesions on his brain, Merckx saw the changes firsthand when he went to Austin in early 1997 and competed with Armstrong in an exhibition bike race. "He hadn't changed much, except he had no hair and had scars on his head," Merckx recalls. "But later he changed. He became thinner, he was different morphologically, and above all, he lost a lot of weight. I think he was completely transformed as a cyclist."

When Armstrong returned to full-time training in early 1998, he spent several weeks in Santa Barbara, California, where his daily massage was given him by Shelley Verses, a highly experienced therapist who worked with several European professional cycling teams. Verses recalls, "One day he told me, 'I'm like thinner than I've ever been. I'm so strong I don't even know what my body can do.' It was like he was in a new body, like a new car. You don't know what the turbos can do yet."

The mostly upper-body weight that Armstrong shed made it easier for him to climb the high mountain passes; but he was always an excellent performer on shorter climbs. In fact, it was in the Ardennes—where this first road stage of the 2004 Tour is taking place—that Armstrong took one of the most significant victories of his early professional cycling career in 1996. It came in a race named the Flèche Wallonne, the Walloon Arrow, which is one of the sport's legendary single-day classics. That race finishes atop a mile-long climb at Huy that has pitches as steep as 18 percent—which means that for every 100 feet of forward progress, the hill rises 18 feet, a height equivalent to almost two stories!

If today's stage had been routed over that climb, known as the Mur de Huy ("Wall of Huy"), it would have probably been given a degree-of-difficulty rating of Category 3, perhaps Category 2. The organizers rate the easiest climbs as Category 4, and the hardest as Category 1. A handful of exceptionally long and steep mountain passes, like Luz-Ardiden, are called *Hors-Cat*, "above-category" climbs. The only ones that merit that highest rating this year are a summit finish in the Pyrenees and two climbs in the Alps. The first few riders across each of the rated climbs are awarded points on a sliding scale in a competition designed to reward the race's best climber. The man gleaning the highest total over the twenty-three days is called the King of the Mountains and gets to wear a red-and-white polka-dot jersey (*maillot-à-pois* in French), which carries its own cash prize and special prestige.

The Borlon climb, where Lisa and Jason Alexander are watching today's race, has a Category 3 rating, while the four other climbs on this stage are rated Category 4. Combining all five climbs with the other hills on the course yields 4,400 vertical feet of climbing for the day, the highest daily total for the opening week. Despite that, the Ardennes climbs are not long enough for the Tour's renowned climbers to gain a true advantage. In fact, the first man over the Borlon and two of the Category 4 climbs—earning enough points to be this Tour's first leader of the polka-dot jersey competition—is Paolo Bettini, an Italian rider with the Quick Step team who has a good record in terrain like today's, but struggles in the high mountains.

Armstrong, who is never far from the front on the climbs, always protected by a couple of teammates, is happy to let Cancellara and his Fassa Bortolo teammates control today's race. They've set a steady, sometimes rapid pace that restricted the five-man break to a maximum lead of 4:25. The lead is down to two minutes on the Borlon hill; and the break is caught on the flatter roads beyond Huy.

———————

Armstrong knew before the start of the racing season that this was going to be a difficult year for him, although perhaps not as rough as the year before. It was in 2003 that Armstrong and his wife separated in February, tried to reconcile in July, and later divorced. And at the Tour de France that year, he experienced a series of setbacks that almost cost him the race. Armstrong went into the event with gastroenteritis picked up from his son, soon developed tendinitis in his hip caused by new shoes and cleats, and had a painful fall in a high-speed pileup on the first stage. He faltered on the climb to L'Alpe d'Huez, after discovering that a maladjusted brake pad had been rubbing his rear wheel rim for a few hours; and the next day he faced a moment of panic when rival Joseba Beloki suffered a terrifying crash right in front of him. Then, chronic dehydration contributed to his losing 97 seconds to Jan Ullrich in a vital time trial; and finally, there was the frightening tumble at Luz-Ardiden, just as he was making the attack he needed to win the race. Armstrong still won the Tour, but by the smallest margin in his five victories—just 61 seconds over Ullrich.

When I spoke with Armstrong at his home in Austin the winter before this Tour, he tried to put his 2003 troubles into perspective.

"I started out with little flare-ups last year on the Tour, but I've never broken bones, never had major injuries, somewhat been fine. . . . Just the personal and marriage stuff was, I suspect, harder on me last year than it's gonna be this year. A *lot* harder. Last year was tough," he concedes, "*very* tough."

I ask him how he copes with a life that his coach Carmichael says "would drive me nuts." "I'm able to focus," Armstrong replies, "'cause I know how important my job is. I know how much I want to win. I think that inherently I'm just an optimistic person. I know that regardless of how tough times can be, or how miserable a day or a period can be, my life is just not that bad. . . . And so I try to remember those things. But a family, marriage breakup is a tough thing to live with, ride with, and sleep with. I could *not* handle that very well. And it showed. But once you find clarity there, and find honesty and truth, and some form of happiness, then . . . it's a lot better. A *lot* better. And I have that now. It's unfortunate; it's not been the most pleasant experience that I've ever been through. Now it's finished though . . . I'm glad it's over."

Armstrong says that the toughest aspect of the divorce was helping his three young children, particularly Luke, the oldest, understand what was happening. "We had some trouble earlier in the year, because we were still spending a lot of time together as a family, and that was hard on him, because it was confusing," Armstrong explains. "So we stopped doing that. But we wanted to, because our idea was to stay close and stay friends and do certain things together."

He adds that his mother comes down from Dallas and helps out when he has the children, who shuttle between their parents' houses on adjacent streets. "Luke talks about, this is Dad's house, that's Mom's house," says Armstrong, starting to smile with pride. "He's an incredibly bright little boy; it's unbelievable how sharp he is.

"I *will* say this, that the whole divorce thing is not what I ever envisioned. But I'm closer to my kids now than I've ever been. When they're here, they're my responsibility. So many times as a father, you rely so heavily on your wife, their mother. And now . . . I'm a single dad. It's great. We are so close, this little foursome. I mean, I like to be around them. I love them so."

As we talk there are constant interruptions. "They're coming in fast and furious now," Armstrong says, when his cell phone and BlackBerry buzz at the same time. His publicist Mark Higgins drops by with a pile of books and posters that need his autograph. And Armstrong's ginger cat, Chemo, needs something too. When he sidles up to him and meows, his keeper explains, "Because I've been gone, he's like, 'C'mon, just be kind.'"

The champion becomes most animated when his blonde-haired twin daughters, Grace and Isabelle, wearing identical pink, sequined T-shirts, come down the stairs after their nap. He shouts to the one carrying a doll: "Hey! Hey! Come here, Little Goddess! That's what the T-shirt says. Come here, Grace. Is that your baby?"

I ask Armstrong if he's making extra efforts because when he was growing up he didn't really have a dad. He denies this connection and says about his children, "I could never envision not being in their life. I like to be around them."

Armstrong has no memories of *his* father, Edward Gunderson, a route manager for the *Dallas Morning News* newspaper, who left his teenage bride before their son was two years old. Lance later adopted the name of his stepfather, Terry Armstrong. But he had a strained relationship with this man who would discipline him with a wooden paddle. When he was 14, Lance discovered that his adopted father was having an affair. He kept the shocking news to himself, but his mother soon found out too, and divorced for a second time.

This intensified the already close mother–son relationship, and it was Linda who encouraged the teenage Armstrong to pursue athletics, initially swimming, and then the swim–bike–run sport of triathlon. After finding national fame as a triathlete at age 16, Armstrong turned to cycling full-time. Carmichael, who was then the U.S. national cycling team coach, remembers inviting the 18-year-old Armstrong to a training camp with the senior team riders. He wanted to see how the young prodigy could cope in a four-man team time trial, an event in which the team of riders works together by taking turns pacing each other to go as fast as possible, and the team with the fastest time wins.

"I wanted him to do some workouts with those guys, and Lance was like, 'What if they can't hold my wheel?' I'm like, 'What do you mean?'" Carmichael remembers with incredulity. "He's like, 'Well, fuck it, what if they can't hold my wheel?' And I'm looking at him to see if he's joking, but he was dead serious, you know. And he was right. They *couldn't* hold his wheel."

Once Carmichael realized Armstrong's immense physical talents, he told him he could be a world champion if he trained right and learned how to strategize. To find better training terrain, Armstrong moved out of his mom's home in the Dallas suburbs to Austin, where he could ride in the Texas hill country. It was there that he hooked up with JT Neal, a sports coach, masseur, and genuine good guy who helped out young athletes. Besides giving Armstrong a solid base for his training, Neal rented him a $300-a-month apartment near the University of Texas campus, which meant that the 19-year-old Armstrong could live comfortably on the $18,000 stipend he was making as an amateur cyclist on a team sponsored by Subaru and Montgomery Securities. Even so, it was a difficult time in Armstrong's life: new home, new town, and the need to make new friends.

I ask Armstrong if Neal, a slim, lively, always smiling man, then in his fifties, was like a father figure. "Well, JT did everything for me so, yes, he was," Armstrong agrees. "He was great at trying to remove some of the junk you get bogged down with at that age, and just helped me manage my life. He was a good man. Interesting character. Yeah, yeah, a little eccentric, but that's what made him great. He could tell stories for hours. . . ."

Neal, as his personal masseur and all-around helper, went on the road with Armstrong to races, even after he turned professional for the Motorola team in late 1992. The fatherly advice he offered and the time Armstrong spent with Neal's family played a big role in developing the future champion's character, particularly his softer side. In his autobiography one of the dedications is to "JT Neal, the toughest patient cancer has seen."

"He was sick for a long time, for years," says Armstrong. "He died October second '02. My mom told me; she was very close to him and his wife. I remember it was hot outside when we went to the funeral."

In the decade since he first met Neal, Armstrong had won the world championship that Carmichael predicted, battled and beaten cancer, married and had three children, won four Tours de France, started a successful cancer-fighting foundation, been elected *Sports Illustrated*'s Sportsman of the Year, become known the world over, and was about to go through a divorce. He and Kristin got back together just before the 2003 Tour, and she and the children were in Paris to help him celebrate his fifth victory. But the marriage officially ended that September.

Armstrong has always dated beautiful women, and once single again it was inevitable that he'd soon be dating another. Perhaps, given his superstar life that's saturated with special events and TV appearances on every talk show from Jay Leno to David Letterman to Paula Zahn, it was also inevitable that his new woman would be as famous as he is. In October 2003 he met rock singer Sheryl Crow at a benefit in Las Vegas. "We just kind of fell in together like we'd known each other for a long time," Crow recalls in her Southern twang. "We have a lot of similar characteristics and speak the same language. We're both really driven. We both have a wacky sense of humor. We both take what we do seriously, and we're both *extremely* competitive and ambitious."

Their relationship grew quickly and was soon public knowledge. It helped that Armstrong's mom and Crow hit it off, while Armstrong was well received by Crow's parents, Wendell and Bernice, when he and Sheryl spent Thanksgiving Day with them in rural Kennett, Missouri. "They love him," Crow tells me. "It's amazing how similar he is to my family. Grew up in a really small town, a kind of rural town. We're all Southerners and both have a tight-knit family. So everybody's happy."

Back in Austin that December, Armstrong enthusiastically describes his just-completed trip with Crow to Europe. He always had ambitions to be a rock musician, and he vividly remembers a Rolling Stones concert he went to in San Antonio in December 1994, where he met the band backstage. "I was talking with Sheryl about that in London because she's good friends with all those guys," says Armstrong, who adds that the Stones' Bill Wyman and Ron Wood came to play with Crow at her London gig. "Woody's hilarious," he chuckles. "Charming old guy. He's hilarious. He's like . . . ," Armstrong changes to a slow, hushed cockney accent. ". . . 'Oy, me, what you do-oo must take such doo-ration.' And I said, 'Ronny, do you mean endurance?' 'Yeah, and that too.'"

As we talk, Armstrong reaches down to stroke Chemo, who's softly mewing for attention. The five-time Tour winner is relaxed and comfortable in his Austin home, happy to have his mother and children around him. It's a cocoon that he knows will be there whenever he returns from his frequent travels. He feels a similar ease when he's surrounded by his teammates, riding in their big silver-and-blue bus that transports them between hotels and race starts and finishes. Those twin comfort zones, together with his growing relationship with Crow, give Armstrong the support he needs to deal with the exhausting and multiple demands on his time.

Carmichael has an interesting take on how Armstrong manages everything demanded of him. "A lot of it is, he *likes* it," Carmichael says. "He likes the stimulus, people all over him. I *have* seen him crack, but he's amazingly good at compartmentalizing things. This is the way *I* have to deal with him. He'll sit down and go, 'Okay, call me at this time.' And if I don't call, or I'm late, my phone's ringing, like 'Come on, what's going on?' I think he's the same with the media: You've got twenty minutes. You don't have twenty-one minutes, or nineteen. And at twenty minutes the timer goes off and he's done. But that time he spends is quality time. He's not distracted. That's one thing he's really good at, and he's always been that way."

The second half of the stage from Liège turns out to be harder than expected. The rain does come, there are frequent crashes, and a strong head wind blows in to make life even more unpleasant. Despite the awful conditions, the speed never drops, averaging 27 miles per hour for the day. Two riders even manage to break clear with 30 miles remaining to the Charleroi finish. They are CSC's rugged Dane, Jakob Piil, and Rabobank's Marc Wauters, an equally resilient Belgian. Both have won Tour stages in the past at the end of long breakaways, and they seem perfectly matched as they race hard through the rain on roads that dip and climb through wooded hills and grimy red-brick towns into the industrial belt east of Charleroi.

Piil and Wauters race to a lead of almost two minutes, with 15 miles still to go. But then the Fassa Bortolo team, which has the double goal of defending Cancellara's yellow jersey and setting up its renowned Italian sprinter, Alessandro Petacchi, for the stage win, steps up the pace of the peloton. Two other teams with hot finishers, Lotto-Domo (for the Australian Robbie McEwen) and Quick Step (for the Belgian Tom Boonen), join in the pursuit.

As the speed increases and the gap to the breakaways contracts, the risk of accidents multiplies. No one wants to be left behind by the pack, while the sprinters are moving forward, to be well positioned should Piil and Wauters be caught. And there *is* another crash, this one about two miles from the finish, when a dozen riders tumble— including high-profile Italian sprinter Mario Cipollini, who's riding the Tour for the last time, and the ever-dangerous Aussie Stuart O'Grady. They still manage to catch the peloton, but they are too late to contest the sprint.

Piil and Wauters, desperately close to holding off the pack, are overtaken just inside one mile to go. It's time for the sprinters, who are dismayed to see that the finishing straight is not as straight-forward as it looked on the map. Set along a suburban street lined with corner stores, Greek tavernas, pizza shops, and gas stations, it narrows between tall row houses toward the end, and it is progressively uphill. Four Fassa Bortolo riders head the charge, hoping their man Petacchi has the juice to win. But he doesn't look comfortable.

"I think Fassa Bortolo was surprised," says the Estonian sprinter Jaan Kirsipuu, who was just behind Petacchi at this point. "It was a very difficult finish, uphill and a strong wind." A Quick Step rider then leads out the sprint, but he turns to find that his sprinter, Boonen, is not there—his chain has derailed.

With the three favorites for the win now out of the running, the big Norwegian champion Thor Hushovd comes to the front. He looks strong, but is challenged by AG2R team veteran Kirsipuu. And coming with a late charge, weaving his way between riders who have slowed, is the adroit McEwen. His arms stretched out and his body low, the fearless Aussie gives his bike a final throw forward and beats

Hushovd to the line. But Kirsipuu is just out of his reach. It's an unexpected stage win for the bulldog 34-year-old from Tartu, Estonia, who's not the fastest of sprinters, yet may be the most tenacious. Although he's never finished the Tour, this is the fourth time he's won a Tour stage.

————————

Armstrong crosses the line in 48th place, away from the dangers of the sprint. But as at any bike race that finishes in a mass sprint—where virtually the whole field arrives together—he and the other riders in the pack are clocked at the same time as the first man across the line. So Armstrong, Ullrich (32nd place), Mayo (34th), Basso (49th), and Hamilton (52nd), along with the other 173 finishers in the peloton, are all given stage winner Kirsipuu's time of 4 hours, 40 minutes, 29 seconds.

This means that on overall time, the gaps between riders remain the same as they were yesterday—except for those who earn time bonuses at the day's three intermediate sprints and at the finish. Race leader Cancellara took second place at two of the sprints, each worth four seconds. For this, he has eight seconds deducted from his overall time, meaning he is now leading Armstrong by 10 seconds. The Norwegian Hushovd of the French team Crédit Agricole, who was fifth in the prologue, 10 seconds behind Cancellara, has also picked up some sprint bonuses: six seconds at an intermediate one, and eight seconds for his third place at the finish. With these 14 seconds deducted from his time, he moves up into second place overall, only four seconds behind the leader.

Armstrong rarely concerns himself with time bonuses. His main goals today were to stay sheltered by his teammates and avoid the crashes, and he succeeded on both counts. After crossing the line, he briefly stops for his soigneur (his personal helper and masseur) to wipe his face and wrap a dark blue towel around his neck, before he swiftly pedals off, weaving past gawking fans, on his way to the team bus that's parked down a side street. "I was very nervous today, with the rain, wind, and crashes," Armstrong says. "It was typical Belgian racing." His first long day in the saddle is over. He'll clean off in the bus, and put on dry clothes before reaching the team's hotel 20 miles away.

Ullrich tells the journalists at his team bus, "This was a shitty day, really stressful with all that rain." He then jokes, "The only problem is that they'll have to wash my jersey, it's in a filthy state!"

The stains on Hamilton's uniform are not just from the mud splashed up by the peloton's wheels. I know from listening to Radio Tour, the in-race information service that reports every incident as it happens, that Hamilton was delayed about 55 miles from the finish and needed four teammates to pace him back to the peloton. After he crosses the finish line, I run alongside him and see blood on his left knee. "I got tied up with a U.S. Postal guy," he tells me. "We went down pretty easy." On reaching his bus, he adds, "It was a better stage 1 for me than last year." That was the stage where he fell in a massive, bloody pileup and broke his collarbone. Better indeed.

STAGE RESULT: 1. Jaan Kirsipuu (Estonia); 2. Robbie McEwen (Australia); 3. Thor Hushovd (Norway); 4. Danilo Hondo (Germany); 5. Jean-Patrick Nazon (France), all same time.

OVERALL STANDINGS: 1. Cancellara; 2. Hushovd, at 0:04; 3. Armstrong, at 0:10; 4. Jens Voigt (Germany), at 0:15; 5. Gutierrez, at 0:16; 12. Leipheimer, at 0:23; 13. Sastre, same time; 16. Ullrich, at 0:25; 18. Hamilton, at 0:26; 29. Mayo, at 0:29; 69. Basso, at 0:37.

Revitalized

JULY 5: *This looping 122.5-mile course starts in Charleroi and has a 30-mile section through French territory before returning to Belgium on rolling terrain. The last five miles follow the Meuse River with a finish in downtown Namur. Sprinters are favored to win the stage, which should have little influence on the overall standings.*

His legs appear first, his torso still hidden, as he walks crablike down the steep steps of his T-Mobile team's bus. You can see every sinew of his calf muscles and bulky quadriceps. When his face appears, the spectators lining the barriers across the road start to applaud. *"C'est lui. C'est Ool-risch!"* They've recognized Jan Ullrich, who has an anxious look on his face. The start of the Charleroi–Namur stage is only ten minutes away.

The 30-year-old German superstar now goes through a pre-race ritual. He places the water bottle he carried with him from the bus into his bike's bottle cage, and hands a warm-up top to an assistant. He removes his sunglasses, puts on the helmet handed to him by his helper, and then puts his glasses back on. Ullrich poses for a photo with a small boy, and then personally looks over his bike. First, he checks the front brake, to make sure the pads are evenly spaced. Next, he studies the rear wheel, flicks open the hub's quick-release lever, tightens the skewer, and locks it back in place. He spins the rear wheel to ensure that the rear brake pads are not touching the rim.

With his bike ready, Ullrich mounts it, signs two autographs, and then rides slowly away, heading toward the sign-in area near the start line. He takes a shortcut between the team buses, bounces his bike up and over a couple of curbs, and rides along behind the spectators before cutting through a gap in the barriers. The race announcer spots him, and as Ullrich bounds up the steps of the podium, his introduction is made over the loudspeakers: "Arriving right now is the winner of the Tour in 1997, five times second in six participations, the Olympic champion . . . *Yan Ull-rique!*"

As the sun comes out in Charleroi, Ullrich turns to acknowledge the applause, gives a brief smile, and remounts his bike. Before he rides off, press photographers take some shots, and television reporters ask a couple of questions. He signs more autographs for more young boys, and on hearing some German fans call his name—"Ulle, Ulle"—he rides across the street to shake their hands and sign some photos.

"I've remained normal, accessible to the public," Ullrich says. He believes that's one reason the German public chose him as their Sportsman of the Year in 2003, ahead of Formula 1 world champion Michael Schumacher. Ullrich's accessibility and his gripping one-on-one Tour battles with Lance Armstrong have made him a popular figure, not only at home, but throughout the world. His fans rave about his incredible strength in the mountains, and his raw power and dynamic style that make him such a threat in the time trials. And despite placing only fifteenth in this year's prologue—perhaps due to a slight cold—people are saying, "Jan is looking great this year; he has the beating of Lance."

At six feet and 160 pounds, the barrel-chested Ullrich is easily the biggest of the Tour's main contenders. He's a good-looking man, with a wide freckled face, strong jaw line, soft brown eyes, and wavy, reddish brown hair. On the "big" days at the Tour, he has the look of a warrior: grim, unshaven, and introverted. But when he smiles, his whole face broadens and he has the air of a chubby choirboy.

Today's stage is not a "big day," although with rain still in the air and a roundabout route that traverses a few large towns before heading into pastoral countryside and over some low, rolling hills, the favorites will again have to be wary of crashes. Ullrich is aware of the dangers but he's at ease here in Charleroi, a city not that different from his hometown of Rostock in northeast Germany, where his mother, Marianne Kaatz, still lives. Both cities date back to medieval times, have populations of 200,000, and are showing signs of renewal from urban blight—after becoming notorious in the recent past for strikes, riots, and crime, following the loss of their former industrial prowess. That's a little like Ullrich himself, who came back revitalized after a series of career-threatening setbacks in 2002.

His problems began that January, when a recurrent knee tendon injury flared up and stopped him from racing. Surgery was seen as the only answer. "The hardest thing was that after the first operation, there was not much light at the end of the tunnel," Ullrich tells me in the spring of 2004. "I started riding again, had some problems, started again, got into some more problems, and it was only after a second operation that I could see I'd be able to race again."

During his darkest period, in May 2002, when the knee pain just wouldn't go away, Ullrich was feeling desperate. Rather than talking things over with his companion of many years, Gaby Weis, he looked for another means of release. As if he were unbottling years of unspent—not misspent—youth, he turned to alcohol. After one night of drinking with some male friends at a wine bar in Freiburg, Ullrich backed his Porsche into a bicycle rack. He was arrested for drunk driving, his driver's license was suspended, and he was given a hefty fine. Talking about the fallout from the incident in his autobiography, *Ganz Oder Gar Nicht* ("All or Nothing"), Ullrich wrote, "I was afraid that Gaby did not want me any more. But she just said I had to change a few things, and put an end to the alcohol. She sneered, 'You are a professional sportsman, Jan! Aren't you embarrassed?'"

Embarrassed or not, it was hard for Ullrich to change. A few weeks later, still not knowing how the second knee operation would turn out and afraid his racing days were over, the German was on the roam again, at a discotheque where he took the drug ecstasy. The following day, by chance, an anti-doping medical inspector turned up at the rehab center in Bavaria where he was having physiotherapy. Ullrich knew that this out-of-competition drug test would show up positive, because ecstasy contains amphetamine, a banned drug in Olympic sports. After the inspector left, the then 28-year-old Ullrich fled to a farmyard and sat down and cried uncontrollably, terrified that his girlfriend would definitely leave him this time. But, like the forlorn heroine of a country western song, Gaby stood by her man.

Ullrich's cycling career was still in jeopardy, though, because he had no idea whether his knee could again sustain the strain of riding thousands of miles a month. "It wouldn't have been good to end my career in such a way," he reflects, leaning forward as he talks. "So I always told myself if my knee works and accepts the hard work again, then I'll continue."

The knee *did* heal and he was able to resume riding that fall. But because of the doping offense, Ullrich was given a six-month suspension by the International Cycling Union, and, far more significantly, he lost his million-dollar-a-year leadership spot on the mighty

Deutsche Telekom team. Ullrich felt insulted by the team's offer that he come back at half his old salary and he was determined not to return. "They too often took me for a child," he says, "so I wanted to prove that I can stand on my own two feet. I didn't have any need for them anymore."

With the help of his longtime agent Wolfgang Strohband and his Belgian confidant Rudy Pevenage, who was Telekom's top trainer, Ullrich joined another German squad, Team Coast. It was a bitter separation, particularly for Pevenage, who had been best friends with Telekom's team manager Walter Godefroot, a fellow Belgian. Things looked better for Ullrich, though, especially after Gaby told him that she was pregnant with their first child. He started training with renewed vigor, and vowed to be in good shape when he returned to racing in April 2003.

But Ullrich's troubles weren't over quite yet. Just after he returned to racing, his new sponsor, Coast, went bankrupt, and Strohband and Pevenage had to scramble to find another. They made a temporary deal with the Italian bicycle manufacturer Bianchi, which enabled Ullrich to compete at the 2003 Tour de France. Finally, eighteen months of nerve-racking experiences were behind him. He was healthy, riding well, and had just moved into a beautiful new home with Gaby in the Swiss village of Scherzingen, overlooking Lake Constance. "I needed to get away from Germany where my house was on the tourist circuit," he says. The couple's happiness was enhanced when the pregnant Gaby agreed to be induced two weeks before her mid-July due date, so that Jan could be present and head to the Tour as the proud father of a daughter, Sarah.

That year's Tour started well for Ullrich: He took fourth place in the prologue time trial, five seconds faster than Armstrong. Then his makeshift Team Bianchi took an unexpectedly high third place in the fifth day's team time trial, just 43 seconds behind Armstrong's U.S. Postal squad. It looked like Jan would again be Lance's nemesis, as he was at the 2000 and 2001 Tours, when he was the only man able to challenge the American. But, unknown to the world until weeks later, Ullrich almost quit the race the next day, when he suffered severe stomach cramps and dizziness.

"I was lucky it was a flat stage," he tells me. "I had fever, I was ill, sick, and I was definitely at the limit of my abilities. But you train a whole year for it and prepare yourself a whole year, then you want to fight to continue in the race. And that's what made me go on."

The sickness was still affecting Ullrich when he tackled the infamous L'Alpe d'Huez mountain climb, and conceded a minute and a half to Armstrong. But he bounced back four days later to give Armstrong his biggest beating in an individual time trial in five years. Ullrich then finished ahead of the Texan on the first of three mountain stages in the Pyrenees to come within 15 seconds of taking the yellow jersey from him. Critics said he should have attacked Armstrong earlier than he did that day and he might have won the Tour, but Ullrich does not believe he made a mistake. "I did what I could, when I could," he says, looking directly into my eyes. Perhaps Ullrich would have raced differently if he had known what Armstrong's coach, Chris Carmichael knew. "That was the most dangerous moment," Carmichael told me. "Lance was totally vulnerable, you know. Ullrich should have won the Tour de France that day." Instead, Armstrong ultimately and dramatically reasserted himself as the strongest in that Tour; but the fact that Ullrich finished as the runner-up, only a minute back, made his comeback from his humiliating experiences of 2002 even more compelling.

The public loves to root for an underdog, and that's why Ullrich has become more popular than ever as he heads into this 2004 Tour. His adoring fans in Charleroi are typical of the thousands of spectators who gather at stage starts in city centers like this one. These crowds put enormous pressure on the riders—not only the Ullrichs and Armstrongs, but also the support riders, and especially the newcomers. Liberty team rider Christian Vande Velde describes the anxiety he and his teammates feel during the early stages of the Tour. "A stage like this can be terrifying, with the manager yelling in your ear the whole time, the speed, the cobblestones. Terrifying. Everyone's scared, and that really brings us together," says Vande Velde, recalling the last time the Tour came through Belgium, in 2001. "I remember walking to the start line in Antwerp with Victor Peña [his then Colombian teammate]. He didn't speak English very well at the time. He said to me, 'I'm scared-ed, so scared-ed.' I said, 'Me too, man.'"

The fears that Vande Velde, Ullrich, and the rest have today are engendered by potential crashes when the massive pack of 187 nervous, speeding riders, still feeling each other out, has to contend with narrow roads lined by dense crowds, along with tight corners, roundabouts, and bad road surfaces. Today's complicated course heads into France before circling back into Belgium for what should be a mass finish that favors the sprinters—muscular riders who have a lightning-fast kick in their legs. While they have no hope of winning the Tour itself—since they rarely have the endurance and climbing skills to match their speed—the sprinters have the sharp acceleration and immense leg strength (and usually several teammates to break the wind for them in the closing miles) to win individual stages, especially on flat courses like today's. Most of the field, especially overall contenders like Ullrich, Armstrong, and Hamilton, will be happy just to survive the day unscathed; but sprinters like Ullrich's veteran German teammate Erik Zabel will be taking insane risks on the run-in to Namur in the hope of ending the day with a win.

On a stage where there are no real difficulties and the riders on the sprinters' teams are still fresh and strong, it's difficult for a small group to escape. That doesn't mean that no one tries. And CSC's Piil is again one of six aggressors who break away after 20 miles of the looping 122-mile course. With him are three Frenchmen, a German, and an Irishman. It's not a move that is going to worry Armstrong or

Ullrich, as none of the riders is a potential threat. So once again they let Fassa Bortolo control the pace of the peloton, keeping the break-aways on a tight leash after they head into the ancient city of Mons, at 30 miles, with a five-minute lead.

———————

Like Armstrong, Ullrich had a difficult childhood. He reveals in his book that one of the few good memories he has of his father, Werner Ullrich, was when he taught him to ride a bike at age five. But his dad was an alcoholic who went on to strike Jan, his older brother, Stefan, and their mother. "I was six when my father flogged me," Ullrich re-calls. "And to this day I have a small scar that reminds me of him." Shortly after that flogging incident, his father left home and never re-turned.

With his father gone, Ullrich's life became more settled. "We moved from a little village near Rostock into the city, where we had a small apartment in a three-story house." Jan was the middle of three boys, two years younger than Stefan and five years older than Thomas. He looked to Stefan for guidance, while their mother worked hard as a state agricultural administrator to give her sons as happy a childhood as possible—at a time when poverty was the norm in East Germany. Becoming an athlete was the best passport to pros-perity for a child in the German Democratic Republic, so Ullrich be-came part of the country's elite sports program. He started at an age when Lance Armstrong was still tooling around Richardson, Texas, on what he calls an "ugly brown BMX bike with yellow wheels."

"I was nine years old when I first raced, and started to train," Ull-rich remembers. "I did my 20 to 30 kilometers a day under good con-ditions. My brother Stefan was more into track and field, but I did some races with him, so we trained a lot together."

Jan Ullrich won his first bike race at age 11, and two years later he became the East German national scholastic cycling champion in track racing (a cycling discipline that takes place on a banked oval, usually built of wood or concrete). That breakthrough win earned the 13-year-old Ullrich a place at SC Dynamo, a sports school in East Berlin. There, he met coach Peter Becker, a strict disciplinarian, and made friends with a skinny youth called Andreas Klöden, who was eighteen months younger than Ullrich and came from Mittweida, a city in southeast Germany. Under Becker's influence, both cyclists thrived, with Ullrich winning the national youth and junior championships on both road and track.

Two years after the Berlin Wall fell in 1989, Ullrich moved to the West, with Becker remaining as his personal coach. Wolfgang Strohband, now Ullrich's manager, dipped into his own pocket to set up Ullrich and nine other East German cyclists in Hamburg. Strohband was hoping that his riders would be good enough to compete at the 1996 Olympics.

Ullrich continued his progression as a top amateur cyclist and enjoyed a growing popularity in Germany. A startling moment he relates in his book occurred in 1993, when just before the start of a race in downtown Berlin, he heard someone call out his name—and it wasn't a fan. "My father was standing there," he says. "He scribbled his phone number on some notepaper and I put it in my racing jersey. It rained during the race, and when I looked later I only had a soaked piece of blank paper." He hadn't seen his father in thirteen years, and he hasn't seen him since.

That August, in Oslo, Norway, the 19-year-old Ullrich won the world road race championship for amateurs, one day before a precocious Lance Armstrong, 21, won the professional title. The American was already on a fast track to fame, and Ullrich was not far behind. Ullrich says his goal then was simply "to become a professional cyclist and win some races." Many urged the young German to turn pro right away—akin to basketball player LeBron James going to the

NBA straight out of high school—but in Oslo, Ullrich met Pevenage, who urged him to wait a year before turning pro. He did wait, and then signed for Pevenage's team, Deutsche Telekom.

The youthful Ullrich didn't meet Armstrong at the 1993 world championships; and their paths barely crossed again until they both started the 1996 Tour de France. That was the year Armstrong pulled out of the race ten days in (and less than three months before his cancer was diagnosed), while Ullrich, on his Tour debut, went on to ride strongly in the mountains, win an individual time trial, and finish second overall. The following year, while the Texan was home recovering from cancer, the German *won* the Tour de France—and he was fully expected to become the next cyclist to win it five times. Instead, the talented Ullrich made mistakes when leading the 1998 Tour, and came in second to the charismatic Italian climber Marco Pantani. Injuries from a pre-Tour crash kept Ullrich out of the race in 1999—the year that Armstrong won the first of his five consecutive titles. It seemed as if Ullrich had been offered his moment, never fully seized it, and now it was Armstrong's time.

Many see Ullrich as having more brute strength than Armstrong and view this Tour as the German's fourth and final chance to beat the American. So why has he lost to him three times? "Well," says Armstrong matter-of-factly, "because he's been the second best in the time trials . . . second best." Coach Carmichael has a different take. He believes that Armstrong has always beaten Ullrich because of his client's psychological strength. "They're both very gifted athletes," Carmichael confirms, "and it's hard to differentiate them from a straight physical side. They're both damn good. But where you really see the difference is mentally. I've never seen an athlete quite like Lance. He's not afraid of losing. He realizes you've just got to go for it, take big risks. Ullrich hasn't quite shown that same attitude."

The relative strengths of Armstrong and Ullrich won't come into play on this Charleroi–Namur stage, in which they're simply focused on staying in the shelter of their teammates, avoiding the wind, avoiding crashes, and perhaps avoiding each other. There's an element of drudgery on days like this, with no real incentive except to finish the stage safely and look forward to a quiet evening. When a sportswriter for the *Denver Post*, John Henderson, came to report the Tour de France for the first time in 2003, he asked, "Why do they have all these flat stages at the beginning? They're boring. Why not have all mountain stages? They're much more fun."

The choice is not as simple as that though. The Tour would be impossibly difficult if every day took place in the mountains—and the same riders would probably dominate stage after stage. A week of flat stages offers every rider a chance at a stage win; and mass sprints are among the most spectacular and exciting stage finales of the Tour. "Besides," I told Henderson, "these early stages give the favorites a chance to feel each other out, find their rhythm, get their bearings. Wait till the team time trial on Day 5. That's when you'll see the race begin to explode."

———————

It's January 2004 and Jan Ullrich, the prodigal son, has come back to Team Telekom, now named for its cell-phone division, T-Mobile. The lavishly funded German squad believes that he is the only man who can dislodge Armstrong from his perch. Ullrich is back on his former team in a position of strength, not humility. In the two years since he last suited up in the team's pink colors, he has become a much more mature and confident person, especially since becoming a father. "I want to be at home as much as possible with the little one," he says. Ullrich has returned to T-Mobile on *his* terms: a reported two-million-dollar salary, having his brother Stefan as one of the team's mechanics, and bringing two of his closest teammates with him from Bianchi. He also links up again with his old friend, Klöden, who has been with this squad for his entire professional career, starting in 1998.

The only downside to Ullrich's return is that team manager Godefroot won't allow Pevenage to be part of the team. Godefroot is still bitter that his once best friend followed Ullrich to a rival team in 2003—even if it was a short-lived arrangement. Ullrich retains Pevenage as his personal trainer, but he isn't being paid by T-Mobile and he's not allowed to travel in the team's vehicles.

T-Mobile's January media event on the Spanish island of Majorca is built around Ullrich. About two hundred journalists have been invited from all over Europe to attend the glitzy presentation, due to take place at lunchtime in a nightclub called Gal Dent. This trendy, upscale, and out-of-the-way spot is reached by a narrow country road that wanders past yellow-stone farmhouses and winter-bare vineyards. The club itself is underground, built into the cathedral-like caves of an abandoned limestone quarry.

For the team presentation, Gal Dent has been transformed into a pink palace, lit up by neon pink tubes and cubes. Bass-heavy techno music throbs through the caves as the journalists gather to witness the show. But sadly, no dancing girls prance on stage through the disco smoke, just a succession of athletic men wearing the dark-pink-and-white Lycra cycling uniforms of T-Mobile. The presentation has the feeling of a revival meeting, with the German emcee doing his version of a Southern Baptist minister as he tries to whip up enthusiasm from the audience. His delivery falls flat with the travel-weary reporters, who are already eyeing the hot buffet being prepared in the adjacent room. And when Ullrich finally appears through the artificial smoke, he's greeted with a smattering of applause rather than the wholehearted enthusiasm that the team's marketing people had envisioned.

A few hours later, both Ullrich and a small group of invited sportswriters are more comfortable when they sit down in the team's training center at the exclusive Robinson Club Cala Serena. The bar lounge overlooks a small, rocky inlet on Majorca's southeast coast, and wood logs crackle in a spacious fireplace. The "new" Ullrich is relaxed and chatty, unlike the pre-2002 Ullrich who rarely opened up to reporters. (At a press conference during his winning Tour of 1997, he deferred to his team captain, Bjarne Riis, rather than answer questions himself.) He's also looking pleasantly plump.

Along with his reputation for being naturally reserved, Ullrich is infamous for not sticking to an athlete's regimen in the winter. Those long, cold months generally find him indulging in chocolates and his favorite Black Forest gateaux, leading to excess pounds that he has a hard time shedding in the spring. A couple of extra pounds will dramatically decrease his power-to-weight ratio, and that could handicap him by a minute or so on a climb like L'Alpe d'Huez. So putting on weight—and not taking it off again—is Ullrich's most potentially self-destructive act. Riis, his former teammate and now the respected CSC team manager, offers a simple explanation: "He does too many kilometers in training, and his body gets tired. And when your body gets tired you want to eat. And he eats too much."

Some analysts fault Ullrich for not doing all it takes—and doing it soon enough—to win the Tour. Things had looked different this year when he began serious Tour preparations in November with a training camp in Italy, rather than waiting for January as he used to. He said at the time, "I've never gotten so much pleasure in restarting training." But at Club Robinson in January he says, "I've always been a guy who did my own kind of preparation for big goals." And when I ask him if his training is as scientific as Armstrong's and whether he uses a specific trainer, Ullrich replies in his precisely spoken German, "I think *we* [indicating himself and other veteran riders] are the best trainers. We have so much experience and we've done this for many years, so learning from that is maybe the best scientific basis."

Riis, an expert trainer himself, doesn't agree with that theory. He feels that Ullrich is hurt by his lack of scientific training. "Ullrich won't win the Tour until he uses the right program, and not before." Ullrich is well aware that he has to change his ways. "In previous years, maybe my training was not a full 100 percent and it didn't go as it should have gone," he says. "The support staff can give us advice and recommendations, but the hardest thing is to put it into daily action."

A couple of months later, when I meet him at a Barcelona hotel during a five-day Tour warm-up race in Catalonia, Ullrich looks as if putting it into daily action was indeed beyond him. He appears to be as heavy as he was in January, even though he has been competing in races for several weeks. I get firsthand confirmation of his lack of condition the next day when I go to watch him race in the rugged foothills of the Spanish Pyrenees. After driving through snow showers on a narrow, twisting back road, I reach the bleak mountain town of San Lorenzo de Morunys. On this frigid afternoon, Ullrich, a blank look on his face, pedals by in a group of a dozen tailenders, a quarter-of-an-hour behind the race leaders. I hop back into my car and follow Ullrich's group on their final 10 kilometers, as they slowly climb a steep, winding road to the finish at a small ski station. Few of the cycling fans clustered by the roadside recognize Ullrich, who's wearing a plastic rain jacket, as he battles his way upward. Three T-Mobile teammates shelter him from the gusting wind and encourage him to go faster, but their leader is at his limit. He frequently stands on the pedals to get extra power, working hard. Salt coats his lips, and his face is flush from the effort. At the finish, where the puddles have iced over, Ullrich wraps a thick towel around his neck and dons a heavy jacket, like a boxer after a fight. If this is what it takes to shed his surplus pounds, then Ullrich is on the right track. He had better be. The Tour de France is only three months away.

———

In late April Ullrich needed a break from racing. Still overweight and having trouble finishing races, he went back home and began a more intensive training regimen. This included riding a stationary bike in his wine cellar, which he had converted into a hypoxic chamber, simulating high altitude—like the hypoxic tent Armstrong uses at training camps and during races, both to aid recovery from hard efforts and to restore his body's natural level of red blood cells. And for the first time, Ullrich also followed another precept of his rival: He held a training camp in the Alps, where he scouted the courses of the three Tour stages due to take place there in July.

Following that camp, Ullrich had shed most of his excess pounds, and he showed increasingly good form at the seven-day Tour of Germany, where he finished seventh, and the nine-day Tour of Switzerland, which he narrowly won in late June. It may not have been a Tour de France–level performance—Ullrich faltered on the main mountain stage, and won by only one second over Swiss veteran Fabian Jeker—but it was a sign of his improving physical shape. Ullrich's morale was further boosted when his team manager Godefroot and personal trainer Pevenage shook hands during T-Mobile's preliminary survey of the team time trial course—although Pevenage officially remained persona non grata.

Unlike Armstrong, Ullrich doesn't expect the total support of all his eight teammates on every stage. That's why his friend and teammate Zabel—another former member of the East German national team—is allowed to shoot for stage wins, as he plans to do today. Zabel, 34, is nearing the end of a Tour de France career that has netted him a dozen stage victories and six green jerseys as a six-time winner of the sprinters' points competition, a record. But to win a stage at this Tour, Zabel will have to be an opportunist. He no longer has the kick that made him top dog from 1996 to 2001. What he does have is the experience and know-how to avoid crashes, follow the wheels of the younger sprinters, and perhaps surprise them in the final 100 yards.

The Namur finish offers the German a good chance: The six-man break is hauled back with 12 miles still to go; late-afternoon sunshine has dried out the humid roads; and the other teams are doing the pacesetting needed to stop any late breakaways.

Racing into Namur alongside the grass-banked Meuse River, Zabel is well positioned among the first dozen riders in the long line of racers being pulled along by, of all people, race leader Cancellara. The young Swiss has had his moment of glory and now is back to team duties, which in his case means setting as fast a pace as possible for his Italian teammate and star sprinter Petacchi, the man who won four of the five Tour stages he contested in 2003 before dropping out due to sickness. Petacchi, who is now vying for the mantle of "world's best sprinter," previously shared by Zabel and Mario Cipollini, still has a good position as Cancellara peels off the front, his job done, with 400 yards to go. The yellow jersey's two-minute effort was the best he could do, but not good enough to please Petacchi. "We weren't able to stretch out the peloton as much as we'd have liked," he says, knowing that the strength of his sprint lies in his teammates pushing the other sprinters to their limit in the final miles. "Our speed wasn't high enough."

Also, the long final, curving left turn is not a finish that suits Petacchi, who prefers straight sprints after a gradual buildup of speed. Instead, it's perfect for a rider with keen bike-handling skills and a fast acceleration, someone like yesterday's runner-up, McEwen, who now bolts through on the inside at what Petacchi calls "an extraordinary speed." The Aussie wins easily, several bike lengths ahead of the big Norwegian champion, Hushovd.

The older generation has been left behind: Zabel is seventh, Petacchi eighth, and Cipollini tenth. As for the race favorites, Ullrich, Armstrong, and Hamilton again arrive safely in the pack, among the 178 riders all given the same time as McEwen. Hushovd's 12-second time bonus for second place takes him ahead of Cancellara on overall time, which means the yellow jersey is now his to wear. He's the first rider from Norway to have this honor.

The sprinters bring excitement to these early stages of the Tour, as well as danger. At the moment that McEwen made his dash to victory on the inside of the curve, two riders drifted out to the right, collided and fell in a heap. Frenchman Jimmy Casper and Norwegian Kurt-Asle Arvesen were both stunned by the impact and took a while to stand up, but they just had superficial cuts and bruises. Theirs was one of five crashes in the day, and a dozen riders will be tending knee, elbow, and shoulder wounds in the night.

There are no injuries among Ullrich's T-Mobile men, who return with their leader to a hotel in Nivelles. It was through here, almost two centuries ago, that Napoleon Bonaparte's army marched on its way to Waterloo to fight a battle that would be its last. Ullrich will be taking the same road in the morning, as Waterloo is the starting point of the next stage. It will be a day when he will have to show his strength to match Armstrong and his Postal team on a course that includes some infamous cobblestone roads in northern France.

Some critics say that the German has the strength but lacks the ambition to defeat Armstrong, a thesis that Ullrich decries. "I'm always ambitious before a race," he states in an interview given at the start of this Tour, "but not in the same way as everyone. I like winning, but not necessarily for myself. When my buddy Andreas Klöden won the German championship last week, I felt the same emotion as if I'd won the race. But it's not only ambition and tactics that win the Tour. Lance also has his weak points. So I don't think he's unbeatable."

STAGE RESULT: 1. McEwen; 2. Hushovd; 3. Nazon; 4. Hondo; 5. Stuart O'Grady (Australia), all same time.

OVERALL STANDINGS: 1. Hushovd; 2. Cancellara, at 0:08;

3. McEwen, at 0:17; 4. Armstrong, at 0:18; 5. Voigt, at 0.23; 13. Leipheimer, at 0:31; 14. Sastre, same time; 17. Ullrich, at 0:33; 19. Hamilton, at 0:34; 31. Mayo, at 0:37; 73. Basso, at 0:45.

The Little Corporal

JULY 6: *This 130.5-mile stage starts from the battlefield at Waterloo and follows a mainly flat, meandering course through Belgian and French Flanders to Wasquehal in the suburbs of Lille. Key challenges are the steep Mur de Grammont climb after 38 miles, and two short sections of cobblestone farm roads with 40 and 16 miles to go.*

Looking down from the 133-foot-high conical hill built to commemorate the Battle of Waterloo, I'm watching the Tour de France's own 4,500-strong "army" assemble for another day of competition. It's a virtual moving city, comprising all the people needed to make the Tour happen and report it to the world. And it takes about sixteen hundred vehicles to move this entourage from one stage to the next.

Since early morning, on a day of blustery winds and occasional sunshine, thousands of race fans have been taking up prime viewing positions at the staging area in the center of Waterloo. This is where the Tour's official speaker, Daniel Mangeas, a fast-talking Frenchman in his fifties, introduces the 186 riders as each of them signs the *fiche de départ*, to prove they are officially starting the day's stage.

To the side, set up on an athletics field, is the race sponsors' tented village, constructed overnight. It's here that local dignitaries, invited guests, race personnel, promotion people, reporters, and television crews gather to read the morning's newspapers, socialize over a free buffet, and perhaps grab a glass of wine. Many of the racers also drop by the village. They come for scheduled interviews, to get a haircut at the tented barber's shop, or to drink espresso at the Grand'Mère coffee bar; while the Spaniards in particular rush over to the France Telecom compound to make free phone calls.

Right now the publicity caravan's hundreds of colorful floats and loudspeaker vehicles are leaving town. As they pass by the battlefield, the sinister soundtrack from *Spiderman 2*, the catchy Grand'Mère coffee jingle, and the thumping beat of disco music from various sources all merge into a dissonant symphony that wafts up to my perch 226 stone steps above them. It's like a scene from the animated Tour cult movie, *Les Triplettes de Belleville*.

The caravan stays an hour or so ahead of the race on this and every stage, to keep the crowds entertained until the peloton comes through. Meanwhile, 100 miles away in Wasquehal, 300 workers are putting the final touches to the massive infrastructure needed at every stage finish: four miles of crowd barriers; bleachers for several thousand spectators; double-deck TV commentary booths and VIP boxes; a 100,000-square-foot technical area to park the 100 TV production trucks, satellite dishes, and miles of cables; and a press room at an indoor tennis facility big enough to seat 500 journalists.

At about 11 o'clock in Waterloo, the twenty-one Tour teams begin to arrive—the riders in their grand luxury buses, the support staff in three or four separate station wagons mounted with spare bikes and wheels on custom racks. Most of the accredited race followers, VIPs, and media people have already parked their cars and headed to the tented village.

The hill I'm standing on was constructed from 10 million cubic feet of earth dug from the barley, rye, and clover fields where the bloody Battle of Waterloo was fought. An estimated 54,000 men were killed here on a single day, June 18, 1815, when the imperial French army of Napoleon Bonaparte was defeated by allied forces led by Britain's Duke of Wellington. It was the deadliest battle the world had yet seen. Looking up from my viewpoint, I can see the face of the 15-foot-high, cast-iron statue of a lion, the symbol of the British Army, which crowns a granite platform on this grassy memorial mound.

Waterloo marked the end of Napoleon's bid to build a French empire that would have covered Europe. Right to the end, his troops affectionately called him "the little corporal," a moniker he acquired during his officer training years in Paris. His Imperial Guard, an elite fighting force of seasoned troops, came to Waterloo undefeated. They were intimidating in their royal blue-and-white uniforms, particularly the cavalry division. "I shall never forget the sight," wrote a corporal in the opposing Scots Greys, when he saw this armored division charging his regiment at Waterloo. "The *Cuirassiers*, in their sparkling steel breastplates and helmets, mounted on strong black horses, with great blue rugs across the croups, were galloping towards me, tearing up the earth as they went. . . ."

Those French horsemen galloped across fields I'm looking at to the south of the hill, while the men of the Tour now arrive from the north and then turn west along what was the front line of the British army in 1815. Before reaching the foot of the mound and the official start of the stage, the cyclists ride past the cracking muskets of soldiers—actors dressed as Imperial Guards—and hear the rousing pipes-and-drums music of a Napoleonic-era band. Another stage of the Tour de France is underway.

———————

Modern sport's equivalent of the powerful, blue-cloaked Imperial Guard is Lance Armstrong's U.S. Postal Service squad, known as the Blue Train, that's made up of riders from America, the Czech Republic, Portugal, Russia, and Spain. When they're defending their leader's yellow jersey, these blue-uniformed athletes on white-and-blue bicycles race tightly together at the head of the pack to discourage the opposition from breaking away. They have led Armstrong to five straight Tour de France victories and are ready to go into action again on this challenging 130-mile stage across the Flemish plains of Belgium and France.

The day will also test the pink-clad riders of T-Mobile, racing to support their German general, Jan Ullrich. But the men who most need to prove they are up to the task of protecting a contender for the overall victory are wearing the green-yellow-and-white jerseys of Phonak Hearing Systems, a Swiss-based team competing at the Tour for the first time. *Their* leader is Tyler Hamilton, the fearless 33-year-old American who has moved quickly though the ranks since being just a "little corporal" in Armstrong's personal army only three years ago. Hamilton now commands his *own* force of riders—five from Spain and one each from France, Germany, and Switzerland—who will do all they can during the next twenty days to derail Armstrong's Blue Train. The odds against the hard-riding Hamilton winning the Tour are 6 to 1 according to prominent London oddsmaker William Hill, compared with the 2-to-1 odds of Ullrich and 1 to 1 of Armstrong. A straw poll of race insiders shows strong support for Hamilton, though, a very different result from the all-Armstrong forecasts of previous years. Many are predicting Hamilton will win because of his courage and the fact that he prepares for the Tour just as thoroughly as Armstrong. And in the pre-race list of favorites published by the influential *L'Équipe* newspaper, Hamilton was given the same four-star rating as Ullrich, behind the five stars given to Armstrong.

To compete on equal footing with such thoroughbreds, the less-powerful Hamilton will have to maximize all of his resources: fitness, recovery, climbing expertise, time-trialing skills, strong morale, and a 100-percent dedicated team. One of Hamilton's immediate concerns is that he has never raced on "real" cobblestones, the large gray granite bricks shaped like loaves of bread that pave two sections of the back roads he'll be racing over this afternoon. Hamilton trained on these roads a couple of days before the Tour start, so he knows what to expect. "The first section's hard. It's almost three kilometers, and it seemed like it went on for a long time," says Hamilton, as he shows me round, quarter-sized blisters on each of his palms that were caused by the severe impact of his bike vibrating over the cobblestones. "I didn't wear gloves." The Colorado-based racer also knows how different the cobblestone sections will be under race conditions, when raging speeds, a big pack, and dense crowds lining each side of the road make crashes almost inevitable. It's the first section of real cobblestones that the Tour has included since the 1980s. One of the chief critics of sending the Tour over the cobblestones was five-time winner Bernard Hinault, who became a technical consultant to the organizers after he retired from racing in 1986. He said that the dangers of crashing, or getting blocked by a crash, were too great and falsified the outcome of the Tour.

Now, for at least one year, the cobblestones are back, and the contenders will be relying on their teammates even more to get them safely through the stage. "I have the best team," Hamilton says before the race, and many Tour analysts agree. Phonak showed its strength, unity, and top form just a few weeks before the Tour at the famed Dauphiné Libéré. "This is a great bunch of guys," Hamilton says. "I have every confidence in them."

The feeling is mutual. Hamilton has proven himself to be a solid team leader and he engenders the unequivocal respect of his team-mates. On this challenging stage they are prepared to do all they can to place their American boss near the head of the peloton as it funnels into the narrow back roads leading up to the first section of cobble-stones. To be caught at the back and risk being dropped or getting de-layed by a crash would be a disaster for Hamilton, whose challenge to Armstrong relies on his gaining seconds whenever he can, not losing them.

———————

"This stage with the cobblestones could catch a lot of people out," Hamilton says as he points at a thin black line curling across the top of a map opened on his laptop. It's only mid-December, but he is al-ready studying the Tour de France route, including this third stage starting at Waterloo that cuts across southern Belgium before looping into northern France. He closes his PC and then gives me a short tour of his new home, a large but simply furnished modern house in the mountains near Boulder, Colorado. Hamilton and his wife Haven are still adjusting to the extra space compared to their other home, a 150-year-old clapboard in Marblehead, Massachusetts, close to their families. "We've been looking here for three years," says Hamilton, who also lives in Gerona, Spain, during the bike-racing season, be-tween February and October.

The Hamiltons' homes reflect their own traits: unpretentious, or-derly, and extremely welcoming. Tyler's round face always looks well-scrubbed, while his thick black hair has that slicked-back, straight-out-of-the-shower appearance. He has sleepy gray eyes, a small mouth, and an easy smile. His clothes have an old-fashioned, natural feel: an unbuttoned white shirt and zip-up beige jacket in the spring, a thick turtleneck sweater and thin leather jacket in the winter.

Haven was a marketing executive when she met Tyler, an economics major, at an East Coast bike race in 1996. She has put her career on hold to work as her husband's do-it-all assistant and, typically, is out running an errand this afternoon. The other member of the household, their aging golden retriever Tugboat, is biting into a toy stuffed-leather buffalo. When the white wooly innards emerge, Hamilton mildly scolds his dog and says with feigned annoyance, "Tugs is *always* doing this."

Beyond the split-level living room's ceiling-to-floor picture windows, darkness is falling across the snow-etched ridges of the Front Range, and a couple of thousand feet below the Hamiltons' castlelike home lights start to flicker on like fireflies across the northern Denver suburbs. Hamilton closes the French doors from the patio. The day's warmth had suddenly dissipated when the sun dropped behind nearby Bighorn Mountain. "It's high up here," he says with boyish excitement. "Seventy-six-fifty."

The thin air at this 7,650-foot elevation allows Hamilton to follow the universal coaching motto: Live high, train low. The theory is that an athlete produces more oxygen-carrying red blood cells when sleeping at high altitude, while his muscles get stronger by training in a lower, oxygen-rich atmosphere. So Hamilton bikes down to Boulder each day to train in an altitude more than 2,000 feet lower, and gets the added benefit of a great climbing workout when he returns home. "I like to be able to finish the day riding up here from Boulder," he says. "It's hard, twenty-three-hundred feet of climbing. I like that. I've always loved the mountains. Grew up skiing."

Hamilton's parents, who met on the ski slopes of New Hampshire's Mount Washington, instilled in their two sons a love for adventurous sports—along with a fierce competitive spirit. "I never liked to be beaten," Hamilton recalls. "If I got beaten, I came back the next day and tried harder. I never liked people to see that I was hurting, either. If they knew I was hurting I didn't give up." The Hamilton brothers raced skis and dinghies, and also did a little cycling. But for Tyler, cycling was never more than a summer-time prep for ski racing, especially after he won a ski scholarship to the University of Colorado at Boulder. He had the potential to become one of the country's top slalom skiers until his winter sports ambitions suddenly ended one day in the fall of 1990.

Hamilton can still feel the pain of that day. He and the other CU ski team members were training on mountain bikes at a local BMX course. In his usual high-risk style, the New Englander was speeding over one of the sharp little humps called whoop-di-whoops when he lost control and went flying through the air. He tried to pull the bike straight and was still holding the grips when the front wheel hit the ground, and Hamilton was launched over the handlebars.

"The first thing that hit was my head," he says. "The helmet shattered. It totally knocked the wind out of me, and I couldn't breathe for a minute. Really scary. Finally, I started to breathe okay, so I stood up, which I shouldn't have done."

What Hamilton didn't know was that the fall had fractured his third and fourth vertebrae, and by standing up so quickly he had risked severing his spinal cord. As it was, he adds, "They were just percussion fractures, but I was in bed for close to two months.

"I was really upset I couldn't ski. It was pretty hard for me. I needed something, so I started just riding my road bike, putting in some base miles, not really knowing what I was training for. I never ski raced after that. But that's really how my cycling took off. That next summer when I started racing I was ten times stronger than I was before."

Physical strength and undaunted perseverance define Hamilton the bike racer. He is also known for being one of the nicest guys in the peloton. Some are even saying he's too nice to win the Tour—but not those who know him best.

One of his former teammates, Christian Vande Velde, told me, "Tyler has a lot of fire inside him . . . particularly from the standpoint of how he can make himself go to the depths of pain that not many human beings ever see. It comes from somewhere, and I don't know how that gets triggered when he gets on a bike. He definitely has a Jekyll and Hyde personality. When the race is going hard he can push himself further than anyone I've seen in my entire life."

Hamilton will have to show some of that spirit on this challenging stage from Waterloo to Wasquehal. A breakaway is made right from the Waterloo start by Dutchman Bram De Groot of the Rabobank team and Jens Voigt of CSC. Voigt, a lean, long-limbed, 32-year-old German, is riding his seventh Tour. He loves to make marathon attacks like this one—attacks from the start that challenge him to stay ahead of the pack for long distances—and he is already leading the "most combative" rider competition in this year's Tour. Though they're on different teams, Voigt and De Groot share the workload: First one of them sets the pace while his companion gets a minute or so to ride in his slipstream, and then the other takes his turn at the front. Only by sharing the pacemaking can they hope to maintain a high speed and stay out in front for as long as possible. Maybe until the end.

The pair has already been together for about ninety minutes when they reach the Mur de Grammont, a Category 3 hill that's famous in racing circles for its sharp grades and cobblestone approach through the hillside town of Geraardsbergen. Almost four minutes behind the leaders, a sharp acceleration is made on the steep hill by the Italian Paolo Bettini, who is trying to increase his lead in the King of the Mountains competition. Hamilton is among the twenty or so riders who respond to Bettini's attack and top the climb a few seconds ahead of the pack. But the pack regroups, and Voigt and De Groot push up their lead to six and a half minutes approaching the border town of Tournai. They're still 30 miles away from the first feared section of cobblestones. The tension is increasing for all the contenders, including Hamilton.

After swapping sports in 1991, the 20-year-old Hamilton progressed rapidly as a cyclist. He won the national collegiate championship in 1992—the year that Lance Armstrong was expected to win a cycling gold medal at the Barcelona Olympics—and in 1993 he was selected for the U.S. national amateur team. By 1995, Hamilton had signed up as a professional cyclist with the California-based Montgomery–Subaru squad, which was the genesis of the U.S. Postal Service team. But any thoughts Hamilton might have had of Tour de France glory didn't surface until 1997, the year when Armstrong was recovering from cancer. "That was a big year for me as it was my first year racing in Europe," Hamilton remembers, "so I was as green as anyone could be. I felt like I was just out of college in '97, still had a college mentality. But after I finished the Tour for the first time and crossed the finish line on the Champs-Élysées, I thought to myself, I really want to come back and try to be a factor in this race someday.

"In '98, I was quite a bit stronger, able to climb quite a bit better and time-trial better—and I was *serious*. For me, the diet was a big thing; from 1997 to '98 I lost about ten pounds."

That's a significant weight loss for someone who's under five-foot-eight. "I probably weigh now about 140 pounds in the winter," he adds. "During the Tour, maybe down to 135, 132 pounds. Your Tour weight is not something you can hold all season."

For his size, Hamilton's 1998 weight loss was equivalent to the fifteen pounds shed by Armstrong during his cancer treatment. Their weight loss gave each of them an increased power-to-weight ratio, which pays off big on long alpine climbs and in hilly time trials.

This was evident at the 1998 Tour, when Hamilton gave the world a glimpse of his great potential by placing second to Ullrich in a difficult 36-mile Tour de France time trial at Correze. Given his talent and drive, Hamilton might have developed into the U.S. Postal team leader, but Armstrong had joined the squad that year, so Hamilton reverted to the lesser role of *domestique*—a team man who works for his leader. It was a situation that didn't displease him.

"When I worked for Lance in his first Tour victory, in 1999, I was able to still finish in 13th overall and take a couple of top fives in the times trials. After that I thought, 'Wow, after doing the work, man, if I were a leader on a different team maybe I could have been in the top ten.' That gave me a lot of confidence about my future. Certainly, I thought it was best to stay with Postal and continue to learn from the best rider in the world."

Hamilton's cycling education accelerated in 2000 when he moved to Nice, to live less than a mile from Armstrong's then summer home overlooking the Mediterranean. "We had the same race program, so we pretty much trained together every day," Hamilton says. "Before that, I thought I trained hard and I was serious, but not until that year did I learn how much further I could push myself. There were a lot of days that I was training with Lance that were much harder than race days, *much* harder. Haven will tell you, there were so many days I came home just completely wasted."

The tougher training helped Hamilton become a more resilient racer. "As you could see," he says, "in 2000 I won the biggest race of my career to that date, the Dauphiné." The Dauphiné Libéré, an eight-day race in the French Alps, is considered a mini version of the Tour de France. To win it, Hamilton rode strongly in the time trials and mountains; but it was the guidance of his teammate Armstrong that made the difference. During a key stage into Digne-les-Bains, the two friends broke away from the pack on a steep climb to finish first and second, and crossed the line with both holding their arms high in celebration. Hamilton has a framed photo of that finish hanging in his Marblehead home.

Despite their friendship, and Hamilton's unselfish riding to help Armstrong win the Tour each year, the New Englander wanted something more from his cycling career. Midway though the 2001 season, he remembers, "I felt I could look three years back and three years ahead and see myself in the same exact position, same role in the team. I made my decision to leave the team before the Tour ended, even though we were on our way to winning the third consecutive Tour de France." Armstrong didn't stand in his friend's way when Hamilton signed a two-year deal with the Danish team, CSC. "I felt it was a good opportunity to go out on my own," Hamilton explains.

———————

The personal relationship between Hamilton and Armstrong has continued to evolve in the couple of years since the student prince parted ways with his master, and they are still friends. During the cycling season, the two men live on separate floors of the same medieval mansion in Gerona, Spain, that has been divided into plush apartments. Yet they rarely see each other there, and communicate more by text messaging than in person. And at this 2004 Tour there seems to be a tension between them that didn't exist before. I hear an undertone of perhaps envy and irritation when I ask Hamilton about Armstrong's repeated victories at the Tour.

"People are like, 'Oh, Lance is going to win,'" Hamilton says. "But there's no guarantees, you know. Every Tour victory has been hard. Last year was extremely hard. They're all difficult, even if he's won by six minutes. Just because he's that much stronger than everybody else doesn't guarantee *any*thing, because there's a lot that can happen."

Indeed, a "lot can happen" on this tension-filled stage from Waterloo to Wasquehal. The small group that both Hamilton and Armstrong were in over the summit of the wall-like hill at Grammont was quickly caught by the pack, but the two leading contenders never stray far from the front of the peloton, always keeping a few team-mates in front of them and one or two others behind. Their teams have to be superaware and ready in case their leader falls or has to stop with a flat tire, so they can quickly pace him back to the group. And as they draw closer and closer to the cobblestones, it's vital that their leaders be at or very near the front of the peloton to avoid crashes that can injure or delay them.

———————

Hamilton left Armstrong to join CSC in 2002 partly because of the confidence shown in him by his new team's owner and manager, Bjarne Riis, who in 1996 became the first Dane to win the Tour de France. "Bjarne wanted me to be one of the team leaders," Hamilton says. The balding, blue-eyed Riis quickly elevated the goals of his American recruit. "If you can get the motivation, then you can do anything," Riis said, after working with Hamilton long enough to sense how far he could go. "We have good chemistry between us. I know him and what he needs." Hamilton began training under Riis's former coach, Luigi Cecchini, who is based in Tuscany. Together, they decided that Hamilton would attempt to win the 2002 Giro d'Italia—the three-week Tour of Italy—as a prelude to targeting the Tour de France in 2003.

Hamilton didn't know how wild his ride would be at the 2002 Giro, starting with its steepest climb, the Colletto del Moro, on the fifth stage. At the top, Hamilton was the only rider still alongside the three favored Italian stars. "It was my first big test of the season and I knew I had to be on my game," Hamilton recalls. "You can't fake it over a climb like that, it was so steep. Then, on the descent, I felt something weird happening with the rear wheel when I was pedaling, but there was no time to figure it out. I was just sprinting out of the final corner of the descent, so we still had a lot of speed. I got out of the saddle, and I was pushing with all my might when, all of a sudden, *snap!* Before I knew it I was on the ground."

The freewheel mechanism on his bike had locked up, causing the crash. Hamilton was quickly on his feet and grabbed a replacement bike from a teammate, but a broken humerus bone and ruptured tendon in his left shoulder made it tough for him to continue—yet he did. To counteract the pain, he clenched his teeth harder and harder each day for the remaining fifteen stages. "I just ground them down," Hamilton states, adding that he later had to have eleven teeth capped. "I honestly didn't have a choice, there was that much pain. Whether I was riding my bike or resting in bed, I was suffering."

Somehow transcending the excruciating pain, Hamilton won the Giro's vital time-trial stage and finished in second place overall, an impressive accomplishment in a race that is almost always dominated by Italians. The only American who ever did better was a specialist climber, Andy Hampsten, who won the Giro in 1988, while Greg LeMond once came in third. What's more, Hamilton proved to Riis and his CSC teammates that not only was he a leader, but he had the gritty qualities needed to win the Tour de France.

While people sense a contained rage smoldering in Lance Armstrong, they are equally struck by the calm demeanor of Tyler Hamilton. But his easygoing manner only masks an intensely competitive nature, raw determination, and incredible drive. And as different as he and Armstrong might be, they share one crucial quality: an extraordinary ability to endure and transcend pain. Armstrong is renowned for this, while Hamilton's gutsy performance at the Giro proved that when it came to suffering, he was anyone's match.

In the spring of 2003, Hamilton fully acquired the status of international sports star when he became the first American to win the Liège–Bastogne–Liège classic, one of only four so-called "monuments of cycling." These prestigious single-day races are the most keenly contested events in the world. Winning one is a feat that not even Armstrong has achieved. Hamilton followed up that break-through victory the following week by winning another notable race, Switzerland's six-day Tour de Romandie. So, only six years after he lined up at the Tour de France for the first time, Hamilton was now a serious contender for its ultimate prize, first place in the final overall standing, or General Classification (GC). "I was in the best shape of my life, I was so ready for this, my seventh Tour de France, the Tour that I was going to do 100 percent for the GC," he says. "I was ready. It was my year."

The 2003 Tour de France *did* start well for Hamilton: He was one second faster than Armstrong in the prologue time trial in Paris. But on the following day, Hamilton encountered the unfortunate fate that seems to befall him more than it does any other leading racer. When the 198-strong pack sped through a downhill right–left curving chicane a quarter-mile from the finish of the stage into Meaux, two riders touched wheels and set off a chain-reaction pileup that led to a monstrous, mind-jarring wreck.

"There was a body lying right in front of me," Hamilton said that evening. "I really had no time to react. Before I knew it, I was on the pavement. I landed on my head and my back first. All the abrasions I have are on my back . . . but my collarbone's broken at the front. I think I hit my shoulder and my head at the exact same time."

The CSC team physiotherapist, Ole Kaere Føli, worked on his broken shoulder for two hours that night and another ninety minutes in the morning. Hamilton's fractured collarbone was braced with bandaging, his handlebars were padded with three rolls of absorbent gel tape, and, true to character, he took the risk of continuing in the Tour. Three weeks later, despite riding the entire race in pain, the New Englander finished the Tour in fourth place—only six minutes behind Armstrong.

It was then that the media started speaking of the American explosion at the Tour. In its 100 years, only two Americans, Armstrong and LeMond, had ever won the race. But now it looked as though the 2004 Tour would have *two* Americans as the leading contenders. In fact, if anyone could beat Armstrong, the odds were on the scrappy Hamilton rather than the imperial Ullrich.

———

What very few people knew during the 2003 Tour was that Hamilton was already contemplating leaving CSC. At this point in his career it made sense. He wanted to have an entire team devoted to his goal of winning the Tour, rather than having some teammates (as at CSC) harboring ambitions to win stages or place well in the overall classification.

"I'd been thinking about it the last week of the Tour," Hamilton confesses, as he sinks deeper into the leather couch at his Colorado home. "I hadn't decided 100 percent . . . but I was definitely leaning towards Phonak. Knowing that I was going to leave CSC made all the success in the Tour a little bit more . . . "

He can't find the right words to describe how he felt about leaving a team that was on its way to winning three stages and the overall team title at the 2003 Tour.

He tries again: "When I finished the Tour, I was happy. Sure, it was over, and I'd got fourth, won a stage, but even when I finished second in the last time trial, and passed two guys on overall time to finish fourth, there was something holding back the happiness, because I knew most likely what was going to happen. I was gonna leave. And it was hard. And when I had to tell Bjarne, it was awful. We both cried."

Speaking softly, Hamilton chokes out, "It was terrible, just terrible. It was probably one of the worst days of my life. But sometimes you have to do what you think is best for you and your career. It was awful, awful. I told him after the Tour. I told him face-to-face."

"It was a big surprise for me. I had no idea," Riis said, when I asked him about that post-Tour meeting with Hamilton. "What are you going to say when you hear that? You say nothing. You're just shocked, you know. You just don't know what to do."

Did Riis understand why his star pupil decided to leave? "No, no," is his sad reply. "I'll never understand."

———

After the emotional parting between Hamilton and Riis—who both say they remain friends—Hamilton signed a contract that fall with the Phonak team in Switzerland. Phonak offered him not only an increased salary, but the opportunity to choose as many new riders as he wanted to strengthen the team for the Tour.

Hamilton is convinced that he made the right decision. "One, it was an educated risk. Two, I'm not afraid to take a chance like this," he says. "But I have a problem with people doubting it. It's fine if they say that we're a so-so team. I can't wait to show 'em. We're a very strong, very strong team."

Hamilton says this in January 2004, as we sit at the bar of the Hotel Esmeralda in Calpe, a scenic beach town on Spain's Costa Blanca. He has just come from dinner with his new Phonak teammates at their preseason training camp. Between sips of *latte*, he proudly lists the riders on his team, starting with the well-known Oscar Sevilla. This rosy-cheeked, round-faced young Spaniard is sitting in the lobby with his friend, the robust José Enrique Gutierrez. They've come to Phonak after spending the first six years of their pro careers on a Spanish team, Kelme. Sevilla, whose specialty is climbing, won the Best Young Rider award at the 2001 Tour de France. He'll be a critical aid for Hamilton during the stages in the Pyrenees and Alps, while

Gutierrez should show his strength as a support rider throughout the Tour.

Hamilton says he handpicked eight of the riders on the twenty-four-man roster, including his French buddy and former CSC teammate Nicolas Jalabert. "I asked him to come with me," says Hamilton, and then recounts a conversation he had with Jalabert after the American crashed and shredded his hand at a race in the Netherlands a month after the 2003 Tour. "After I went down, he was there with me," recalls Hamilton, whose immediate and typical reaction was to get back on his bike and chase after the pack. "Blood was pouring out of my finger and dripping down on my wheel, so Nicolas said, 'Tyler, this isn't the Tour de France. You don't have to go until you keel over.'"

A couple of years younger than Hamilton, Jalabert, with his closely cropped ginger hair, round nose, and prominent chin, looks more like a boxer than a cyclist. He comes from the rural Tarn region of southern France, and his older brother, Laurent Jalabert, was a national hero who won more than a hundred bike races before he retired in 2002. His brother's fame doesn't bother Nicolas, who is satisfied with his role of domestique. He's a ten-year veteran of pro cycling and has often raced on cobblestone roads at events in Belgium and northern France. Jalabert is one of the teammates whom Hamilton will rely on the most at the Tour de France, especially to help him survive stages like this one from Waterloo. He's expected to protect Hamilton from the wind when the pack reaches the first section of cobblestones, which they are now rapidly and apprehensively approaching.

———

To witness this critical part of the Tour, I've driven with a fellow journalist a half-hour ahead of the race and parked in Wandignies-Hamage, a hamlet of small brick houses and tiled roofs, just beyond the end of the mile-and-a-half section of cobblestones that starts in the village of Erre. We walk back to the granite cobblestones, where the road is only ten feet wide and sunken on the sides, pushed down by two centuries of horses hauling cartloads of beets, potatoes, and coal. The resulting hump down the middle of the road is a danger to bikes and cars alike. Just as we arrive, a television crew's minivan speeds past and hits the hump with a loud bang. Spectators give the driver a sarcastic cheer. There are probably 10,000 fans lining this one section of cobblestones. One of them, Tina Müller from Dortmund, has a white Ullrich flag wrapped around her waist. "What do you think of Jan's chances?" I ask. "I hope," she says, "but I think Armstrong's very strong. Jan's ill now, I read in the paper, but I hope he gets very good." She's right to be concerned, as Ullrich's cold has worsened into mild bronchitis.

In a group of French teenagers, two are budding bike racers. One tells me he likes Ullrich, the other Armstrong. "Who do *you* think will win the Tour?" I then ask a veteran race follower from nearby Valenciennes. "*Le Tour*? I would really like if someone other than Armstrong wins this year," he says. "I don't know who will beat him, but I hope it's a new name."

That's an opinion I'm hearing more and more. The media did such a pre-Tour overkill on Lance, with his picture plastering nearly every cover, that many people are hungering for a new name, a new hero.

As I walk along the cobblestone road, I hold a small scanner to my ear, listening to the updates on Radio Tour, the official race information service transmitted on a private waveband. It reports that the main pack is 12 miles away, coming through the town of St. Amand-les-Eaux, more than six minutes behind the two breakaways, Voigt and De Groot. American Levi Leipheimer has flatted and stopped for a wheel change; four of his Rabobank teammates wait to pace him back to the pack. Then comes the news that "U.S. Postal, Crédit Agricole, and Euskaltel-Euskadi are leading the peloton, which has greatly increased its pace since leaving St. Amand."

Champion Lance Armstrong reveals both his intensity and his fun side as he sets out on his quest for a record sixth Tour de France victory.

Jan Ullrich believes he can put behind him three second places to Armstrong.

They say Tyler Hamilton is the one man who has the measure of Armstrong.

Paparazzi perfect. The Basso family, Ivan, Michaela, and Domitilla in Provence.

Andreas Klöden proves an excellent stand-in for friend and teammate Jan Ullrich.

Prologue winner Fabian Cancellara takes an emotional yellow jersey.

Lance throws down the challenge in the Liège prologue, finishing second.

A pre-cobblestone crash sinks Iban Mayo on Day 4 to Wasquehal.

Eagles soar for Ivan Basso as he beats the champ at La Mongie.

Ullrich inexplicably falls apart on Day 14's climb to La Mongie.

Thomas "Ti-Blan" Voeckler saves his yellow jersey by 22 seconds on Day 15.

Fifteen minutes later, the Radio Tour speaker gets animated: *"Attention, attention!* The *maillot jaune* (yellow jersey) has fallen, but he's about to set off again. Riders from Illes Balears, Saeco, Quick Step are on the ground, along with the *maillot à pois* (best climber), Bettini, who's getting help. Cipollini, too, is on the ground, and Iban Mayo is in the ditch. Two from Crédit Agricole are also down, Hushovd and Christophe Moreau. The crash happened at kilometer 139. The peloton is split into four parts right now as team riders wait for their leaders."

The crash occurred on an open stretch of road, some of the men falling in a deep farm ditch, just over four miles before reaching the cobblestones. The teams of Armstrong, Ullrich, and Hamilton are pushing the speed up to almost 40 miles per hour on this stretch that zigzags through the streets of small villages. It's a serious situation for pre-race favorites Mayo and Moreau, who could be facing the end of their chances of making the podium in Paris. But Hamilton's scouting trip has paid off: He avoided the crash and his whole team is working hard for him.

I relay what I've heard to two race fans standing next to me. They're from Adelaide in Australia, and are watching the Tour for the first time. "How many wide will they come down here," one of them asks, "at least four or five?" "No," I reply. "One at a time." "One at a time? Wow, that'll be good." "They'll be going crazy fast down here," I tell them. "You'll see people like Postal's George Hincapie and Viatcheslav Ekimov on the front."

Radio Tour announces that the two breakaway riders have entered the cobblestone section. We look to the south and see four helicopters hovering low over the cornfields. Race cars and police motorcycles arrive to clear the way, kicking dust into the air. But the crowds are soon back in the road, straining to get a first look at Voigt and De Groot. Suddenly the two leaders appear, riding on the dirt and gravel shoulder, avoiding the stones, and forcing the fans to jump backward out of the way. Voigt looks to be the stronger, but both are clearly weary from racing hard at the front for the past four hours. Claps and cheers merge with the sounds of car wheels thundering over the cobblestones, Klaxons blaring, people shouting and running, and chopper blades chattering.

Less than three minutes later, we hear the chase group approaching. Radio Tour says they're racing at a frenetic pace in single file. We all look up the road again. Some point their fingers. Others shout, "Here they come!" The crowds part to let the racers through. They *are* going crazy fast, their wheels bouncing on the cobblestones, their arms vibrating, their eyes staring straight ahead. Three blue uniforms are at the front—U.S. Postal men Hincapie, Ekimov, and Armstrong! And Ullrich is right behind Armstrong! Next in line are the famous Italian racer Michele Bartoli, French sprinter Jean-Patrick Nazon, and the German sprinter Erik Zabel. I also spot four from Phonak in this front line of about twenty riders: Santos Gonzales, Oscar Pereiro, Nicolas Jalabert, and Hamilton. There's a small gap before the favored Italian, Gilberto Simoni, races by. Then a much bigger gap before the next group of about forty hurtles past, many of their mouths open from the effort, their faces darkened by the dust kicked up from the road. This group contains Liberty's Roberto Heras, Rabobank's Leipheimer, and CSC's Ivan Basso. The wearer of the yellow jersey, Hushovd, and his teammate Moreau head another chase group 1:20 back, while Mayo, paced by two teammates, is just over two minutes behind the Armstrong group.

"I was excited to be on the cobbles," Armstrong later says. "But getting to them was the problem . . . stressing about it the night before and starting the race. And the final kilometers before the cobbles were really hectic."

———

When all of the riders have passed we jump back in our press car and follow the tailenders for a few miles. During this time, Armstrong's team decides not to push the pace because of a blustery headwind, and the front two groups merge. But their pace soon picks up again, as the teams of Armstrong, Ullrich, and Hamilton work hard to catch the day's main aggressors, Voigt and De Groot, and to increase their advantage over those behind. At the same time, Mayo's men pace him up to the second chase group containing Hushovd and Moreau, and they set off for the finish, still 30 miles distant, two minutes behind.

By now we have turned off the course onto an *autoroute* and driven at almost 100 miles per hour toward Lille, where Wasquehal is situated. After navigating through a maze of suburban streets, we arrive at the stage finish and run to the finish line to watch the final miles on televisions set up in the press area. The front group, now ninety strong, is steadily gaining on the one behind, a sixty-man bunch in which the three team riders from Euskaltel (for Mayo) and two from Crédit Agricole (for Hushovd and Moreau) are fighting a losing battle. The look of defeat on these riders' faces heightens as they approach the second stretch of cobblestones, much shorter than the first but just as challenging. Here, a Slovenian on the Alessio-Bianchi team, Martin Hvastija, tries to race clear of the front group. His move brings an unexpected reaction.

"When Hvastija attacked, I took a photo I never expected to take," says Graham Watson, a veteran race photographer from England. "Lance Armstrong was leading a break on the cobbles. And he was *smiling*!"

The Texan's acceleration doesn't last for long, but it triggers a series of more breakaway attempts over the remaining 15 miles. At the same time, the impetus drops from the chase efforts of those behind. Over the final miles, only Euskaltel's Unai Etxebarria, a Basque born in Venezuela, is pedaling at the head of Mayo's group and that two-minute gap becomes almost four minutes by the end. "Mayo can't win the Tour now," says a colleague. "And he's going to lose more time to-morrow in the team time trial." Mayo himself is furious that Armstrong and his team raced so hard after the Basque crashed. His anger fuels the Spanish media's anti-Armstrong stance, and antagonizes the Mayo fans even more.

The stage into Wasquehal finishes just like the last two days: a chaotic sprint between those willing to risk crashing in search of a win. As in Namur, 24 hours before, McEwen dashes away on the left of the road, but he hasn't taken into account the gusting wind blowing from that side. The wind slows him in the final 50 yards, while two men battle past him on his right: Ullrich's teammate Zabel and French sprinter Nazon. Zabel appears to be the strongest, yet in the very last seconds the Frenchman bursts by him to take an exciting victory.

Nazon, 27, almost quit cycling at the end of 2002 when Fdjeux.com, a team sponsored by the French national lottery, discarded him. He was eventually picked up by a low-budget squad, Jean Delatour, where Nazon was seen as one of its few potential race winners. It was a good transplant, and Nazon ended the 2003 Tour de France by winning the prestigious final stage on the Champs-Élysées. As a result, he had no trouble getting a more lucrative contract for 2004. A third team, AG2R, hired him to be an eventual replacement for their aging star, Jaan Kirsipuu. To have both men win stages so early in the Tour is a huge bonus for their sponsor, a French insurance company.

As for McEwen, he says he's disappointed not to have won the stage and acts with indifference when told that the six-second time bonus he earned for third place has given him, for now, the yellow jersey. "Oh yeah?" he says. The Australian knows that taking the race lead is purely symbolic for a sprinter like him, who lacks the climbing abilities to keep the jersey once the Tour hits the mountains.

The mood is very different over at the U.S. Postal team bus. As the riders arrive from the finish, there's an exciting buzz about how well the team has performed on the cobblestones, particularly Hincapie and Ekimov. Both Hincapie, 30, a native New Yorker from Queens, and, Ekimov, 38, a Russian who lives in Spain, are regular contenders at the springtime Paris–Roubaix classic, which includes more than 30 miles of cobblestones. Hincapie's strong riding and experience in the spring classics is vital in helping Armstrong get through this first week of the Tour unscathed. It's no wonder that he is the only team-mate Armstrong has had at his side throughout his Tour-winning reign, and that the Texan calls Hincapie his "best bud."

In the Postal bus on the way to their hotel that night, there was ex-citement in the air, which served them well on the eve of the team time trial. "Everybody was congratulating Triki because he was in the first group," Hincapie says, referring to his lightly built Spanish teammate, Manuel Beltran. "I think he was the most nervous of any-body, and he's not known for riding the cobbles. José [Azevedo] was like, 'I don't need to ever ride the cobbles again.' Chechu [Rubiera] was telling me I was a god, and that 'I have so much respect for you.' The Spanish guys were really, really impressed with the cobblestones. They just couldn't believe it."

Tyler Hamilton's Phonak team also came through this stage in good shape. Before getting onto his team bus after the finish, Hamil-ton tells me, "I felt good. . . . The team was strong today; they did what they needed to do." He then talks about his first experience of racing on rough cobblestones, which are called *pavés* in French. "With forty kilometers to go before the first pavés, it was really stressful in the group," he says. "It's unfortunate that a guy like Mayo loses that much time. I feel bad for him. Sure, it's great that I put time on him, but cobbles are for Paris–Roubaix. I'm glad I wasn't on the wrong end of the split, though."

How close Hamilton came to being on the wrong end he'll never know. Moments after leaning his bike against the bus and climbing aboard, the rear tire on his bike explodes. There's a small slit in the tire's sidewall, something that could only have happened on the cobbles. He said that the team rode with slightly wider tires today, with lower air pressure than usual. If there had been more air, the pressure would most likely have burst through the sidewall during the race. You could call it good fortune, or good planning. But maybe it was just a sign that Hamilton's long series of accidents in major races was coming to an end. He'll need good fortune in tomorrow's team time trial, another critical stage. What does he think of his Phonak team's chances? "I think we're strong, really strong. I'm happy."

STAGE RESULT: 1. Nazon; 2. Zabel; 3. McEwen; 4. Tom Boonen (Belgium); 5. Kim Kirchen (Luxembourg), all same time.

OVERALL STANDINGS: 1. McEwen; 2. Cancellara, at 0:01; 3. Voigt, at 0:09; 4. Nazon, at 0:12; 5. Armstrong, at 0:16; 9. Leipheimer, at 0:24; 15. Sastre, at 0:29; 18. Ullrich, at 0:31; 20. Hamilton, at 0:32; 42. Basso, at 0:43; 101. Mayo, at 4:23.

In the Trenches

JULY 7: *A rolling 40-mile team time trial between the medieval cities of Cambrai and Arras, passing through twenty communities across a rural landscape. Heavy rain showers and strong wind gusts challenge the fortitude of every team. This is one of the Tour's "big" stages.*

Heavy rain pummels the taut canvas roof above my head. The impact is so loud that I barely hear a clap of thunder crashing over the slate rooftops of ancient Arras. Suddenly, out on the wet cobblestone square, an assistant with the French team, R.A.G.T. Sémences, is shouting, directing his drenched cyclists into the press tent where I'm standing. The riders, who've just finished their 40-mile team time trial, scuttle in from the storm pushing the same cumbersome, disc-wheeled time-trial machines they used in the prologue, and walking like ducks on their metal-cleated shoes, trying hard to stay upright.

They crowd the tent and fill it with animated chatter: "Those last turns on the cobbles were crazy!" . . . "What time did we do?" . . . "I think it said 1:17:40." . . . "Not so bad, huh?" . . . "It was tough in that head wind."

They peel off the tops of their sodden skin-hugging green-white-and-orange uniforms, grab towels from the trainer, and start talking into mikes thrust in their faces by reporters from French TV and radio, who've squeezed their way into the tent in search of some colorful quotes. "We've all seen the rain, but what are the conditions like out on the road?" they ask.

While some of the riders tell their battle stories, the young R.A.G.T. team assistant, who has a diamond eyebrow piercing, collects the riders' helmets, hands them each their individual bag of dry tops and trainers to change into, then gives them directions to ride to their team bus: "*Suivre la direction l'autoroute. C'est environs cinq bornes.*" *Cinq bornes?* Five kilometers? Three miles? One of the riders protests: "I can't do *cinq bornes* like this." "Well, maybe it's just three or four," the assistant equivocates. "Just stay with me, and I'll see if there's room for you in the car." "No, it's okay, I'll ride. . . ."

After racing with all their power through cold rain, risking falls on slick roads, and being forced to change clothes in the damp outside air—are they really being asked to go back into the rain and ride their bikes another three miles to reach their parked bus? No wonder American journalists have dubbed R.A.G.T. "the ragtag team." Management that forces its riders through such indignities, and risks them catching colds, or worse, is a team that has poor organization. And poor organization is a recipe for losing at the Tour de France.

In contrast, Lance Armstrong's Postal team has its bus parked just around the corner from the finish line. When his men finish, they will be in their bus within seconds, where hot showers and warm, dry sweats await them. The American team's smooth organization is a vital part of Armstrong's bid to win another Tour, and that organization has to be especially good in today's stage, the only team time trial in this year's Tour.

Besides Postal, only a handful of teams—T-Mobile of Germany, Phonak of Switzerland, CSC of Denmark, Rabobank of the Netherlands, and perhaps Liberty Seguros or Illes Balears of Spain—have the necessary strength of riders and backup personnel to win this demanding stage. "The team time trial is very emotional. It's unbelievably terrifying at the beginning because you know that you have to be at your very best and fit in with the others," says Christian Vande Velde, an American who this year switched from U.S. Postal to the Liberty team. "An individual time trial is one thing, it's only you; but when your whole team is surrounding you and relying on you, there's a lot more shit."

The parameters are simple: Each team of nine riders begins separately at five-minute intervals, riding together as fast as it collectively can. To rev up the speed they ride in a tight formation called a pace line—in which they fly like geese angled into the wind, one slightly behind the other, taking turns at the front to set the pace. It is critical that at least five of them be together at the end, since the team's finish time is that of its fifth rider to cross the line, which determines its standing in today's stage. Each rider on the winning team has that time added to his individual overall time, so it plays a huge role in a contender's final overall position in Paris.

Under a new rule being introduced this year, the other teams are given the time of the winner plus a progressive time penalty: 20 seconds for the runner-up, 30 seconds for the third-place team, 40 seconds for fourth, and so on down to the last team, which is penalized three minutes. The only exceptions to this scoring system are for riders who finish adrift of their teammates: They are given the actual time they take to complete the course. This could be a much larger time penalty, and is the reason why no team wants to leave behind a rider who gets a flat tire or falls during the race, especially if that rider is one of their best hopes for a high placing in the final overall standings.

———

Three minutes before the R.A.G.T. team finishes its team time trial in Arras, the CSC squad is getting ready to start from the medieval Aristide-Briand square in Cambrai. As in the individual time trial, the strongest teams are seeded at the back of the field.

The nine men on the esteemed CSC team wear red uniforms that have the big white initials of the Computer Services Corporation and a stylized eagle emblazoned on the chest. The eagle symbol was added by team owner and manager Bjarne Riis, whose nickname in his racing days was the Eagle of Herning, his hometown. A benevolent, brainy boss, Riis can spot talented riders better than any other team director, he's a smart recruiter, and he has become a brilliant team manager who knows how to get the best out of his riders on a slim budget. When his former team leader Tyler Hamilton told Riis after the 2003 Tour that he was leaving, Riis was distraught. Still, he knew immediately who could take Hamilton's place: the 26-year-old Italian Ivan Basso.

Basso was ready to leave the Italian team, Fassa Bortolo, which is managed by Giancarlo Ferretti, a bullish, balding, godfatherlike figure in his early sixties who has *ciclismo* ingrained in him, body and soul. When I asked Ferretti his assessment of Basso at the end of 2002, he said, "Over the whole season he didn't win a single race and, taking into account his potential and qualities, that's a bit of a waste." Yet that was a year when Basso, then 24, took the Best Young Rider award at the Tour de France, in which he finished eleventh overall. Basso was given a much higher salary for 2003, but Ferretti's opinion of his star pupil deteriorated, even though Basso stepped up to finish seventh at the Tour. At the time when Riis came knocking on Basso's door, Ferretti said, "I can't keep on paying so much to a rider who never wins." Basso says he signed with Riis because the Dane was the first one to talk to him, even though other teams, including Armstrong's, offered him more lucrative contracts.

Ivan Basso is a down-home kind of guy. He proudly wears his wide, gold wedding band, as well as his thin, black sideburns. He's not like the bulk of young Italian racers, whose long hair and sharp outfits come straight from Milan Fashion Week, and whose fast cars are the ones that pass you at 200 kilometers an hour on the *autostrada*. No, Basso moves to a slower-beating drum. Just under six feet tall and weighing a little over 150 pounds, he talks with a soft but firm voice, showing the quiet confidence that has distinguished his cycling career. He has been patiently learning his craft rather than prematurely itching to grab the glory.

In contrast to his flashier peers, Basso is a family man. He's close with his parents and he married young. When I first interviewed him in Colorado, in November 2002, he was thrilled that he and his wife Michaela were expecting their first child, a daughter Domitilla, that February. When we parted, he was off for a visit to GapKids. Family was again on Basso's mind when he came to this 2004 Tour de France. Not his daughter or wife, but his mother, Nives, hospitalized with cancer.

"I know she will be watching me on television," says Basso, whose mother and father, Franco, are both cycling enthusiasts and encouraged him when he took up racing in his mid-teens. He showed early talent for the sport, and his parents were always there to watch him: when he came in second at the world junior championship at San Marino, Italy, at age 17; and when he won the world under-23 championship three years later at Valkenburg in the Netherlands.

Basso started his first Tour de France in 2001 at age 23. That experience abruptly ended after a week, when he crashed on a slick mountain descent while in a breakaway. He still finished the stage in fifth place, but a broken collarbone prevented him starting the next day.

"Of course, I'm sad that I've had to quit," Basso said at the time, "but I'm happy to have discovered a race that really suits me. I know that I am a rider for the Tour de France."

When I spoke to him in 2002, after he placed eleventh at his second Tour, Basso said, "I believe that by preparing even better for the Tour, I really can finish in the top five. I don't have the same motor that Armstrong does. So, to be at 100 percent for the Tour, I have to train in a specific way, not follow the training regimen of another athlete. Not even Armstrong's teammates follow the same training regimen that he does."

After his seventh place in the 2003 Tour, Basso came back this year with the ambition of finishing on the podium—first, second, or third—in Paris.

When I spoke to Riis a few weeks before the Tour, he said that Basso, who was showing erratic form, would be ready for the Tour, as he had planned an extended training camp for the team based near his Tuscany home. Riis added that besides Basso, he was confident that his Spanish climbing specialist, Carlos Sastre, could finish in the top ten, and that with riders like Jens Voigt of Germany, Jakob Piil of Denmark, and Bobby Julich of the United States, he had "a good team for the team time trial."

Cambrai, where the team time trial starts, was on the front lines in World War I. For ten days in November 1917, British tanks pounded the German fortifications in Cambrai, without breaking through. One of the German soldiers defending the city was a young writer, Ernst Jünger, whose first book, *Storm of Steel*, featured that siege. "The breath of battle brushed us and made us shudder," he wrote. "The war had grabbed us like a strange intoxication. And it was under a rain of flowers that we parted, tinted with roses and blood."

No blood will be shed among the squads battling each other in this team time trial, but the Tour has its own "strange intoxication" and an aura of war—especially on an afternoon of apocalyptic rainfall on a course that weaves between fields of wheat and barley, where poppies and wild roses bloom at the roadside, where every village has its war memorial to *"nos disparus,"* where gray concrete blockhouses are a grim reminder of the German war defenses, and where each intersection seems to have signs pointing to cemeteries filled with the graves of thousands of British, Canadian, Australian, South African, and German troops killed in the dark days of trench warfare.

In sporting terms, there will be hidden dangers waiting like land mines in today's stage. On back roads awash with water, gravel, and sand, puncturing the wafer-thin treads of racing tires will be one hazard. Crashes are another, perhaps caused by a bike sliding out on a turn where narrow tires, only three-quarters of an inch wide and inflated to bursting point, fail to grip the slick surface.

To help the riders after crashes or flats, each team has mechanics riding in a pair of support vehicles that carry spare bikes and wheels. After a rider flats, a mechanic runs from the car, removes the old wheel, inserts a new one, and then pushes the rider back into action, all within 20 to 30 seconds. It takes a slightly shorter time for a mechanic to unclamp a bike from the roof rack, run to the rider, and replace a wrecked bike.

Things start badly for the CSC team. Soon after leaving Cambrai, Basso gets a flat front tire and needs a wheel-change. Then his German teammate Voigt punctures his rear tire and gets a replacement bike. Each time, the other team riders slow down, with a couple of them almost stopping, before pacing their colleague back to the group. Each time, they have to accelerate back to top speed, return to their tight riding formation, and refocus on their pedal cadence and gear size. They're usually pedaling between 80 and 90 revolutions per minute and using the highest gear where the chain is on a 55-tooth chainring at the front and an 11-tooth cog at the rear, a combination that moves the bike about thirty-five feet with each revolution of the pedals, for a speed of about 1,000 yards a minute—the equivalent of ten football fields.

Riders are constantly shifting gears on this opening 11.7-mile stretch between Cambrai and the first time check at Metz-en-Couture, because they have to climb seven short hills, for a total elevation gain of 445 feet. CSC's problems put it only twelfth best at this time check, almost a minute slower than the fastest team, Illes Balears, which goes through Metz-en-Couture in a time of 21 minutes, 22 seconds, at an average speed of 33 miles per hour.

Perhaps the Illes Balears riders are inspired by the bright red kerchiefs they have knotted around their necks in honor of San Fermin's Day—which is celebrated today by the Running with the Bulls in Pamplona. Pamplona is where the team's management is based, even though the title sponsor is the Balearic Islands provincial government, which uses the cycling team to promote its Mediterranean vacation islands of Majorca, Minorca, and Ibiza. The top riders on this team are the Spanish champion Francisco Mancebo and the young Russian pair Vladimir Karpets and Denis Menchov.

The rain has intensified in the half-hour since Illes Balears passed the Metz checkpoint, so by the time Tyler Hamilton's Phonak team comes through, its time split of 21:52—while 30 seconds slower than Illes Balears' time—is still excellent, and proves to be the best among the last ten teams to start. It's a performance in line with Hamilton's expectations that Phonak will win this stage and score a psychological victory over Armstrong's Postal team. The one negative so far is that teammate Nicolas Jalabert flatted and has been left behind. "We agreed to wait for anyone who had trouble in the first six miles, but Nicolas flatted after that," explains Hamilton. He and his team director figured beforehand that the half-minute lost by waiting for a still fresh rider in the opening stretch would be overcome by having nine strong men for the full distance. Had they known what was about to happen, they might have waited for Jalabert.

Just one mile after the Metz checkpoint, Phonak faces another quandary when two of its Spanish riders hit problems. Santos Gonzales's handlebar clamp has worked loose and he needs a new machine, while Santiago Perez gets a flat and needs a new wheel. With almost 30 miles still to go, Hamilton realizes that it could be disastrous to ride the rest of the time trial with only six men. From the back of the line he shouts "Stop!" to override the instructions that riders hear through their radio earpieces. Hamilton himself waits to pace Gonzales and Perez back to the rest, but the American underestimates the speed of the chasing Spanish riders, who go straight by him, blown by a strong tailwind, on an open stretch of road between fields of beet and chicory. As a result, Hamilton has to make a big effort to chase back on his own.

Before the Phonak men can regroup, they have to wait again when the powerful José Gutierrez flats. But they don't wait 15 miles from the end when Oscar Pereiro is the fourth Phonak man to puncture. The team has clearly made a mistake in choosing to ride the lightest time-trial tires, which give more speed but not the resilience of a slightly heavier tread. It's a gamble that hasn't paid off in the wet conditions.

Meanwhile, five minutes behind Phonak, the CSC riders hope that their two early punctures are the end of *their* dose of misfortune for the day. But they're wrong. Fifteen miles into the time trial, they are trying to make up for lost time as they race rapidly into Bertincourt. From scouting the course, they know that there's a tricky left-right-left-right-left series of turns through this village of old brick houses. Manager Riis shouts to his men through their earpieces, warning them to take it easy.

"I know I have to go slow," Basso says later, "but all of a sudden I am on the ground. I don't have time to think. It's instinct to stand up right away." Basso lost his balance coming out of the second turn and slid into the curb. The two riders behind him also crash, but like Basso, Julich and the Danish champion Niki Sørensen pick themselves up, ignore their abrasions, and reenter the team's pace line as fast as they can.

With their triple delays, both CSC and Phonak have conceded at least a minute, probably more. But they still have the second half of the course to make up some time, and even challenge the other top teams. Maybe they can take inspiration from the people of the small town they now race through. This is Bapaume, whose name comes from the French *battre des paumes* ("clap hands"), something the locals did in the Middle Ages when travelers arrived in town after making it through the surrounding bandit-infested forests.

The forests have long since been cleared, but the locals have proven to be as feisty as those ancient travelers, rebuilding their town thirteen times over the past millennium. In World War I, Bapaume was occupied by German forces in 1914 and remained on the front line through the nearby Battle of the Somme. It was the scene of bloody fighting, was taken and retaken several times, and was left as a field of ruins at the end of the war in 1918. Perhaps CSC and Phonak can rebuild their challenge as the course turns to the north for the final 17 miles, where the cold northeasterly wind will become more of a hindrance than an aid.

It was because of the day's strong winds that Jan Ullrich's T-Mobile team decided not to fit the rear disc wheels that every other team is using. Carbon-fiber "solid" discs reduce the turbulence caused by regular spoked wheels and give a bike a better aerodynamic performance. But T-Mobile manager Walter Godefroot judged that strong crosswinds would accentuate the one negative of discs: They can catch the wind and make bikes difficult to handle. It appears to have been a bad decision, because T-Mobile, with no delays, comes through Bapaume only a few seconds ahead of the much-delayed Phonak.

Both teams have suffered today because of choices they made over equipment. Their choices may well hurt them in this stage against Armstrong's team, which is the final one to leave Cambrai.

———————

To protect them from the downpour, race officials hold golf umbrellas over the heads of the nine Postal riders, who line up at the start side by side. In a bizarre tableau, local young women who'll be taking part in a later beauty pageant hold the riders' saddles to keep them upright until the timekeeper gives the signal to go. As soon as they're riding, along the aptly named Avenue de la Victoire, the nine men in their blue-and-white helmets, long-sleeved navy skinsuits, and red waterproof shoe-covers snap into their tight, one-behind-the-other formation. Postal won this equivalent stage in 2003, and wants to win again.

Armstrong loves the team time trial, and he knows how to get the best out of his team. His usual strategy is to start relatively slowly and push the pace in the second half. That's confirmed by Postal team director Johan Bruyneel, who says, "It was planned that we would take no risks and not start very fast, but there was a lot of rain that slowed us down a great deal at the start. It's probably a combination of those things that after 10 kilometers we were 27 seconds slower than T-Mobile."

That time difference acts as an incentive for the team, says Bruyneel. "When I saw the time difference I told them to go faster. It was planned to go faster, but I told them they had to go faster than planned." As a result, the Postal men fly through the first official time check at Metz-en-Couture in fifth place, now 9 seconds *ahead* of Ullrich's men, and 21 seconds ahead of CSC, but still 7 seconds behind Hamilton's Phonak squad and 37 seconds behind the feisty Illes Balears.

With the wind at their backs, the Postal men are now into their rhythm, averaging an amazing 35 miles per hour despite contending with the harsh conditions and constant undulations, and having to ride slowly on the sharp turns through the many villages of single-story brick houses and roads made slick by the mud washed from the fields. Former Postal team member Vande Velde well remembers the influence that Armstrong has on his riders: "Lance is definitely the motivator, like yelling obscenities and screaming at us, trying to get us going, to be more excited. 'Let's go!' he shouts, just pushing to get everything out of the guys he possibly can."

The goading from Armstrong and Bruyneel has the desired effect, with team riders George Hincapie, Viatcheslav Ekimov, Pavel Padrnos, and José ("the Ace") Azevedo taking turns at the front, setting the pace alone, sometimes for as long as a mile. By the time they get to the second time check at Achiet-le-Grand, four miles after Bapaume, U.S. Postal has the fastest time of 46:30. That's 39 seconds ahead of Ullrich's T-Mobile men. Phonak, despite its troubles, and with only six riders still together after Pereiro flatted, is 50 seconds behind, while CSC is a minute-twenty-three back. And the early time split of 46:58 set by Illes Balears is still holding up in second place. Those red San Fermin kerchiefs seem to be working miracles, except for a puncture for Mancebo that caused the team to wait.

The Postal win is not yet in the bag, however. There are another 14 miles to go. Postal still has eight riders together while Phonak, which has emerged as the main challenger, is down to only five after the valiant Swiss, Martin Elmiger, rode himself to a standstill. On the straight, flat, open road heading north toward Arras, two Americans are leading the dance: Armstrong paces his team for as long as a kilometer at a time, completing one of these turns in less than a minute (that's almost 40 miles per hour!), while Hamilton is constantly urging on his four teammates and taking long pulls himself.

Phonak keeps up the pressure all the way into Arras, even around the last two slick left turns that lead onto the large, uneven, and very slippery cobblestones of the Grand'Place—a magnificent town square that's surrounded by seventeenth-century Flemish-style buildings featuring arcaded walkways. The crowds are still using the yellow umbrellas they bought from the Tour concession booths, but early-evening sunshine makes a tenuous appearance just as Hamilton's band of brothers crosses the line in 1:13:10, putting them temporarily in first place.

The New Englander stops outside the press tent to say a few words: "We finished with just five guys, but we still had a great ride. I'm proud of my guys. We were fantastic. We didn't give up and we fought to the bitter end. It's a shame; we could have been a lot faster. Take off a minute—the time lost to bike and wheel changes—and see how we shaped up to the strongest teams."

At this moment, Phonak *is* the strongest team, eight seconds ahead of Illes Balears and 12 ahead of T-Mobile. There are just three more teams to come. Basso's heroic CSC squad finishes next, 39 seconds behind Phonak. It's followed by the weary Fassa Bortolo team of Fabian Cancellara, almost four minutes slower than Hamilton's men. And then, just a few seconds behind the Italian squad that started five minutes before them, the victorious Postal riders arrive. Armstrong's men eased up a little in the final few miles, knowing that the win was locked up and not needing to gain any more time—remember, the winning margin is not important because there are fixed penalties for the beaten teams: 20 seconds for Phonak; 30 for Illes Balears, 40 for T-Mobile, and 50 seconds for CSC.

All of the Postal team riders are smiling as they bump over the wet cobblestones before the line. Hincapie, at the front, reaches back with his left hand to shake Armstrong's right hand. The boss obliges, but later admits he was reluctant to take his hand, scared of falling. "In this race, I'm always scared. And when you factor in the rain, the wind . . . the last few days for me have been really traumatic."

His trauma has been exacerbated by a just-published best-selling book in France, *L.A. Confidentiel, les Sécrets de Lance Armstrong*, which intimates that Lance and his team have used performance-enhancing drugs. "It's a tough thing for the team and for him to go through," Hincapie confirms, when asked about the book. "But he takes that and turns it into energy. When for the first time we were up in the time splits, he just started screaming at everybody. He's just a ball of energy, almost like it's his first Tour de France. He was just completely consumed by the race, and by the fact that we were going to win the team time trial, and it was going to be an amazing team effort, not just a Lance Armstrong effort."

To the American fans' delight, the stage win gives Armstrong the overall race lead, several minutes ahead of the previous leader, Robbie McEwen, whose Lotto-Domo team finishes this stage only eighteenth of the twenty-one teams. It's the sixtieth time in six years that Armstrong slips on the yellow jersey. But what's even more noteworthy is that his American teammates are right behind him in the overall standings: Hincapie in second and Floyd Landis in third. As for Armstrong's main rivals, Hamilton has moved up to eighth place in the overall standings, 36 seconds behind. Ullrich, who says he was having nasty memories of the crash he had in similar conditions at the 2003 Tour's last time trial, is sixteenth at 55 seconds; and Basso, who hurt a hip in his fall and had a hard time pedaling after that, is twenty-sixth at 1 minute, 17 seconds.

Two hours after the finish, the Postal team gathers in the dining room of the hotel where they're staying the night: the secluded l'Univers, an elegant stone building with an inner courtyard that began life as a monastery in the eighteenth century. There's a mood of muted celebration and optimism among the squad's entourage. Armstrong has the yellow jersey, but he says he has no intention of defending it for the moment. After all, the first mountain stage is still one week away, and there's no point in tiring out his teammates, who would have to ride hard at the front in all of the next six stages to keep their leader in yellow.

However, team director Bruyneel is not against one of Armstrong's teammates, specifically Hincapie, taking the lead. "Of course, our objective is not now to retain the yellow jersey," he says. "But if George can smell the good break and get in there, he has a free ticket. No problem."

Would Hincapie take a chance at taking over the yellow jersey from his boss? "Oh yeah," he says. "It is the Tour de France, though . . . and it's so difficult to get in breakaways. But if the chance was there, I'd definitely take it. That would be very cool."

STAGE RESULT: 1. U.S. Postal-Berry Floor, 1:12:03; 2. Phonak, 1:13:10; 3. Illes Balears, 1:13:18; 4. T-Mobile, 1:13:22; 5. CSC, 1:13:49.

OVERALL STANDINGS: 1. Armstrong; 2. George Hincapie (USA), at 0:10; 3. Floyd Landis (USA), at 0:16; 4. José Azevedo (Portugal), at 0:22; 5. José Rubiera (Spain), at 0:24; 8. Hamilton, at 0:36; 16. Ullrich, at 0:55; 21. Leipheimer, at 1:08; 26. Basso, at 1:17; 92. Mayo, at 5:27.

The Yellow Jersey

JULY 8: *From one cathedral town to another, this 124.5-mile stage from Amiens to Chartres heads south through the hilly farmland of Picardy, crosses the Seine River valley, and closes on flat roads through the wheat and corn fields of the Beauce region. Strong easterly winds and heavy rain showers add to the day's challenges, making this a day propitious for breakaways.*

Standing on the smooth flagstone floor of Notre Dame Cathedral in Amiens, I can hear the silence. This 83,000-square-foot edifice is higher, longer, and wider than its Paris namesake and considered "one of the world's supreme creations." More than a hundred slender stone pillars reach 138 feet above my head to the unseen rafters, while a surprising number of tall, stained-glass windows bring in the gray light of a cool, humid day. Two other visitors are present. One is praying in the *"zone de silence,"* to the left of the elaborate, 700-year-old wrought-iron choir screens. The other is walking the thin, curving black line of the cathedral's famed labyrinth. The few muffled sounds that filter into this sacred haven come from the Tour de France: the strident horn of a team car leaving the start early, the perky jingle of a publicity vehicle leaving late, and the amplified voice of a hawker selling *"le collection officiel du Tour!"*

I join the spectators outside the cathedral on the Rue Victor Hugo—a street named for the nineteenth-century French poet and novelist who described Amiens Cathedral as "a marvel." If he were here today, he might well marvel at *le Tour.* As an advocate for social justice and the common man, Hugo would appreciate this sporting event that democratically carouses through the streets of peasant villages as well as the cities of the rich, becoming, for the moment, an integral part of everyone's life. And he would enjoy the enthusiasm for the race I hear in the voices of these noontime fans, who are happy to watch the Tour departing their city before taking in a quick lunch, maybe the regional specialties of duck pâté and leek pie, washed down with a bottle of blonde *Arrageoise* beer. The locals are so excited by the race they even applaud the press vehicles of *France-Soir, L'Équipe,* and their local *Voix-du-Nord* newspaper that depart Amiens just ahead of the riders.

The first few miles of every road stage are like a parade, as the peloton rides behind the slow-moving, bright-red sedan of race director Jean-Marie Leblanc, until clearing the city limits. So the pack is moving slowly when it turns into the Rue Victor Hugo, and the fans can easily pick out the different riders, particularly those in distinctively colored jerseys. They all applaud the man near the front, Armstrong, who has a broad smile on his face and a yellow, long-sleeved rainproof top over his brand-new yellow jersey. They get a longer look at another rider, Thomas Voeckler of the Brioches La Boulangère team, who's wearing the blue-white-and-red jersey that's

awarded annually to the winner of the French national championship.
Voeckler has just suffered a flat rear tire, and he stops at the corner,
removes the rear wheel, and waits for his team car to drive up with a
spare. He's probably thinking "better now than later" as he appraises
the puncture, for the 25-year-old Frenchman has big hopes for this
day. His team mechanic changes the wheel and pushes Voeckler back
into action. He has an easy task of joining his fellow competitors before they all reach the rolling start, four miles down the road, where
Leblanc tells his driver to accelerate as he waves a small tricolor flag,
signaling to the riders that the stage from Amiens to Chartres is under way.

As soon as the flag drops, another man wearing a tricolor jersey,
Dutch champion Erik Dekker of the Rabobank team, lifts himself out
of the saddle, stands on the pedals, and sprints away from the field.
He's soon caught, but his acceleration triggers a series of attacks,
fierce and unrelenting, most of them featuring riders from the French
teams, Boulangère, Cofidis, and Fdjeux.com, along with CSC of
Denmark. "Every day of the Tour is a world championship," says
Armstrong. "You've got about eighteen teams that want to win a
stage, so there's always somebody playing to win."

About six miles into the race, a breakaway group of eight riders
forms and moves a hundred yards clear. Hincapie is among them.
Perhaps this is a chance for the 31-year-old New Yorker, who lives in
North Carolina, to gain a little prestige beyond that of being Armstrong's "best teammate." Because his boss is now wearing the yellow
jersey of race leadership, Hincapie does not have to work in a breakaway. Every team respects this basic protocol of the sport, that a
leader's teammate can race defensively by riding at the back of any
group. And since Hincapie is lying second to Armstrong in the overall

standings, he would automatically take over the yellow jersey if his group managed to stay clear of the pack until the finish.

Hincapie was in a similar break in the opening week of the 1998 Tour between the Breton ports of Roscoff and Lorient, where he came within two seconds of taking the yellow jersey. That was his last chance for Tour glory; every year since then he has been a selfless worker for Armstrong. Today, though, Hincapie has been given the green light by Armstrong and Bruyneel to go with a break like this one, which has no riders who could pose a long-term risk to the defending champion's bid for another Tour win.

Unfortunately, says Bruyneel, "when George got into that break, the T-Mobiles chased." That's because Ullrich's team was reluctant to give *any* of Armstrong's men a free ride. As a result, Hincapie's eight-man move is caught just before a small hill, where the pack finally slows down a little. The stage is still less than 10 miles old, but when the road levels out after the short climb, the day's winning break moves clear. Fdjeux rider Sandy Casar is the first to accelerate. He wants to make a big impression on this stage because some 70 miles down the road, in his hometown of Mantes-la-Jolie, his family and friends are waiting for him, brandishing a twenty-foot-wide banner that says, "*Salut Sandy Casar.*"

There are many miles and challenges before reaching Mantes though. First, Casar has to prolong his attack on this windswept ridge that commands wide views over the green, undulating countryside of Picardy. He's soon joined by two men who have figured in many long-distance breaks over the years: CSC's Jakob Piil and Cofidis's Stuart O'Grady of Australia. Then, two other chasers manage to cross the growing gap—Sweden's Magnus Bäckstedt of Alessio-Bianchi, who's a renowned hard worker, and the ambitious Voeckler. Within a couple of miles, after speeding downhill into the village of Croissy-sur-Celle, the five men have a half-minute lead.

"We decided to let this move go clear. It was ideal for us," explains

Postal's Bruyneel, "five strong riders from five different teams and none of them dangerous on general classification." The Postal director knows that each of the five men in the break has up to eight teammates in the pack, perhaps forty riders in all, who will now ride defensively by disrupting the efforts of rival teams to organize a chase. Also, the riders who crashed or made big efforts in yesterday's team time trial, including Hamilton's and Ullrich's men, will be happy to have a less stressful stage today.

As a result, Bruyneel's team restores order by moving to the front of the peloton, and setting a steady pace that's just fast enough to discourage an all-out pursuit. This allows the break to quickly gain ground: five minutes as they crest a short climb at Crèvecoeur-le-Grand, ten minutes as they pass the massive yet unfinished Gothic cathedral in Beauvais, and almost 15 minutes as Casar and Voeckler lead the breakaways over the Category 4 Mont des Fourches hill, the day's high point at 813 feet elevation, 44 miles into the stage. Will their lead keep on growing? At what point *does* it start to matter?

———————

As the breakaway riders continue their adventure, race followers begin to recall similar situations in Tours past. Surely Armstrong and Bruyneel must be remembering a break they let get out of control in 2001, when thirteen riders gained thirty-five minutes on a hilly 138-mile stage to Pontarlier. What they might have forgotten, though, is that one of that break's driving forces was O'Grady, who is also in today's break, and who ended up in the yellow jersey at the end of that cold rainy day.

O'Grady, who does poorly in mountain terrain, wasn't a threat to Armstrong's overall victory at the 2001 Tour. But another man in the infamous Pontarlier thirteen was a little-known rider from Kazakhstan, Andreï Kivilev. The Kazakh wasn't on the Postal team's "A list" of challengers, but he *was* a surprisingly good climber and strong enough not to lose too much time to Armstrong in the mountains.

Armstrong and I had talked about the Pontarlier break a few months before the 2004 Tour. "I guess we dodged a bullet that day," he said. "We would never let that happen again. Had Kivilev not lost eighteen minutes on a stage a few days before that break, he would have had the full thirty-five minutes. . . ." Armstrong was referring to an earlier stage on which the Postal team made a huge effort that split the peloton into two halves. Kivilev finished with the rear half of the pack that day, and thus conceded those eighteen minutes.

"I remember the day we created that split," the Texan continued. "Everybody on the team asked me why we did all that work, and who was so important at the back. I said, '*Kivilev* was in the back.' 'Kivilev? Ha, ha, ha,' they replied. Three days later he gets thirty-five minutes, and I said, 'Guys, remember that? You remember you all yelled at me the other night?' So you've got to look at guys like Kivilev."

When the 2001 Tour ended, Kivilev took fourth place, nine minutes and 53 seconds behind Armstrong. If the Kazakh hadn't lost those eighteen minutes in the earlier stage, he might well have won the Tour—or, at the very least, Armstrong would have had to summon up a phenomenal effort to make up another ten minutes.

Tragically, Kivilev was killed when he crashed at the Paris to Nice race in March 2003. His death was the catalyst for a new International Cycling Union rule that made helmets mandatory in every bike race.

There are no guarantees that the move by O'Grady, Piil, Bäckstedt, Casar, and Voeckler will carry them to the finish of this Amiens–Chartres stage. In fact, that looks unlikely when three miles after the Mont des Fourches summit the Lotto, Quick Step, and

Gerolsteiner teammates of sprinters McEwen, Boonen, and Danilo Hondo suddenly increase the pace of the peloton. If they don't get a chase organized now, they won't get another chance.

So the three teams decide to make a classic cycling move, the *echelon*: On the dead straight road, with the wind coming from the left, the first rider moves at great speed along the left center of the road. His colleagues then form an angled pace line, each one slightly behind and just to the right of the rider in front, so that each gets some shelter from the wind. Once the first rider has ridden hard for perhaps five seconds, he drops back a few feet to allow the rider on his right to take his place. As each rider drops back after his turn at the front, they form a parallel line of riders, with the front line moving to the left and forward, and the second line of riders taking shelter from the first and moving back and to the right. From above, you would see a constant counterclockwise rotation of the two lines, similar to the formation geese use when flying against the wind.

If the echelon, which is probably composed of twenty to thirty riders, is formed correctly, it is impossible for any others to jump into it. The trailing riders are forced to ride single file in the right-hand gutter—getting no shelter from the wind and working twice as hard as those in the echelon. They *can* start a second echelon, which forms maybe 100 yards behind the first. That's what happens right now, and a half-dozen echelons are soon spaced at regular intervals down the road.

This is exactly what occured on that stage in 2001 when Postal put on the pressure at the front, and the rear echelons steadily lost ground, with the gap finally extending to the eighteen minutes conceded by Kivilev and ninety other riders. The same thing could happen today, because the echelons are moving perhaps 10 mph faster than the five-man break, which could quickly be caught. Instead, the echelons are abandoned when the course bears left onto a more sheltered road that leads into a town with several sharp turns. O'Grady and his four companions, now riding in steady rain that has just started, retain a healthy lead.

Soon after the peloton slows at the day's feed zone—where each rider grabs a small cotton shoulder bag of provisions to replenish the supply of nutrition bars and instant-energy gels carried in his jersey's rear pockets—the sprinters' teams once more increase the pace. The pack splits into several echelons, but a mass pileup in heavy rain ends the acceleration just as the pack leaves Magny-en-Vexin, a small town of creeper-clad brick-and-stone houses. Dozens are involved in the crash, including Roberto Heras, Alessandro Petacchi, and three of Armstrong's teammates. The pace slows so that the fallen and delayed riders can return to the regrouped peloton. All of this allows the five leaders to push ahead to a lead of 17:20. That's too large a gap for the sprinters' teams of McEwan, Boonen, and Hondo to close in the remaining 40 miles, so it's now left to Armstrong's Postal men to stop the gap from becoming too huge. They're remembering what happened with Kivilev and, as Armstrong said, they'll never again let a break gain *too* much time.

Of the five breakaways, the highest placed is Thomas Voeckler, the young French racer who started the stage exactly three minutes behind Armstrong, 59th in the overall standings. Second best is O'Grady, 120th overall and a full 3 minutes, 49 seconds behind Voeckler. The youthful French champion's claim to the race leadership becomes a certainty 10 miles out of Chartres, where the five are still together, with a fifteen-minute lead. That's when the riders catch their first glimpse of the twin 375-foot-high spires of the city's breathtaking cathedral that appears to be floating above the wheatfields to their left. "To do its beauty justice," wrote Victor Hugo, "you'd need whole volumes and millions of exclamation points."

By the time the breakaways reach the base of the black crags on which the cathedral stands, they have each made separate, but failed attacks. The five come together again as they top the ridge on the opposite side of the valley from the cathedral, and prepare to sprint for the stage win. All of them are tired from their five hours at the head of the race, battered by the wind, numbed by the rain, and depleted by the many climbs. The giant Bäckstedt, six-four, 198 pounds, is hurting so bad he can make only a token acceleration before dropping his head in exhaustion. But O'Grady uses the Swede's short effort to get up to sprinting speed, and he battles past a dogged Piil to take a jubilant victory.

O'Grady is thrilled. "This is a massive relief after everything that's happened in the last few months," he says, referring to a doping scandal that enveloped his Cofidis team all year long. Although the Aussie, new to the team, is not implicated, several of his teammates have been sacked after admitting to using banned drugs. O'Grady said that in April he lived through "the hardest ten days of my life," when his beloved grandfather died, he crashed in a race and broke a rib, and his team suspended its entire racing program because the media furor over the doping scandal became so bad.

While O'Grady talks about "going back to basics" and "racing with new heart" since he returned to Europe after his grandfather's funeral in Australia, Voeckler, the new leader of the Tour, says he's only just realized what he can achieve in cycling. "Last year, in my first Tour, I was overwhelmed by the speed," he admits. "Things only started to click at the Classique des Alps race a few weeks before this year's Tour. I found myself in the winning break with great climbers like Mayo and Sevilla, and it somewhat surprised me that I could stick with them."

Voeckler was born in a small town near Strasbourg in northeast France, and at age seven moved with his parents to a fishing village on the Caribbean island of Martinique. Tragically, his father was lost at sea on a solo transatlantic voyage; but the teenage Thomas went on to become a proficient sailor before taking up cycling at age 13. He also learned to speak Creole from his black buddies, who nicknamed him "Ti-Blan," or "little white guy." His family still lives in Martinique, which is officially part of the French Republic, but Voeckler moved back to the mainland in the late-nineties to pursue his dream of becoming a professional cyclist.

A bit of a romantic, Voeckler always wanted to win a bike race on his birthday, June 22. He finally achieved that feat eleven days before this Tour, when he celebrated his twenty-fifth by winning a mountain stage of the four-day Route du Sud race, after sharing a daylong breakaway with Casar—who was with him again in today's marathon move. Then, a week before the Tour, Voeckler won the 140-mile French national championship race.

But nothing comes close to wearing the yellow jersey. And today, after his group finishes twelve and a half minutes ahead of the peloton, Voeckler gets the thrill of pulling the Tour leader's yellow jersey over his champion's tricolor outfit.

Why yellow? The idea came to race founder and director Henri Desgrange during the 1919 Tour, the thirteenth one he had organized, after he heard complaints from roadside spectators that they had a hard time identifying the man leading the race. Desgrange decided to award a special jersey, and he chose yellow because the newspaper he edited, *L'Auto*, which also sponsored the Tour, was then printed on yellow newsprint. Today, his "HD" initials adorn the shoulders of every yellow jersey, reminding us of his pioneering efforts.

Desgrange was a larger-than-life figure who helped create the Tour's mythical image by penning fiery prose on that yellow newsprint. He once wrote a cyclist's training manual called *La Tête et les Jambes* ("The Head and the Legs"), which spelled out the need for a successful racer to have a smart brain as well as strong legs. He would have appreciated Voeckler's strategic attitude. After donning the yellow jersey, with a nearly ten-minute lead over the now sixth-placed Armstrong, the talkative "Ti-Blan" says, "I heard Armstrong say he wasn't going to defend the jersey, so that gave me some ideas."

Later, a journalist points out to Armstrong that Voeckler could be another Kivilev, and that the mountain stage the young Frenchman won at the Route du Sud included four Category 1 climbs in the Pyrenees. "I guess I didn't know that," the five-time champion admits, "but I think we're confident with the gap." At least it isn't thirty-five minutes!

———

Besides Desgrange, credit for creating the first Tour also goes to Géo Lefèvre, *L'Auto*'s lead cycling writer in 1903. Lefèvre's ideas probably evolved when he attended the Lycée Marceau, an elite high school here in Chartres. Like anyone else seeing the city's exquisite cathedral for the first time, he couldn't help but be inspired by the beauty, design, and immense scale of a structure built almost a thousand years ago. Bold projects breed bold ideas.

At a November 1902 meeting in the Paris offices of their newspaper, editor-in-chief Desgrange asked for ways to boost the paper's fortunes, as the publication was in danger of losing a circulation war to its rival sports daily, *Le Vélo*. In response, the then 25-year-old Lefèvre outlined a plan for a new bike race "longer and harder than all those that already exist," and encompassing the whole country. "And what name will this race have?" asked a skeptical Desgrange. Lefèvre shot back, "*Le Tour de France, pardi!*"

Now, a century later, *le Tour* has finished in Chartres for the first time, and another 25-year-old Frenchman, Thomas Voeckler, has realized *his* bold idea of leading the race that Géo conceived. Voeckler is the new *maillot jaune*, the yellow jersey.

STAGE RESULT: 1. O'Grady; 2. Jakob Piil (Denmark); 3. Sandy Casar (France); 4. Thomas Voeckler (France), all same time; 5. Magnus Bäckstedt (Norway), at 0:03.

OVERALL STANDINGS: 1. Voeckler; 2. O'Grady, at 3:13; 3. Casar, at 4:06; 4. Bäckstedt, at 6:06; 5. Piil, at 6:58; 6. Armstrong, at 9:35; 13. Hamilton, at 10:11; 21. Ullrich, at 10:30; 31. Basso, at 10:52; 95. Mayo, at 15:02.

Dangers in Angers

JULY 9: *This 122-mile stage from Bonneval to Angers is one of the flat-test of the whole Tour, heading west along the Loire River valley, through towns dominated by impressive châteaux. Strong head winds will make life hard for breakaways, and likely cause a mass sprint finish.*

A wall of riders suddenly falls before him. Tyler Hamilton slams on his brakes. Haunting memories flash through his mind: last year's crash, the broken collarbone, the pain.

Well into the final mile of this stage into Angers, and racing along the residential Rue du Maine at 40 miles per hour, Hamilton was right where he should be, near the front of the tightly packed peloton, not far from his rivals Armstrong and Ullrich. "I was thinking, 'Oh, wow, only one K to go.'" He knew he was just one kilometer from the finish because that's where the organizers erect a 20-foot-high, four-legged tubular plastic archway that straddles the street. "I could *feel* there was going to be a crash. You could just feel it. It was very nervous. And just as we were going under the archway I thought, 'If they crash in the front, we'll all get the same time.'"

Hamilton was referring to Article 20 of the race regulations, which states: "In the event that a rider suffers a fall . . . after passing the final kilometer sign . . . then the rider concerned is credited with the same finishing time as that of riders he was with when the incident occurred." If a crash occurs *before* one kilometer to go, the victims receive their actual time—even though it might take them several minutes to extricate themselves from a crash, check their bike for damage, maybe have a wheel changed, and ride to the finish.

To think about this rule at the precise moment he is about to crash affirms how focused Hamilton is on winning the Tour. He doesn't know what his fate will be, but he's reassured knowing he won't lose any "race" time.

Losing time is the last thing on Robbie McEwen's mind. The Australian sprinter who took the third stage into Namur is ready and eager to win another. "I thought, 'I feel fantastic,'" he says. "I really thought that I would win today." Approaching the one-kilometer-to-go mark, McEwen is riding at the very front of the group, just to the right of a big Austrian rider, René Haselbacher, who is setting the pace for his Gerolsteiner team's top sprinter, Danilo Hondo.

Haselbacher, who crashed in a sprint finish at the 2003 Tour and almost took McEwen out, has a reputation for taking big risks in mass sprints. Right now he is trying to squeeze past the leaders on the far left of the 20-foot-wide street. Before making his move, he doesn't see that the aluminum crowd barriers present a threat. To make enough room for the archway's legs on the tiny sidewalk, the barriers along this block have been moved from the sidewalk to the street. This has narrowed the roadway by two feet. Also, two of the barriers angle slightly farther out into the street to go around the heavy base of one of the legs. "I felt that it was getting narrower and narrower," says Hamilton. "It's crazy to send 180 guys down a street like that when we're racing flat out." He has a good point, because it was also the Tour organizers' poorly designed stage finish at Meaux twelve months ago that exacerbated the damage caused by the terrifying crash that Hamilton can't put out of his mind.

At the crash site in Angers, an on-duty police officer later tells me, "A racer hit one of the barriers on the left just as they went under the archway." That rider was Haselbacher. In trying to race through a gap down the left side of the street, he hits the protruding barrier, his handlebars break, and he's sent cannoning into the riders on his right. Most of them come down, including McEwen, who confirms, "Haselbacher bounced into me." At least a dozen riders on the right get through unimpeded, including the previous day's winner, Stuart O'Grady, who says, "I heard the crash right behind me, the sound of twisting carbon and alloy."

Near the back of the peloton, a tall, skinny Dane, Michael Rasmussen, nicknamed "Chicken," is taking no chances. "I hit my left hand yesterday, and I have a few bruises on the usual spots, hips and knees. So I stayed in the back today just to stay out of trouble in case of crashes. That gives you another few seconds to slow down. I actually heard the crash before seeing it. A lot of noise. Just like metal against metal and pavement."

Instantly, Rasmussen and everyone else grab for their brakes, but as Hamilton says, "There's not much you can do when you're racing at 60 kilometers an hour and twenty guys crash in front of you. There was a fallen rider right there. To avoid riding into him I just jammed on the brakes. If there'd been a camera there, it was a crash they would have kept on replaying in slow motion. I spun over the handlebars, flew through the air, and landed on my back." The impact is so violent that Hamilton's helmet splits open, while his entire back, shoulders to hips, slams into the tarmac, before he careens along the pavement on his back, scraping away skin and deeply bruising a half-dozen ribs.

When I visit the crash scene after the race, I see the frightening proof of the pileup: thirty bike-tire skid marks where riders slammed on their brakes. The thin black lines are up to 30 feet long. Most are straight, a few of them snaking, and they all veer toward the curbs to the left or right, where riders tried to avoid the pileup in the middle. "There's no place to go when there are barriers down both sides," Hamilton notes.

An Angers resident, Robert Forvoille, who lives in the neighborhood, tells me: "I was hanging over the barriers watching the riders. They were going very fast, and then they all seemed to fall at once. At least twenty were on the ground. People were gasping, 'Oh! Oh! Oh!' as each rider fell." The policeman, who saw the crash from behind, adds that "the riders completely blocked the street, and I had to clear a way through for the ambulances."

The medical team's main focus was Haselbacher, who was lying on the street, screaming in pain. McEwen, furious at the Austrian, relates, "I walked over to where the medical staff was attending to him and said, 'It was all your fault! You've done it again!'" The shoot-from-the-hip Aussie, who probably phrased his displeasure more colorfully than that, had a right to be angry. Haselbacher's move was reckless. And in search of glory for his team, he endangered the lives and aspirations of many others.

After limping to the finish several minutes behind the rest of the crash victims, McEwen was clearly suffering. It was difficult for him to walk because the skin from his left buttock had been stripped away, and his right buttock was almost as bad. But he was more concerned about a long, deep wound down his left calf muscle that could have longer-lasting consequences. An X-ray didn't reveal any fractures, because the swelling on his back probably hid the two broken vertebrae that were identified after McEwen finished the Tour. No wonder he was in pain for the rest of the race.

Back on the Rue du Maine, Hamilton is the most badly injured of five Phonak riders who fall. After a teammate helps pick him up, Hamilton remounts his bike and slowly rides to the finish. Had he looked down when he crossed the intersection at the Rue de Brest, he would have seen in two-foot-high white letters painted on the street: "HAMILTON. WINNER." Was this still a possibility, or was his dream of Tour victory slowly unraveling?

———————

Armstrong also crashed on this stage, but he was luckier than Hamilton. Just eight miles from the start in Bonneval, the pack was stretched into a long line, racing after a group of breakaways and fighting a strong crosswind that blew across the open wheatfields of the Beauce. With such a wind, every rider battles to stay as close as possible to the man in front of him, with one man's front wheel usually overlapping the rear wheel of the next. It only takes an extra strong gust to make the two wheels touch, and that's what happened: Two riders went down right in front of the defending champion. "I braked as hard as I could, but there was nothing I could do," Armstrong said. He hit the road, but had slowed down enough that he sustained only minor scrapes to his hip and knee.

"I was a little bit behind Lance when he fell," said his American teammate Floyd Landis, who was able to immediately help his leader. That was fortunate because, as Landis added, "Sometimes the radio's not working, and that was the case when he fell." He was referring to the wireless communication system that the Postal team uses to send messages between team director Bruyneel and the riders, to advise them of road conditions and let them know when Armstrong needs help. By the time Armstrong picked himself up, Landis and three teammates were with him, ready to pace him back to the peloton.

Four hours later, 90 percent of the field either falls or is blocked by the disastrous pileup in Angers created by Haselbacher. Unlike Hamilton, Armstrong has enough space to slow down before falling. He dismounts, wheels his bike past the fallen riders, and rides slowly to the finish.

Crashes are an ever-present danger in bike racing. The massive one in Angers marks the twenty-fifth time in the first week of this Tour that riders have fallen. "It was like NASCAR," joked actor Robin Williams, "'They're down! They're back up again!' It was full-contact cycling. 'Be there! Sixty men start, two men leave!'" Some of the crashes are single-rider falls; others involve a few men who fall after their wheels touch; and a few, like this one, bring down dozens. Ninety-nine of the 188 starters have already fallen, some multiple times. One team, Cofidis, has had all of its riders involved in crashes, including the Australian Matt White, a strong support rider who left the U.S. Postal team at the end of 2003 to join a team that would give him the chance of riding his first Tour. Unfortunately, a few hours before the start of the Liège prologue, White crashed over some television cables in the start area when he was looking over the course. He broke his collarbone and couldn't start the Tour.

His team put in a phone call to its veteran Peter Farazijn, who lives in Flanders. He was the only team member able to reach the Liège start in time to replace White. Farazijn wasn't keen to ride another Tour de France, which he last started in 1999. When he got the call on his cell phone, the 35-year-old Belgian was out watching a motor rally near Ypres. He dashed home, grabbed some clothes and his team uniform, and—this being the equivalent of an American footballer getting a last-minute call to the Super Bowl—he was given a police escort to drive at 100 miles an hour from one side of Belgium to the other. He arrived a few minutes late, but his prologue start time was rescheduled, and he rode White's bike and race number (which featured the Australian flag) to 185th place. "When they called me, I thought I might be okay for three or four days and then I'd go back home, but I'm still here," Farazijn says. He would go on to finish the race in Paris in 107th place.

Of the ten riders who dropped out in these opening seven days of the Tour, eight were injured in crashes; one quit due to the consequences of a pre-Tour incident, and the tenth was eliminated for finishing outside the official time limit. The rider who abandoned the race for extraneous reasons was an Australian, Brad McGee. This 28-year-old from New South Wales, who has been tipped as a future Tour winner, came into the Tour with high expectations after two months of excellent results. His team's sponsor, the French national lottery Fdjeux.com, put considerable pressure on him, expecting him to win the prologue time trial in Liège, just as he did in Paris in 2003. Despite a back problem that he had kept to himself, McGee dug deep into his reserves to take fourth place, nine seconds behind Cancellara.

The seriousness of McGee's condition became apparent the next day, on the road to Charleroi, when he lost contact with the main pack in the high-speed finale and arrived six minutes behind the rest. He was reluctant to talk afterward, but did express the pain he was in. "My back is cut in half, and I can't feel my legs," he said wearily. "My feet are numb, and I can't get any power." As for the reasons of his suffering, McGee would only say "home duties." Later, he told a friend that he put out his back a week before the Tour when he was planting olive trees at his new home in Monaco. Contacted a week after he left the Tour, McGee said, "My team doctor said I have symptoms of fibromyalgia. It's like a chronic fatigue ailment, but with mental as well as physical characteristics." McGee's condition is not uncommon in a sport that places harsh demands on its athletes' bodies and minds.

Some are tempted to give up when they're wounded, exhausted, and demoralized. Others ride until they drop. That's the case with Nick Gates, another Australian, who crashed on the first road stage, banged his knee on the handlebars, and, in great pain, courageously rode the last 60 miles on his own. He finished half an hour behind the pack, and was eliminated for crossing the line outside the mandatory time limit.

In the early years of the Tour there were no such limits. Even riders who finished several hours behind the day's winner could remain in the race. In today's more competitive environment, all the racers have to finish within a certain percentage of the stage winner's time. It's a cruel rule, but it's also practical. The Tour roads are completely closed for several hours a day, and they have to be reopened to regular traffic as soon as possible after the race ends. In addition, officials have a short time window to record and tabulate all the racers' times, while the construction crews have to begin dismantling the finish "city" within an hour of the last man coming through.

The time limit for a flat stage is set at nine percent of the race winner's time. Gates arrived more than thirty minutes behind stage one winner Jaan Kirsipuu, 5 minutes and 23 seconds too late. Another reason for the elimination rule is that a rider who finishes outside the limit is probably not capable of continuing in the race for much longer. That was the case with Gates, whose knee injury was serious enough that his team doctor at Lotto-Domo would never have allowed him to start the following day.

Gates's role at the Tour would have been to help his teammate McEwen get through each stage safely and keep him fresh for the sprints. It certainly would have been an important task on this stage to Angers, which McEwen was so confident of winning. The 32-year-old sprinter knew that a mass finish was inevitable on what was the flattest course of the race, especially on a day of head winds when it's harder for anyone to sustain a break. So the six-man breakaway that escaped 13 miles into this 122-mile stage didn't have much hope of success. Still, the six riders stayed together for almost 100 miles before starting to fight among themselves, each one hoping that he'd be able to hold off the pack and win the stage. The last of the six to be caught was a speedy young Spanish rider, Juan Antonio Flecha. He was passed by the stampeding peloton within sight of the kilometer-to-go archway, moments before the crash that changed the course of the entire Tour.

Twenty riders managed to escape the crash by passing through on the right. They continued toward the finish and got ready for a sprint. Specialist sprinters can generate phenomenal power, but only for a matter of seconds, the time it takes to cover about 200 yards at top speed. Usually, teammates help maneuver their team's sprinter into the best position from which to make a final thrust—it's better to remain sheltered from the wind by riding behind your opponents, and accelerate past them in the final 100 yards. But today's sprint, which is uphill for the last half-mile, is hardly usual: There are no teammates to help these sprinters; they've all been blocked or downed by the crash. So it's man against man, as first one, then another tries to sprint clear, with each of them running out of steam on the difficult uphill finale.

In the end, it's Tom Boonen of the Quick Step team—who didn't figure in the sprints the first two days because his chain dropped each time—who proves to be the fastest and strongest. He zips across the finish line outside the ornate city hall of Angers with time to raise his arms in triumph, well clear of O'Grady and Zabel. This is his first Tour and his first stage win—a huge boost to the young Belgian's nascent career. "It's the sort of sprint I love," says Boonen, "even though I was a little scared in the finale. I was most worried about Zabel, who also likes an uphill finish."

Ullrich is the only one of the race favorites who isn't involved in the pileup; he finishes with his friend Klöden just behind the sprinters. Over the next several minutes, all the riders who fell or were delayed in the wreck drift slowly in. Among the first to arrive is the uninjured Armstrong, alongside his faithful Hincapie. Basso, too, isn't hurt but his CSC teammates Julich and Voigt were victims. A battered Hamilton arrives with teammates Gutierrez, Pereiro, and Perez, and heads straight to the white Phonak team bus. The final man to finish is McEwen, who has a dazed look in his eyes when he crosses the line, helped by his tall Belgian teammate, Wim Vansevenant.

While the TV cameras and radio reporters focus on the day's winners and breakaway heroes, a handful of journalists gather outside the Phonak bus. The team's mild-mannered Spanish team director, Alvaro Pino, is angered by the crash. Speaking in French, he says, "All of Tyler's back has abrasions, and both arms. He went down with four more of my men: Bert Grabsch, Martin Elmiger, Jalabert, and Sevilla."

"Who's to blame for this pileup?" he asks. "Just ask the riders. It's those two sprinters, McEwen and Haselbacher. They do the same dangerous things every day. They should put them out of the race . . . send them home."

The team's manager, Urs Freuler, a tall, elegant Swiss with an Inspector Clouseau mustache, is less emotional about the crash. "It's bad luck, no? The riders involved were all in the first twenty, twenty-five riders. It's clear that Tyler's morale is not so good, because he's thinking about last year when he broke his collarbone in a similar fall. But he can move everything and so we hope he will be okay."

One reporter asks Pino, with no regard to his distress about having two-thirds of his riders suddenly injured, how all this will affect their performances in the Pyrenees, which are still a week away. Pino has had enough. He turns his back on her and walks away.

An ambulance, its siren wailing, pulls up nearby. The Phonak bus door opens and Hamilton's top *domestique*, Pereiro, a Spaniard who fell in the early part of the stage, steps out and walks across to get help. He needs an X-ray on a damaged right hand. "We hope he can start tomorrow," says Freuler.

It's now almost 6 p.m., only twenty minutes after the stage finished. The Postal and T-Mobile buses have already pulled away. Spectators are streaming out of downtown, headed home, perhaps to a quiet game of *pétanque*, or for a pre-dinner drink at a local bar or bistro. I check to see if an Indian restaurant I pass will still be open at 10 p.m., the time that the pressroom closes, and when we head out into the dusk for dinner. There will still be a few hours of daylight when Armstrong and his Postal teammates reach their hotel after a 40-mile drive to the little town of Pouancé, which is not far from tomorrow's start at Châteaubriant, where Ullrich's T-Mobile squad is staying. Both of these teams have come through the end-of-race pileup unscathed. Hamilton and Phonak experience a far different outcome. Their team doctor and physiotherapist will have a busy evening in nearby Beaucouzé, where the injured riders will have a restless night.

It takes an element of good fortune to win the Tour. Hamilton has had more than his share of bad luck, and on this day, he once again met up with his all-too-often fate.

STAGE RESULT: 1. Boonen; 2. O'Grady; 3. Zabel; 4. Hondo; 5. Baden Cooke (Australia), all same time.

OVERALL STANDINGS: 1. Voeckler; 2. O'Grady, at 3:01; 3. Casar, at 4:06; 4. Bäckstedt, at 6:06; 5. Piil, at 6:58; 6. Armstrong, at 9:35; 13. Hamilton, at 10:11; 21. Ullrich, at 10:30; 31. Basso, at 10:52; 94. Mayo, at 15:02.

Testing Times

JULY 10: *This 127-mile stage from Châteaubriant to St. Brieuc heads north to the coast of Brittany and is the only day that riders in the 2004 Tour will see the ocean. A hilly finale will make it tough for the sprinters today.*

It's a beautiful day in Brittany. After a week of mostly rain, the sun has gloriously returned, a soft breeze rustles the oak and holly leaves, and birds sing in the swaying gorse and broom grass. Our press car crosses a stone bridge over a shining stream, drives up a short hill that swerves past flower-bedecked granite houses, and speeds down a single-lane farm road, always following the yellow race arrows. With only minutes to spare, we pull into a big grassy field where today's stage starts in Châteaubriant. There's no problem finding a parking space since most of the accredited vehicles have already left. Perhaps they knew beforehand that to get from one side of this small town to the other, the Tour organizers would send us on a 20-mile jaunt through the countryside.

Right then, one of our cell phones rings. It's a fellow journalist: "Have you heard that one of the Lotto riders, Christophe Brandt, has tested positive?" Dark news. This Tour's first doping offense. It deadens the invigorating day. As I run between parked cars toward the team buses, I think about the call and feel saddened. I hear that Brandt broke down and cried. He couldn't understand why he tested positive for methadone at a routine drug test taken in Namur a few days ago. "I was shocked, too," says Lotto team manager Claude Criquielion. "Christophe is one of the most diligent riders on the team."

I find the Phonak bus and talk to Hamilton as he rides to the start line. "How did you get through the night with those back injuries?" "I had to use sleeping pills," he replies. "I can only sleep on one side." Sleeping pills? Perhaps there's a banned product in those, too, I think, getting a little paranoid. But I'm sure his team doctor checked them out.

Hamilton says he hopes the racing won't be too hard for the next two days, so he can start to recover and get safely through to Monday's rest day. With that, he joins a smiling Armstrong and a serious-looking Ullrich, and they head off with the pack for another long stage in the Tour, this one heading north toward the Emerald Coast of Brittany. All of the major contenders are looking for a safe and crash-free day, hoping that the pack will stay together for the finale, the yellow jersey will stay on Voeckler, and they will maintain their high overall standings.

———

We learn more about the Brandt case. He told his team bosses that there had to be a mistake. This was the only time he'd tested positive in five seasons as a professional racer. And he had no idea how traces of methadone—an artificial narcotic used for rehabilitating heroin addicts—had entered his body. But methadone can also be used as a pain-reliever, which is why it's on the World Anti-Doping Authority's (WADA) blacklist.

Brandt's culpability is later confirmed when a urine sample he had supplied in Angers also comes up positive for methadone. A month before the Tour, the 27-year-old Belgian was feeling great. After three weeks racing in Italy, he'd gone home to his wife in Liège to tell her all about his fourteenth place at the Giro, the Tour of Italy. He was considered Lotto's best hope for a high placing at the Tour de France. Now, certain to be sacked by his team, his future in the sport is uncertain.

Although daily drug tests remain a deterrent, they rarely reveal a true cheat. They're more likely to catch out someone like Brandt who unwittingly absorbs a banned drug—he later claimed that his regular nutrition supplement was contaminated with methadone. Unlisted ingredients often show up in supplements, and that's why the athletes and their doctors have to be painstakingly aware of what they can ingest and what to avoid. The WADA list of prohibited substances is constantly growing, so even common nutritional products can contain banned ingredients.

As a result, we see cases like that of U.S. Postal's Czech rider, Pavel Padrnos, who is being threatened right now with expulsion from the Tour. His crime? He's on a list of riders who were caught in possession of "banned substances" at a police sweep on team hotels at the 2001 Tour of Italy, and he's due to be questioned at a judicial hearing later in the year. A few days earlier, the French daily *Le Monde* reported that Padrnos could join two others riders, Martin Hvastija of Alessio and Stefano Casagranda of Saeco, who've been threatened with exclusion from the Tour for being involved in the same investigation.

"I know everything about this case, and we're not speaking about any medicines here," says Postal team director Johan Bruyneel, referring to the product found in Padrnos's hotel room three years ago. "There's nothing. There *is* a small quantity of monitol in [the product they seized], but it's there as a preservative. There is no reason to have any doubts about Pavel Padrnos." Monitol is listed by WADA as a prohibited substance because it can be used as a diuretic, which means that a rider *could* use it to flush out illegal products from his system prior to a drug test. But not if it's solely a preservative.

The European public doesn't show much interest in drug stories involving men like Padrnos, Casagranda, Hvastija, and Brandt. In fact, the French don't even seem bothered that their most popular rider, Richard Virenque—who this year is attempting to win a record seventh King of the Mountains title—was a central figure in the infamous Festina affair at the 1998 Tour. The Festina team was ranked number one in the world before a team assistant, Willy Voet, driving a Festina team car, was stopped on his way to the Tour by French border police. They discovered large supplies of banned drugs, including the blood booster erythropoietin (EPO) and human growth hormone, which the team members (including Virenque) eventually admitted were destined for their use at the Tour. This doesn't stop the French fans from screaming with adulation whenever Virenque passes them on these twisting back roads of Brittany, or on any other stage. Yet while Virenque and the other Festina riders have been largely forgiven, even seen as victims for their doping offenses, the European media and public seem ready to condemn any hint of transgression by Tour champion Armstrong.

When the Festina scandal broke, Armstrong was just making his comeback to cycling after eighteen months of battling cancer and recovering his health. In early 1998, before reporting to the training camp of his new team, U.S. Postal Service, he spent several weeks with his fiancée Kristin at a beach house in Santa Barbara, California.

There he began serious training, taking his first long bike rides since overcoming cancer. After his rides into the San Rafael Mountains or along the coast, he had a massage from Shelley Verses, a soigneur who previously worked with a number of professional cycling teams. She was the first female soigneur on the European circuit, and is highly respected for her skills as a massage therapist and nutritionist.

I asked Verses if she talked about drugs with Lance during his stay in Santa Barbara. "We used to talk about the simplicity in cycling," she replied. "We talked about how the cyclist's body only needs certain things, and how a cyclist's body can't metabolize certain things. . . . I gave Lance oral homeopathics from Germany to take after he left Santa Barbara. Had those products been available here in the States in subcutaneous injectable form, I would have given him those products, 'cause they would have been absorbed faster. The ones I gave him were just plain old cellular homeopathic products that anybody here could buy. We also talked about drugs, mostly just the dangers of what was happening in the cycling world."

Those dangers were emphasized a few months later when the Festina affair broke at the Tour. During the race, French police raided several teams' hotels and hauled a number of riders to police stations where they were strip-searched, interrogated, and held in jails overnight. Their harsh treatment caused an outcry from the other competitors, who staged two sit-down strikes, one delaying a stage by two hours, the other causing a stage to be abandoned. Seven of the twenty-one teams quit the Tour in protest.

During and after that Tour, the European public was bombarded with newspaper and TV stories and even books about illegal drug use in cycling. The Tour organizers responded to the backlash against their sport by greatly increasing the number of surprise early-morning blood tests they would take. And a skeptical media sent news reporters as well as cycling specialists to the 1999 Tour. Lance Armstrong, riding his first Tour after cancer, was their prime focus of attention—especially after he walloped the best continental racers on the opening day's prologue.

Suspicions that the Texan might be using performance-enhancing drugs surfaced before the fifth stage when the sports daily *L'Équipe* revealed from an unnamed source that one of four urine samples taken after the prologue tested positive for a corticoid (as corticosteroids are usually called). Since prologue winner Armstrong was among those tested, the media rushed to conclusions. That evening, the International Cycling Union issued a statement confirming that yes, one of the four samples was above the legal limit, but adding that the rider involved had a medical certificate to use corticoids—which can help asthma sufferers, cure skin disorders, or (illegally) help an athlete recover from fatigue. The Danish racer Bo Hamburger, one of the four tested, who had a certificate to use the drug for his asthma, turned out to be the culprit.

This did not stop the growing cynicism of the French media, and Armstrong knew that questions about doping would keep coming back. In response, on the Tour's first rest day, he made an extraordinary, impassioned statement to a crowded pressroom: "I think we all love this sport, and we're all here for that reason. . . . Now, we can choose to do one of two things. We can try and break down a Tour de France that's been around forever, or we can try and repair it. Unfortunately, there are still some people that want to tear it down. I'm not one of them. I want to be part of its renovation. It's not a crooked sport. It's a healthy sport, a good sport. It's a wonderful sport."

The following day, Armstrong amazed the cycling world by winning a six-hour, 140-mile stage with a mountaintop finish at Sestriere. On that cold rainy evening in the Alps, I was standing near the finish line next to a veteran Italian race follower, watching a TV monitor. When Armstrong rode away from the best Spanish, Italian, and Swiss climbers on that steep mountain road, the aficionado vigorously shook his head and cried out, repeatedly, in English: "Doping!" "Doping!" "Doping!"

Immediately after the finish, I was asked by a genuinely baffled French radio reporter to explain to his listeners how, after coming back from cancer, a "non-climber" like Armstrong could win a mountain stage and increase his overall lead on the runner-up to six minutes. I told him and his listeners: "Armstrong was already a good climber on shorter hills when he was young, and he has lost ten kilos in body weight since then because of his cancer treatment. That's given him the build of a climber, tall and lean, and has increased his power-to-weight ratio by a good ten percent. Last September he showed us that he could stay with the best climbers on long mountain climbs by finishing fourth at the Tour of Spain. This year, he has focused his whole season on the Tour, worked on his power, and trained tirelessly in the mountains near his home in Nice. His victory today doesn't surprise me at all. *Voilà!*"

I could feel that the radio guy didn't believe my explanation. Nor did other reporters in the pressroom that night. When I gave a British sportswriter my opinion that Lance didn't use illegal drugs, he laughed in my face. "You're stupid to think that. That's naïve . . . "

The cynicism was the same at the following year's Tour, in 2000, when a French television network decided to investigate the U.S. Postal team, looking for any signs of "suspicious" activities. One morning during that Tour's final week, the TV crew followed Postal's Spanish doctor and American chiropractor when they drove from the team's hotel in Courchevel. Halfway to the next stage town, the car stopped, and the doctor dumped some trash bags in a roadside bin. The French cameraman then filmed the bags' contents: mostly disposable syringes and used medical products. Many teams get rid of daily medical waste in the same manner; but after Postal's trash-bag incident was shown in a sensational TV documentary, a Paris judge opened a judicial investigation. It lasted some two years and involved testing all of the team's urine samples, which had been kept in cold storage since being taken at the Tour. Nothing irregular was discovered, and the case was quietly closed. The only "suspicious" product found in the medical trash was Actovegin, a filtered extract of calf's blood that the investigators said could be used to oxygenate the blood. The team claimed it helped treat riders' road rash, and was also used by a diabetic member of its back-up staff.

Tyler Hamilton, who was on the Postal team that year, has unpleasant memories of the investigation. "Basically, they were saying we as a team were dopers. . . . I was angry. If I was actually taking whatever that was [Actovegin], I guess I would have felt different. But when you're accused of something you don't even *know* about. . . . Somebody can make a statement, and that becomes fact, and you're guilty until proven innocent. It can be frustrating."

Armstrong continues to feel frustrated and angered by the still ongoing innuendo that he uses performance-enhancing drugs. He has frequently pointed out that he has never tested positive in his twelve years of professional cycling—and he's been tested as much as any cyclist in history. In 2002 he told me, "You think I wanna do something stupid, and see my kid go to high school in ten years and have somebody across the aisle from him say, 'Oh, your dad's that guy that got busted for dope'?"

———————

Brandt has been branded a doper, and his eviction from this Tour engenders plenty of discussion in the peloton. But the riders don't have much time to chat as they race out of Châteaubriant through that bucolic Breton countryside at breakneck speed. The Phonak team riders try to control and slow the pace, to make things easier on Hamilton's injured back, but they can't stop the rush of attacks. The pack's speed is so great—31 miles completed in the first hour—that the Saeco team's Italian leader, Gilberto Simoni, a two-time winner of the Giro, falls off the pace. Demoralized by two crashes he's had in the past three days, a week of rain, and the daunting speeds, Simoni looks ready to quit. But his boss admonishes him on the team radio and orders all of Simoni's teammates to wait. Shortly after they pull him back to the peloton, one of Brandt's Belgian teammates, Thierry Marechal, and Rabobank's always ambitious Erik Dekker make the day's first successful break. They struggle to gain the first minute. Then their fortune improves when the Boulangère team, whose new star Voeckler has held the yellow jersey for two days, moderates the pace of the pack, just as Armstrong's Postal team did on the stage to Chartres. Without the pack breathing down their backs, Marechal and Dekker—neither of whom are threats on General Classification—surge ahead. Within an hour, and with 70 miles left to race, the two breakaways have an eight-minute lead.

In the months leading up to this Tour, Armstrong knew that a book attempting to link him to illegal drug use would be published in June, and on sale throughout France in July. The book, *LA Confidentiel: Les Secrets de Lance Armstrong*, is written by two well-known journalists, Frenchman Pierre Ballester and Irishman David Walsh. To research their book, they spent three years interviewing dozens of people. Ballester, once a cycling staff writer for *L'Équipe*, was the ghostwriter for a "tell-all" book by Willy Voet, the Festina soigneur who was caught red-handed with a carload of banned drugs on his way to the 1998 Tour de France. Walsh, the chief sportswriter of London's *Sunday Times*, is on a crusade to eliminate doping from sport. This book reflects that mission, and it's written with an assumption that most cycling teams turn a blind eye to doping. The narrative has three threads: the story of Lance Armstrong's cycling career; the story of the U.S. Postal Service team and its policies, written from the perspective of the people who work for it; and the authors' views on the widespread nature and dangers of doping in cycling. Doubting the authenticity of Armstrong's repeated victories at the Tour de France, the authors quote extensively from the French newspapers *Le Monde* and *L'Équipe*, as well as from Armstrong's two autobiographical books, *It's Not About the Bike* and *Every Second Counts*. Testimony comes from former teammates and team workers of Armstrong.

The most potentially incriminating testimony is that of Stephen Swart, a former New Zealand cyclist who raced on Armstrong's team, then sponsored by Motorola, in 1994 and 1995. Swart told the authors that he used the banned blood-booster EPO in June 1995. "As I remember it, we didn't speak much about EPO in 1994, but we did the following year," said Swart, who went on to talk about "a program" that he, Armstrong, and teammate Frankie Andreu discussed during a March 1995 training ride in Como, Italy. "We talked among ourselves, deciding what to do. Lance took a full part in the discussion, and his view was that we should go ahead." When Andreu was asked to comment, he said he didn't remember the training ride. "Perhaps Steve had this conversation, but I don't remember it." According to Swart, there was no collective "program," and it was up to each individual to organize himself. Swart said he bought his EPO supplies over the counter at a pharmacy where he lived in Switzerland. The book implies that Armstrong, too, was "on the program," but the authors present no evidence of that.

After the Motorola team lost its title sponsor at the end of 1996, many of its staff moved on to the U.S. Postal squad that Armstrong joined in 1998. Hamilton was with Postal throughout this period. He told me, "I've ridden on three different teams and I can say there is no systematic doping. I can't speak for the other teams, but clearly if you want to dope it's up to you. It's your risk, not the team's. It's in your contract if you're caught positive for something, you're out, no question about it. And that's the way it should be."

More damning testimony for *LA Confidentiel* came from an Irishwoman, Emma O'Reilly, who was a massage therapist with Postal when both Hamilton and Armstrong were on the team. O'Reilly, who eventually became Armstrong's personal soigneur, talked about three incidents that made her suspicious. The first happened in August 1998 when she dropped off Armstrong at an airport in the Netherlands. He asked her to dump a small black bag he'd forgotten to dispose of himself. She said it contained empty syringes used at the weeklong race he'd just finished. The second incident was in May 1999, when Armstrong asked O'Reilly to drive from France to the team's Spanish base, a ten-hour roundtrip, to get some pills for him. O'Reilly describes team director Johan Bruyneel "discreetly slipping a bottle of tablets into my hands . . . with no one seeing me." She says she delivered the plastic bottle containing two dozen pills to Armstrong in Nice, where he lived at the time. The third incident came just before the start of that year's Tour de France, when O'Reilly used some makeup foundation to mask some bruises on Armstrong's arm caused by syringes.

When I asked Verses, the seasoned American soigneur, about these incidents, she was unconvinced of their significance. "It's part of a soigneur's job to dispose of syringes," which are used by all cyclists on a daily basis to inject vitamins and other nutrients in the most effective way. "And I used to drive all over the Continent getting drugs," Verses continued, "*legal* drugs. And I often lent guys makeup to hide bruises. Riders are so vascular because they have no body fat, and they bruise easily." And most people wouldn't understand that these bruises, like the use of syringes, are commonplace.

Perhaps more troubling is a conversation O'Reilly tells the authors she had with Armstrong a few weeks before the 1999 Tour. While he was on her massage table, he told her his hematocrit level—the percentage of red blood cells—was 41 percent, whereas the limit allowed by the International Cycling Union is as high as 50, and the higher the level, the less you have to work to go the same speed. O'Reilly says she replied impulsively, "But that's terrible, 41, what are you going to do?" She alleges that Armstrong answered, "Emma, you know what I'm going to do, I'm going to do like all the others." The inference was that other cyclists used EPO to artificially raise their hematocrit level to close to 50 percent, which can considerably improve an athlete's performance.

The book then details Armstrong's longtime association with Italian sports doctor and coach Michele Ferrari, who has been charged in Italy with supplying elite athletes with banned products, including EPO. Ferrari denies any wrongdoing. "I've never prescribed doping products," he told the court in April 2003, "as I believe that doping boomerangs and affects the health of an athlete who uses it." He also has explained that his work with Armstrong and coach Chris Carmichael since 1998 has been principally to improve the Texan's climbing style, focusing on an increased pedal cadence.

Armstrong, who told me in 2002 that Ferrari had also helped him with altitude training, vigorously defends his association with the controversial doctor. "It's been a hard relationship, a hard topic for us to figure out what to do," he admits. "We've all known him for a long time. And we've known him to be fair, honest, correct, and ethical, so we cannot punish the guy, because that's the person we see.

"We've consulted with him for a long time . . . and they've looked everywhere for [a connection with banned drugs]. Everywhere. Blood, urine—for years. And it always comes up clean. If I were so dirty, and Michele Ferrari were so dirty, and Chris Carmichael were so dirty, and we were all so dirty, don't you think that they would have found it by now? It's not there, so I stand by Michele."

Armstrong has indeed never tested positive, and his current team has said repeatedly that its riders do not use banned substances. Which leaves us with two camps of opposing views. On one side, there are those who truly believe that Armstrong is a drug cheat, but their only "proof" is "he said–she said" recollections, circumstantial evidence, and the assumption of guilt until proven innocent. On the other side, there is the Tour champion and his acolytes, who passionately deny all such charges and rightly claim that Lance is innocent until proven guilty.

———————

In Liège, two days before this Tour began, Armstrong was asked at a press conference for his reactions to the book. Knowing that co-author Walsh was present, he said, "Extraordinary accusations must be followed up with extraordinary proof. Mr. Walsh and Mr. Ballester worked four or five years, and they have not come up with extraordinary proof. I will spend whatever it takes, and do whatever it takes, to bring justice to the case."

Armstrong and his lawyers were in the course of starting libel suits against the book's authors and publisher in France, Éditions de La Martinière; the Paris magazine, *Express*, that published doping-related extracts from the book; and *The Sunday Times*, for a full-page story based on the book's findings. A Paris judge turned down an injunction from Armstrong's lawyers requesting that their client's denial of the book's contents be inserted in every copy.

Besides the book, Armstrong had other drug-related matters on his mind. The most upsetting was the pre-Tour admission by one of his good friends in the sport, British rider David Millar, leader of the Cofidis team, that he had used the banned blood booster EPO on several occasions. As a consequence, Millar was barred from starting this Tour. The Scotsman was the latest "catch" of a French judicial inquiry investigating a drug-trafficking ring that involved several members of the Cofidis team.

Millar told the police that he bought his doses of EPO from a Spanish doctor, Jesús Losa, who was the team physician for Iban

Mayo's Euskaltel team. One of Euskaltel's riders, Gorka Gonzalez, was prevented from starting the Tour when "abnormalities" were identified in his pre-race blood sample that could have been caused by the use of EPO, which is why the Tour had 188 starters instead of 189. Euskaltel sent Losa home during the first weekend of the Tour.

The in-competition blood and urine tests, a growing number of unscheduled out-of-competition tests, and mandatory quarterly medical checkups on *every* professional rider make cycling the most drug-tested sport in the world. This in turn makes it increasingly difficult for drug cheats to escape detection. And now that there's a test for EPO, and more and more riders are being caught positive, the next step in doping could be gene manipulation—which has already been added to the list of prohibited methods and substances, even though there's no evidence that this is happening. Avoiding any specifics, Tour director Leblanc told me he feels that "certain doctors in cycling have gone off track and done things to improve the performance. And that's not medicine. . . . I think the doctors are very much responsible."

Meanwhile, the only real breakthroughs in detection during recent years have been achieved by the police, whistleblowers, investigative journalists, or just plain luck. The shocking admission of guilt from Millar—who defeated Armstrong at the opening time trial of the 2000 Tour and was a favorite to win the time-trial gold medal at the Athens Olympic Games—continued a series of doping revelations in 2004. One of the most worrisome came from a Spanish cyclist, Jesús Manzano, who shared his story of systematic doping in cycling with the readers of *As*, a Madrid sports newspaper.

Manzano was well known to Tour de France followers because of his collapse, believed to be due to heat stroke, at the 2003 Tour. He revealed in his newspaper story that his collapse was caused by a mysterious injection he had been given that morning by a staffer on his Spanish team, Kelme. His accusations against the team, which sacked him at the end of the 2003 season, led to Kelme not receiving an invitation to the 2004 Tour.

The repeated disclosures about systematic doping have made life difficult for every Tour de France rider. "Cycling's taken such a bad hit this year," says Hamilton. "In Spain, where people love cycling, some of my teammates have said people on the road make comments to them just because of one rider, Manzano. France has been the same. You're out there trying to train, and people are harassing you." Tour contender Ullrich observes, "As in life, cheating seems to be part of it, and there will always be some black sheep. It's a pity for this beautiful sport."

Despite the distractions of suspicion, men like Ullrich, Hamilton, and Armstrong must remain centered, to focus their attention solely on winning the Tour. They all have their families and friends to support them in this ambitious goal, while Armstrong has a much wider family to depend on—and to answer to. Most of all, he cannot let down the folks in his cancer community, who see him as the ultimate symbol of hope and inspiration. He knows that they would be devastated should he be identified as a drug cheat.

———————

The two breakaway riders Marichal and Dekker—who have decided that today's the day they will make *their* big effort in this Tour—are 8:30 ahead of the pack when they race through Calorguen, where they are greeted by a Breton band, yellow balloons, and thousands of people in a festive mood. The celebrations are special in Calorguen, because this is the adopted home of five-time Tour de France champion Bernard Hinault, who became a farmer here when his racing career ended in 1986. Returning to the soil—he grew up in a farmhouse at nearby Yffiniac—reflects his family's simple lifestyle. Like many Europeans, his parents never owned a car and have gotten around on bikes and mopeds all of their lives. Hinault remains in the national spotlight, though, because of his other job. As the Tour's public relations chief, he rides with guests in his blue VIP car at the head of the race and orchestrates every day's award ceremonies. The famed champion even helps the winners put on their yellow, green, white, and polka-dot jerseys. When Armstrong clinched his fifth Tour victory in 2003, Hinault greeted the American on the podium, shook his hand, and said, "Welcome to the club." And should Armstrong win his sixth, Hinault's handshake will be just as warm. "Armstrong can win six, seven if he wants, it makes no difference to me," he says.

Hinault could probably have won six or seven Tours himself, but records like that never interested him. He's a dogged individual who holds strong views and sees life in black and white—just like the Badger, the nickname he acquired as a tenacious racer. When asked about the drug abuses in cycling, for which cheats rarely get suspended from racing for longer than one year, he says, "There are still some idiots who dope, but if we made the decision to ban them for life, they wouldn't be there."

As one of his race duties, Hinault heads the panel that chooses each stage's most combative rider. Today, he'll pick Marichal, a modest rider who's won only a half-dozen races in his nine years as a professional racer, who instigated the breakaway with partner Dekker. They are still four minutes ahead of the pack when they reach the coast.

Right then, CSC team director Riis orders his troops to move forward, just after the course turns sharply left at the stubby Cap Fréhel lighthouse, a beacon that warns fishing boats of the bleak 200-foot-high cliffs we can see to our right. With the wind blowing off the steely ocean, bringing in a slashing rainstorm, Basso's men form a perfect echelon and race as fast as they can. Their effort splits the peloton in two. Riis is hoping that some of Basso's rivals will be caught out in the back group. But the only "names" left in the big group behind are points leader Stuart O'Grady and French hope

Christophe Moreau, who call on their Cofidis and Crédit Agricole teammates to chase the main pack in an attempt to re-merge the two groups.

It takes the two teams almost 20 miles of wild riding over roads dipping in and out of small beach towns to close in on their goal. But their 50-second deficit is erased only when the wind eases, which nullifies the effect of the echelon, and the CSC riders decide to halt their collective effort. The CSC acceleration has pulled the peloton past Dekker and Marichal, so CSC now delegates its trusty Piil into a new breakaway, and three others join him. On a long, straight road between rich meadows, the four men gain a half-minute lead that decreases to just 12 seconds by the time they reach Hinault's original hometown of Yffiniac. They're caught as they leave town at the foot of a two-mile-long hill—the same hill that the young Hinault climbed on his red bicycle on his way to school.

"If a truck was passing at the right moment." Hinault remembers, "I'd tuck in behind it, sheltered in its slipstream, so I could climb the hill at thirty miles an hour. It was a risky business, but I liked the challenge, the risk, and the effort."

Thirty-five years on, without a truck to pace them, the Tour riders crest the hill in a swirling mass, seeming to merge with the ten-deep lines of spectators greeting them. Right then, another Hinault, unrelated to Bernard, sprints away from the pack: Sébastien Hinault, who races for Crédit Agricole and lives close by. He joins six others in a new break, with four roller-coaster miles remaining. "I saw that the sprinters' teams weren't too strong today," Hinault says, "so I had to try something." He's right. The long effort by CSC weakened all the sprinters and destroyed their plans, and their teammates no longer have the strength to pursue this new seven-man move.

A steep downhill helps the breakaways gain a 10-second lead as they approach the two climbs and two descents to come before a short rise to the St. Brieuc finish. First, one rider lights out from the break, then another, then another . . . until Spanish champion Francisco Mancebo of Illes Balears gets clear. He's joined by the youngest rider in the race, Fassa Bortolo's Filippo Pozzato, 22, who could be an Italian Armstrong in years to come. The two are caught on the last downhill by one of the orange-clad Euskaltel Basques, Iker Flores, who uses his momentum to start an early sprint for the line.

But the one with the most speed in his long legs is Pozzato. The rangy Italian bolts past Flores for the victory, his hands covering his face in joy. Until yesterday, when his team leader Petacchi left the Tour after a crash, Pozzato was working as a domestique. Now he's a winner, happy that his team manager Giancarlo Ferretti gave him the chance.

By now, Christophe Brandt is home in Liège, where the Tour started a week ago. The Belgian's future is uncertain, mired under the dark cloud of doping. Here in St. Brieuc, the evening sun has cast a golden light on the hilly streets, bringing a bright ending to what has been a difficult day. But for Armstrong, Ullrich, and Hamilton, it was the trouble-free day they hoped for, and Voeckler still holds a comfortable lead and the yellow jersey.

It's fitting that the stage is won by the Tour's youngest rider, under the guidance of the Tour's oldest boss. Ferretti has seen it all. He raced before anti-doping rules existed, directed teams through the decades of denial (to themselves and the public), and now tries to restore romance to his sport. The grizzled Godfather speaks for many when he says, "My most negative experiences have taken place only recently: these moments of persecution with regard to doping. Here in Europe, we feel persecuted by judges, the police . . . everyone, as if we were all criminals. I don't feel like a criminal. I feel like a sportsman, a man who has very much helped his many racers, and who will continue to do so for, I hope, a long time."

*STAGE RESULT: 1. Filippo Pozzato (Italy); 2. Iker Flores (Spain);
3. Francisco Mancebo (Spain), all same time; 4. Laurent Brochard
(France), at 0:10; 5. Sébastien Hinault (France), same time.*

*OVERALL STANDINGS: 1. Voeckler; 2. O'Grady, at 3:01; 3. Casar,
at 4:06; 4. Bäckstedt, at 6:06; 5. Piil, at 6:58; 6. Armstrong, at 9:35;
13. Hamilton, at 10:11; 22. Ullrich, at 10:30; 26. Leipheimer, at 10:43;
31. Basso, at 10:52; 89. Mayo, at 15:02.*

Traditions, Culture, and Beliefs

JULY 11: *This 104.5-mile stage starts at Lamballe, a town just to the east of yesterday's finish. It heads southwest on twisting roads to Mur-de-Bretagne, where the day's steepest climb awaits the riders: one mile at 8.6 percent. The course remains hilly for the rest of the day, with a mile-long climb to the finish in Quimper, but the sprinters are still favored to win.*

The people of Brittany love nothing more than a bike race. For the farmworkers, fishermen, shipbuilders, chefs, and shopkeepers of this wild, rocky peninsula, cycling is almost a religion. They talk about it daily, they know all its history, and they argue passionately about its stars. When the sport was at its zenith just after World War II, virtually every town and village had its own bike race, organized by the *comité des fêtes* that nearly always included the local priest—who made sure everyone attended morning mass before going to the race. Often, the cycling event would be part of a *pardon*, a traditional Catholic festival that features religious parades, Celtic music, folk dancing, and a street fair. Many of these *pardons* are still run, along with scores of other circuit races and multiday stage races, making Brittany one of the most active bike-racing provinces in France. Not surprisingly, it has produced hundreds of top racers, including three postwar Tour de France winners, Bernard Hinault, Louison Bobet, and Jean Robic. The Bretons worship their champions, and flock like pilgrims to see the Tour whenever it visits their rugged region. To join them on this second Sunday of the Tour, I head over misty gray hills to the little hillside town of Châteauneuf du Faou.

The big stone church in the center, where barriers are being placed and banners hung for one of the Tour's intermediate sprints, is closed for renovations. Mass has been transferred to a smaller granite chapel that sits on a promontory high above the curving green valley of the River Aulne. I get there by crossing the marketplace, where a trio of jazz guitarists is strumming a half-decent rendition of "Misty." The chapel's congregation is already leaving, some joining the trio's audience at long tables outside a food tent. A handwritten sign offers "ham on the bone" and "fish couscous."

It's just after 1 o'clock. And while thousands of fans have already taken up prime viewing spots on the hill that leads into town, the racers are only just leaving the start in Lamballe, 80 miles away. They aren't due here in Châteauneuf until 4:18 p.m., according to the Tour's yellow road book. This 198-page manual provides details of every day's stage, with maps, profiles, schedules, and everything else an accredited race follower needs to navigate this moveable beast. For now, though, I'm watching the early part of the stage on a widescreen TV set up in the window of an electronics store. It looks damp and chilly back in Lamballe. All the riders are in long sleeves, while some wear knickers to keep their leg muscles warm in the humid air. Heavy rain is in the forecast: typical summer weather for this most maritime part of France.

Before the race is even a half-hour old, a group of three men break away: Ronny Scholz, a young German on the Gerolsteiner team; Matteo Tosatto, an Italian domestique on Fassa Bortolo; and Piil, the persistent Dane who seems to get into a break every day.

It'll be another couple of hours before they get to Châteauneuf, where main street is slowly turning into a racecourse. Crowds line the barriers, an announcer at the sprint line gives updates on the break's progress, and rock music blasts from loudspeakers fixed to lampposts. Older residents remember when this was the *finish* line for their annual circuit race, forty laps around the town, with a couple of short climbs every lap. "We'd get the best riders from all over Brittany," recalls Pierre Cloarec, a man in his sixties who's standing by the church, reading the sports section of *Ouest France*. "I remember the guy who won here three times, Le Buhotel. He last won in sixty-four, I believe."

Le Buhotel: That's a name I haven't heard for a long time. "He was part of what we called the Breton mafia. There were four of them," I tell Pierre. "I raced here in Brittany for a couple of summers in the mid-sixties. Rode for a team over in Vannes."

Pierre is impressed. "So you raced against those guys?"

"Well, I raced *with* them," I correct him. "They were too good for me. I was just starting out. They were all ex-pros. Won all the prizes and split the cash between them. Controlled everything. The mafia."

"I remember now. Another one was Thomin, right? He lived in this area. I think he won a stage of the Tour once."

"Yeah," I confirm. "The others were Bihouée and Le Bihan. They were incredibly strong. At a race near here, I attacked on a hill where there was a cash prize. Le Bihan cruised up to me like he was on rails.

Didn't say anything, just wagged his finger. I figured I wasn't supposed to be going after 'their' prizes. They made more money as amateurs than they did as pros!"

"Umm . . . François Le Bihan," Pierre contemplates. "There was a big stink in the papers when he died. I think he was only thirty-seven. They said it was the drugs that killed him. A lot of riders went to his funeral."

Le Bihan and his buddies began racing in the early fifties, soon after a war in which amphetamines were issued to the troops to keep them alert. In that time and environment, bike racers popping pills was no big deal. It was already part of the culture—and was an accepted part of the sport's culture as well. Yes, it was doping, but there were no drug tests at races, no lists of prohibited substances. When the French government passed an anti-doping law in 1966 and sent police to test riders at the Tour in Bordeaux, the cyclists staged a protest, led by five-time Tour de France champion Jacques Anquetil. That was where he made his infamous statement: "You can't win the Tour de France on mineral water alone. . . ."

There were pills aplenty, but no drug testing in 1960, when Le Buhotel and Edouard Bihouée raced at the Tour. That was also the year when renowned *New York Herald Tribune* sports columnist Red Smith came to report the race. He didn't write about drugs, but about the riders' amazing courage and daring. One was a Belgian who "plunged over the side, splitting his head and carving up both arms . . . remounted and rode on. Along the curb smiles changed to horror as he passed. 'It's nothing,' he said through a red mask."

Smith was also impressed by the size and diversity of the crowds. After one stage, he wrote: "In the crowd the clergy is heavily represented, priests, friars, nuns. The Tour de France seems to have a special appeal for the religious, probably because the riders hitting sixty [miles per hour] down the bend are shaking hands with the hereafter."

Cyclists know the dangers they face every time they put a leg over a saddle at the start of a race, or even before a training ride. Lance Armstrong has had several "shaking hands with the hereafter" bike moments. The Texan isn't a churchgoer, but he does wear a silver cross on a chain around his neck. It was given to him at the Indianapolis Medical Center by his nurse, LaTrice Haney. She would chat with him about cycling while she monitored his chemotherapy sessions. That cross has seen its share of duty.

Three years after his cancer treatment ended, Armstrong had two bad crashes, both during training rides, not races. In May 2000, while descending a Pyrenean mountain pass at 50 miles per hour, his front wheel hit a small rock in the road, the tire exploded, and he couldn't control the bike as he raced toward a switchback turn. He hit the road with a thump and sustained a slight concussion. Armstrong was lucky, especially as he wasn't wearing a helmet that day. Two months later, he won the Tour for a second time.

Later that summer, while training for the Sydney Olympics, Armstrong was on a deserted country road in Provence with his then teammates Tyler Hamilton and Frankie Andreu. "Lance was in front," Hamilton remembers. "He went around a turn and there was an almighty bang. He'd hit a car coming the other way that was on the wrong side of the road. It was the first car we'd seen in an hour. Lance's bike was wrecked, and I thought he'd be too." This time, Armstrong cracked a vertebra, but he didn't need surgery. Another lucky escape.

The worst *race* crash the Tour champion had was in June 2003 at the Dauphiné. Coming down an alpine descent in a fast-moving line of racers, his rear wheel locked up when he braked for a bend. He fell heavily and went careening down the road. "That was my scariest moment ever on a bike," he later said. This time, he *was* wearing a helmet, and his only immediate injury was a gashed right elbow that needed a couple of stitches. Lucky again? Or was it LaTrice's good-luck charm?

Jan Ullrich makes a quick sign of the cross with his right index finger before he starts time trials at the Tour. "I'm not religious," he tells me, "but I'm not a complete non-believer. I have my own belief in myself, and things that bring me luck. I carry them with me." He wears two items that his partner Gaby gave him: a silver hoop earring and a St. Christopher's medallion that hangs around his neck on a tight leather cord. A silver cross sometimes replaces the medallion. And to boost his fortune, the German also counts on two stuffed animals, a chubby *plüschhamster* and a little elephant.

Ullrich acquired most of his good-luck items after a bad crash at the Tour of Germany in May 1999. He fell with a bunch of other riders on a slick, wet road, and suffered a blow to the head and damaged knee cartilage. That crash stopped him from riding that year's Tour. He had another serious fall at the end of 2000, when he crashed head-first during the Paris–Tours classic and needed surgery on a badly cut lip and nose. Ullrich's most notable fall, seen by millions on live TV, came at the 2001 Tour. He overshot a turn on a steep downhill in the Pyrenees, sped down a grassy bank, and landed in a creek. Amazingly, he was unhurt. But it was a frightening reminder of the real and constant perils of his sport. No wonder he has amulets and animals to protect him.

One man who surely needs protection is the crash-prone Hamilton. I ask him if he's superstitious. "A little bit more each year," he says. "Ever since I crashed at the 2003 Tour I've carried a little vial of salt when I race. Our French mechanic on CSC, Frédéric Bassy, had a friend who's very superstitious. She saw my picture in the newspaper when I crashed, and sent me some water and salt. She said, 'Every day, carry the salt with you and have a sip of the water, and it'll get you through the Tour healthy.' I was pretty low at that point, and said

I'd try anything. So I carried the salt in my back pocket for the rest of the Tour. It seemed to work."

———————

When I return to the shop-window TV in Châteauneuf, Hamilton and the other leading contenders are riding in the middle of the pack, just focused on getting safely through this hard day. The pace is slow as they climb the infamous Mur de Bretagne, a mile-long hill that's steep enough to force the riders out of the saddle, standing on their pedals. A running time check shows that Piil and his two companions are already four minutes ahead, which is why the Boulangère team-mates of Thomas Voeckler are leading the peloton in a steady chase. They can't let Piil get too far ahead, because he's lying fifth in the overall standings, 6:58 behind their French race leader. If Piil gains another few minutes on this break, he'll take the yellow jersey from Voeckler.

Having a Frenchman in the yellow jersey is good for Armstrong: His team can yield, for a time, the burden of controlling the race to La Boulangère. It's also good for the Tour: While Armstrong has worn the *maillot jaune* sixty times in the past five years, the French have had it for only seven days. And it's a treat for the home country supporters: The smiling "Ti-Blan" is their new hero, even though they know that when the mountains arrive later in the week Voeckler will have a hard time defending his ten-minute lead against the Texan.

The fans' freshly written banners say it all: "We love you Thomas!" "Courage Ti-Blan!" He may not be a Breton, but the spectators on the Mur warmly applaud him and his French team as they ride past at the front of the peloton. Midway up the hill, where umbrellas are starting to open in the crowd, the race passes under two huge, black-and-white *Gwenn-ha-Du* flags, the emblem of a free Brittany.

Freedom is not taken lightly by people who have twice been occupied by a foreign power in the past century. Mementos of combat are everywhere. Outside the church in Châteauneuf, a bust of the late Abbée Cadiou overlooks the sprint line. Its inscription: "Shot by the Germans on 6 August 1944." Locals have bitter memories of the young abbot's death, because the town was liberated the previous day, August 5, according to another memorial that faces the marketplace. This one tells us that the 86th Reconnaissance Squadron of the U.S. Armored Division arrived in town that day, but only after twelve of their brethren were killed crossing the river, ambushed by a cluster of German troops hiding near the hilltop chapel.

Turning away from the memorial, I see that festivities are in full swing. It may be raining, but Bretons are used to that. And the Tour coming through town won't mark the end of the day's celebrations. Still to come is a *Grande Soirée Bretonne Gratuite*—a night of music, dancing, eating, and drinking, with the last of five bands due to be playing through midnight.

When the three breakaways arrive at Châteauneuf exactly at 4:18 p.m.—having maintained the organizers' predicted average speed of almost 27 miles an hour—Italy's Tosatto takes the intermediate sprint ahead of Piil and Scholz. La Boulangère is still leading the pack, which has reduced the break's lead to 2 minutes, 40 seconds. The locals vigorously cheer everyone on, with special applause for their old favorite, Virenque, who punctured his rear tire on the hill before town, and is chasing back alone through the wet streets.

This stage has turned into a hard slog, with the persistent rain and hills making this an unwelcome conclusion to a difficult week. Racing in the rain for so many days has put added pressure on everyone. Racers' muscles get numbed by the cold and need extra care from their soigneurs. Their bodies get battered in rain-slicked crashes, causing extra work for the medics. And their weather-beaten, mud-soaked bikes need much longer overhauls each night from overworked mechanics.

By the time Piil and his friends are caught, a frustratingly close six miles from the finish, I'm standing in a drizzling rain on Rue de Stang Bihan, high on a hill above Quimper. This solid city, established by the Romans two millennia ago, is seeing only its second-ever Tour stage finish. The first time was in 1991, when the Motorola team's Australian Phil Anderson bolted across the line first at the head of a four-man break that *did* hold off the pack. That was the day when all nine riders on the mighty Dutch team, PDM, quit the race, apparent victims from a tainted batch of an intravenous nutritional drip called Intralipid. Dark stories of systematic doping circulated that night in Quimper, but nothing was proven and a resulting investigation was inconclusive.

Today, thirteen years later, drug rumors still swirl around the peloton. We're no longer in the "anything goes" era that caused the death of François Le Bihan or that of Britain's best-ever racer, Tom Simpson, at the 1967 Tour de France. Still, despite a changing culture and all the tests and media attention, doping remains a serious issue in the sport. So much so that it makes it hard for race followers to believe that *any* riders are "clean." Yet they know there are some. Maybe the majority.

On the final uphill mile of today's stage, one exhausted rider after another attempts to break clear, only to fail. Then, at the top of the hill, Norway's Thor Hushovd, who looks like a hulking Viking, makes a strong surge for the win. A minute later, I see the young man who came in second, Luxembourg champion Kim Kirchen, bent double over his bike and gasping for air. The 26-year-old Fassa Bortolo rider gave his all in a bold attack over the final 500 yards. Hushovd overtook him with just ten yards to go. "I knew the finish was tough," says Kirchen, once he has had time to regain his breath. "But second place on a Tour stage is not so bad. That's good for the morale, eh?"

If Red Smith were here, he'd *still* be writing about the riders' amazing courage and daring in this marathon Tour that pushes them daily to their physical and emotional limits.

STAGE RESULT: 1. Hushovd; 2. Kim Kirchen (Luxembourg); 3. Zabel; 4. McEwen; 5. Andreas Klöden (Germany), all same time.

OVERALL STANDINGS: 1. Voeckler; 2. O'Grady, at 3:01; 3. Casar, at 4:06; 4. Bäckstedt, at 6:27; 5. Piil, at 7:09; 6. Armstrong, at 9:35; 11. Hamilton, at 10:11; 20. Ullrich, at 10:30; 24. Leipheimer, at 10:43; 29. Basso, at 10:52; 89. Mayo, at 15:02.

Road Trips

JULY 12: *Transfer from Quimper to Limoges and rest day.*

The Tour de France traditionally includes two rest days, giving riders a chance to catch their breath and their helpers a short break from their demanding daily chores. The rest days sometimes come when there's a great distance to travel from one stage to the next. That's the case today, with 340 miles between Quimper, where yesterday's stage ended, and Limoges, close to where tomorrow's stage begins. The 176 riders still in the race were flown last night from Quimper to Limoges. Today, they get to sleep in, go for a brisk ride of two to three hours to keep muscles loose, and then have a light lunch, deep massage, and plenty of sleep. Some do short TV interviews, while others are treated for injuries sustained in the first week. The latter includes Hamilton, whose osteopath is busy working on his damaged back. Meanwhile, for lowly journalists and the rest of the race entourage, this rest day is anything but.

I've been driving with my Australian press buddy Rupert on two-lane roads for five hours, either crawling along at 20 miles an hour behind a line of trucks and holiday traffic, or briefly blasting along an open road at 80 while watching out for the radar guns of *les flics*. At one point on this so-called rest day I've had enough. The traffic has stopped completely. No miles an hour. I then spot a small sign pointing to *centre ville*. Maybe I can cut through the center of town and avoid the jam. I squeeze by the line of cars and turn right. No traffic! The empty street is paradise . . . for ten seconds. Then comes a no-entry sign. I have to turn left, back toward the blocked *route nationale*. I might have leapfrogged twenty vehicles—but it seems worth it.

Any tiny victory magnifies in importance on such a trip, especially when you're hurting. I have a swollen, infected right thumb that I haven't had time to treat, and right now it's throbbing with jabs of pain.

Following the Tour from start to finish for twenty-three days can be a joyful experience, but that joy lessens when you have to undertake so many transfers between stages. Although this Tour is just over two thousand miles long, the odometer on our rented Volkswagen will have clocked exactly four thousand miles when it's dropped off in Paris. Thirty-six towns host a stage start or a finish this year, but only three of the stages finish in the same town from where the next day's race will start. That means that all the other start towns have to be accessed by car. No wonder the racers complain that they seem to be on the move all day, and sometimes part of the night.

Their complaints pale next to the ones my driving partner and I are now voicing, as we look hopelessly for somewhere to stop for a drink or bite to eat on this endless journey from the far west of France to its heartland. One problem with this "in between" part of the country is that the towns are far apart, and in rural France, cafés and small shops tend to close both on Sunday *and* Monday. Today's a Monday. Eventually, still 50 miles from Limoges, we find a town where the traffic is light, a restaurant is open, and there's a place to park. Thank-you, Lussac-les-Chateaux. A cheese sandwich and a cup of coffee never tasted so good.

———————

It was in a town not far from Lussac that a Swiss cyclist named Urs Zimmermann was having a quiet dinner with his soigneur one July evening in 1991. Being an amiable chap, "Zimmi" posed for a local photographer, who was surprised to see a Tour rider in town. The freelancer thought he might make 100 francs from the local newspaper, as the editor would be sure to use the shot. A famous cyclist dining in town—he was third at the 1986 Tour—is big news for a small paper. Zimmi had raced a 150-mile Tour stage that day, and now his Motorola team helper was driving him through the night to Pau, which was hosting the rest day. All the other riders were going by plane the next morning. Zimmi was petrified of flying, so he swapped his air ticket with a team-support guy who would have been in his seat in the car. It seemed like a good idea.

Tour race director Jean-Marie Leblanc takes up the story. "The next day in Pau, someone who'd driven from Nantes showed us a newspaper he'd bought on the way down. There it was: a photo of Zimmermann in a restaurant having dinner. We called in Zimmermann and his *directeur sportif* Jim Ochowicz, and told them that they'd broken one of the Tour's fundamental rules, and that Zimmermann was disqualified from the race. The rulebook clearly states that every rider has to use the transportation supplied by the organizers, and that the penalty for not doing so is disqualification. Sorry, but that's the rule.

"It's not a rule made just to screw the riders, I told them. It's made so that, firstly, everyone is equal, and, secondly, they're safe. If we let someone go into the unknown like that and there's an accident in the night and he's killed, I don't want to be the one who knocks on Madame Zimmermann's door to tell her. . . . So, I was very annoyed. Sorry, but he's out."

The next day, Ochowicz is driving Zimmi to the Pau airport, but decides to go to the start of the race first. When they get there, they see that the peloton is staging some sort of sit-down strike. "It looked as though they weren't going to start without Urs," Ochowicz recalls, "so I said to Urs, 'Get your bike clothes on. Let's go!'"

Leblanc remembers it a little differently, saying that the main reason for the riders' action was to protest a new rule from the International Cycling Union making helmets mandatory. "This was the first mountain stage, with major climbs in the Pyrenees, it was going to be hot, and they refused to wear helmets. The Zimmermann question came up at the same time, and they were playing one thing off against the other." Meanwhile, Zimmi, now in cycling gear, has "started shyly going toward the starting area," says Ochowicz. At the same time the city police commissioner arrives and tells Leblanc that his streets are jammed with traffic waiting for the race to begin, and he'll set the traffic free—and block the race—if the start's delayed any longer.

The race director is forced into making quick decisions: The riders don't have to wear helmets, Zimmi can start the stage, and Ochowicz must report to Leblanc that evening. "The end result," Ochowicz concludes, "I was kicked out of the Tour de France and Urs got to stay. I didn't know about the rest-day transportation rule because the rulebook was in French. But from that day on they agreed to print it in English, too."

———

When I finally reach Limoges and head for the pressroom, race boss Leblanc is holding a press conference. He informs us that the race organizers have decided to exclude two riders from the Tour because of their involvement in the Italian doping investigation that has been proceeding since May 2001. A fax from the prosecutor confirms that Hvastija of Alessio is accused of using a banned corticoid, and Casagranda of Saeco for possession of EPO. No word yet on the other two involved in the case, Padrnos and Zanini.

Continuing stories like this keep doping as a disturbing undercurrent to this Tour. A few months before the race, I had asked Leblanc for his stance on the subject. "What can I say?" he starts. "First, I can confirm that you *can* do the Tour de France without doping yourself. I know. I did it. Two times. I was a 'little' rider, yes. But it's not superhuman. The champion may have pressure to win, but the little riders have pressure not to get eliminated. That can be just as hard."

Leblanc believes that the reduction in the Tour's total distance from 3,000 miles in the fifties to just over 2,000 miles today has "humanized" the event. "Yes, it's still tough," he says, "but there is no need to dope yourself, because it's *not* a competition where record speeds are demanded like track and field. It's a competition where you have a first, a second, a third, et cetera, and it doesn't matter whether their average speed is 24 miles an hour or 27 miles an hour. We don't demand higher speeds. We like a spectacular race, yes, but it's the riders and their staff who choose to race faster."

What he doesn't mention is that today's temptation to cheat is greater than ever because of the huge salaries that a successful racer can command, and because of the added pressure from team sponsors—they want something to show for spending up to fifteen million dollars a year on their teams.

Even riders who don't cheat run the risk of having a career ruined by a positive drug test for something they didn't know they ingested. The list of banned drugs in cycling, and other Olympic sports, has become so long that if ordinary citizens were subjected to frequent drug tests they would probably come up positive more often than not.

This becomes blatantly clear to me in the next few hours. The swelling in my right thumb has now become so bad that one of the Tour doctors sends me to the emergency room in Limoges. I check myself in that evening and wait with some other patients. A 17-year-old youth with body piercings has fallen off his motorbike; a chubby 14-year-old boy crashed his mountain bike; and a man with muddy shoes, who was working in the fields and is now lying down on a gurney next to me, says he can't move his legs. After the others go off for X-rays, I enter an operating room where a young woman doctor lances my thumb and drains the infection. A nurse eventually comes and puts on an antiseptic cream and bandages, before handing me a list of prescriptions for medicines to help heal the wound. These include antibiotics (which commonly contain cortisone-based drugs) and an anti-inflammatory (steroidal drugs). Both ingredients would test positive in any sport's drug test. This just confirms the care that cyclists and their doctors have to exercise when treating any sort of illness or wound. And in the Tour de France their injuries must be healed and their sicknesses cured while they're still competing. No wonder the Tour is often touted as the world's toughest competition.

———————

While I'm in the emergency room, I call my hotel for the night to let them know I probably won't be there till 11 o'clock. No problem, I'm told. After the surgery I head for the hotel, about 20 miles out of town. The reservations were made several months ago, a deposit was paid. As I drive along a winding country road in the dark, I get a call on my cell phone from another journalist in our group. "Bad news," he says. "When we got to the hotel, they didn't have any rooms for us. They've given them to someone else. But the good news is, we've found another place. It's one big room, like a dormitory, with a dozen beds, used by cycling teams when they come here. They're really nice people, and they say they'll keep the restaurant open till you get here."

It's been a long day's night. But at least there's a good ending. The mushroom omelet is the best of the trip. The grilled potatoes are superb. The rosé is just right. And the conversation is excellent. We order another bottle of wine and talk about the Tour with the patron. He wonders whether Voeckler can hold on to that ten-minute lead he has over Armstrong and the other main contenders. Rupert says he admires the young Frenchman's gutsy attitude and thinks he'll probably manage to hang on to the yellow jersey in the Pyrenees, but not by much. The rest of us agree: "Voeckler will lose a lot of time on those two mountain stages, but probably not ten minutes." The bigger question, of course, is how will Jan, Tyler, and Lance's other challengers fare in the Pyrenees. We'll find out in a few days' time.

At 2 a.m. we retire to our dorm room and get out our laptops. There's always writing to do during the Tour, but we're relieved that our "rest day" is over, and that tomorrow—or, rather, today—there will be some actual racing to see.

La France Profonde

JULY 13: *From medieval St. Léonard-de-Noblat, this 100-mile stage takes a looping, S-shaped journey to the east and then north to finish in Guéret, capital of La Creuse. None of the roads are flat, but the hills are short, and the day is expected to end in a field sprint.*

Swooping from a rocky plateau of tall, dark pines, the two racers begin their dramatic descent. Down, down, down they go. No need to brake. Picking up speed. No need to steer. Their bikes glide instinctively through each swishing turn after turn after turn . . . left, right, left . . . ever faster . . . ever deeper into this land of crystalline and granite bedrock. The two cyclists, one Basque wearing orange, the other Italian, in white and black, are a blur in the lush landscape as they race along the skinny, snaking, slate-blue road that parallels a wild little stream called the Gourbillon. With their torsos bent low and forward, their hands gripping the hooks of their handlebars, they plunge past angular crags coated with lichens, past wrinkle-barked oaks and thin green ferns, and on and on, down into the cloven valley of the Creuse River.

Iñigo Landaluze and Filippo Simeoni are the two lucky men on this deliciously exciting downhill run. In five miles they add five minutes to their lead over a peloton that's cruising for the moment, knowing there's still 60 miles to go. The two breakaways motor through St. Quentin-La Chabanne, where a large placard greets them with the words: *"Vive le Tour en Creuse."* France is composed of ninety-five departments, and for the first time the Tour is finishing a stage in the department of La Creuse. This is the grassroots heartland, as deep as you can reach in this pristine land: *La France Profonde*.

———

One of the greatest attractions of the Tour de France is its journey through vast areas of stunning landscapes, dense forests, patchwork farmland, and a wealth of ancient villages and towns whose buildings change in color, shape, and design as you move across the country. The Tour organizers are cognizant of their precious gift, and this stage in La Creuse is a perfect example: a strikingly scenic route that carves a giant "S" through the country's core to simultaneously serve the needs of a modern Tour and the traditions of this beautiful sport.

Today's start bows to tradition. It's not in the burgeoning city of Limoges, but a few miles to the east in serene St. Léonard-de-Noblat. This medieval hilltop town on the ancient pilgrim route to Santiago de Compostela has been the home for fifty years of all-time popular French racer Raymond Poulidor—a heroic yet ill-fated figure who finished on the podium eight times in his fourteen Tours, but never took first place. His autobiography was titled *Glory Without the Yellow Jersey*.

Now in his late sixties, the always-tan Poulidor has thick white hair, narrow smiling eyes, and the widest grin you'll ever see. He's thrilled that *le Tour* has finally come to his town, despite it being four decades since his impassioned duels with five-time Tour winner Jacques An- quetil divided France into *Poulidoristes* and *Anquetilistes*. When it wasn't Anquetil who stood between him and the *maillot jaune*, it was Eddy Merckx. And when it wasn't Merckx, it was misfortune. But Poulidor is not bitter about his "eternal second" legacy. "The more unlucky I was, the more the public liked me, the more money I made. It led me to believe that to win would make no difference."

Poulidor's popularity with the fans endured because he continued racing until he was 40, and even then he finished on the Tour podium. You still see *"Allez Popou"* signs held up at the Tour, where, ironically, he does public relations work for Crédit Lyonnais, the bank that sponsors the yellow jersey, and dishes out its little lion mascots to every race leader! And yes, Poulidor is wearing a yellow shirt today, as he is introduced to his hometown crowd before the stage to Guéret. It's a warm, overcast but breezy afternoon, a perfect day for a bike race.

———————

With a population of only four thousand eight hundred, St. Léonard wouldn't appear to be large enough to afford the asking price for hosting a stage of the Tour de France. But the town has prospered of late, thanks to its revitalized porcelain, papermaking, and tanning in- dustries, and the historic buildings that attract growing numbers of visitors. Its candidature to host a stage was also helped by the egalitar- ian selection methods used by the race promoter, Amaury Sport Or- ganisation.

Veteran race director Jean-Marie Leblanc explains how a different course is chosen each year. He says the only "given" is the finish in

Paris, while the starting city for the whole race is named almost two years in advance. Then, about eighteen months before each Tour, his selection committee combs through the applications of some ninety French communities, looking to see if they will fit into a course that takes in the Alps and the Pyrenees and follows the parameters of twenty-three days, including two rest days, and a maximum distance of 3,500 kilometers (2,175 miles).

"We don't choose stage towns because of their politics, nor for financial reasons, because we ask the same amount from every town," Leblanc says. "We don't set the price too high—it's 120,000 euros (about $150,000) right now—because we don't want to attract only the big cities. But it's high enough that only the serious candidates come forward. We also like to take the Tour to different regions of the country, like this year we have Brittany that wasn't included last year. Each gets its turn, because we believe that the Tour belongs to every citizen. And then we like to visit a different country each year—Belgium this year, and probably Germany in 2005."

Turning to the selection of the stage towns for today's stage, Leblanc says, "There are two tales. First, Guéret is the capital of La Creuse, which is the only department in France that has never had a stage of the Tour. It hasn't been possible because of the lack of hotels there; but with new *autoroutes* in place, people can stay in other cities, like Limoges. So we're very happy because they're very proud. And so we have a small town of *La France Profonde* that will see the Tour.

"As for St. Léonard-de-Noblat, the mayor sent me their candidature about two years ago. When I saw that, I thought . . . umm . . . St. Léonard . . . Poulidor . . . we have to go there! And so we have a stage, mostly in La Creuse, a department that's not very rich, doesn't have many people. It's good."

Leblanc's choice of stage towns has a big impact not only on the Tour, but on France itself. On leaving Poulidor's St. Léonard at the start of this hilly but not too demanding stage, everyone sees a large, hand-painted banner strung across the street: *"Merci Raymond et Jean-Marie!"*

"The stage itself is not very long," Leblanc concludes. "A hundred sixty kilometers (100 miles), not flat, very up and down, some fine roads, beautiful countryside, and so I think it will be a stage for breakaways."

Breakaways, maybe, but the sprinters have a chance, too.

Breakaways are the last thing on the agenda for Armstrong, Ullrich, and Hamilton. After their rest day, the Tour favorites are simply pleased that there's no rain in the forecast, so they can use this less challenging race as a warm-up for the climbing stages soon to come. However hard they've trained, all the contenders have doubts about how they will cope with the Tour's always harsh transition from the plains to the mountains.

"It's like going into the unknown," says Ullrich. "It's exciting. I can't wait to be there because at last we'll find out where everyone's at. If I feel good, then sure I'll attack. You have to."

The fans, too, always anxiously await the mountain stages. They are awed by the rocketlike speed with which these flat stages end, but their anticipation heightens each day as the Tour approaches the mountains. It is there that the teams will fight their most desperate battles. And it's there that the true mettle and chances of each contender will finally be revealed.

In 2003, Ullrich suffered on the early mountain stages because of a sickness he was recovering from. His fans are worried that the cold he picked up at the beginning of this Tour could affect his climbing once more.

Hamilton's big worry is his back injury. Chiropractic treatment can relieve pressure and ease tension in the body, but a crash as traumatic as the one he had at Angers usually needs time to heal. He's concerned that he hasn't had enough time. When I ask for an honest assessment of his back, he gives me a guarded, "It's a *little* better."

Armstrong, on the other hand, has had a first week of racing that he calls "close to perfection." Still, repeated days of racing in the rain can lower anyone's resistance, including that of a five-time champion. So even Armstrong is wary, especially in a year when his climbing form has been erratic. On a freezing Sunday morning in March, at the Critérium International race in the Ardennes, his performance was disappointing. He made his team ride hard up a switchback hill to soften up the opposition, but *Armstrong* was the one who suffered. He placed only seventeenth in that race's summit finish. And in April, on an 80-degree day in the Appalachians of Georgia, he struggled to finish third on the steep, narrow climb to Brasstown Bald Mountain, a peak that likely would be given a Category 2 rating at the Tour. Then, in May, we saw Armstrong at his best: On a steep but short hill to a summit finish at the French port city of Sête on the Mediterranean, the Texan scored an explosive solo stage win. But short and steep is not the same as long and steep, so Armstrong still had concerns in June. He was expected to win the uphill time trial of the Dauphiné race. Instead, he appeared to struggle in the heat on the 13-mile climb to the summit of Mont Ventoux—which Armstrong calls "the hardest climb in France." He placed only fifth, 90 seconds slower than Hamilton and almost two minutes behind stage winner Iban Mayo, who broke the Ventoux course record that day.

"Two minutes is a lot," Armstrong conceded at the time, "but it's a long way to go to the Tour de France." Wasn't he concerned about his form? "I probably expected to go a little faster today," he admitted. "As for being worried, I'm worried *every* year before the Tour de France. For me, it's a constant struggle to try and find the best condition, and you learn a lot more from poor performances or disappointing performances than you do from successful or surprising ones."

The short climbs on the stage to Guéret are not challenging enough to test the contenders' condition. One of these hills, though, is one too many for Jaan Kirsipuu, the sprinter who won the opening stage into Charleroi. He gets dropped by the pack and abandons the Tour. Later, standing in the doorway of his AG2R team bus, the bulky Estonian says, "With the mountains coming up, it's now the turn of the other riders on the team to get serious and assume some responsibility."

Out on the road, breakaways Landaluze and Simeoni are dead serious. They emerge from their thrilling run down to the Creuse valley with an eight-minute lead over the pack. Neither of the two riders is of any concern to Armstrong and company, at least not today. Simeoni and the Texan have some off-the-bike issues to settle, but those can wait.

In their only previous Tour appearances, Landaluze finished outside the top one hundred in 2003, and Simeoni came home in 55th in 1998. But both are potential stage winners, and they're going to ride with all their might in an attempt to reach Guéret before the pack. With no wins to his credit in four seasons of racing on the Euskaltel team, Landaluze is determined to open his account today. And while Simeoni came to this Tour as a domestique for Mario Cipollini, his aging team leader quit during the first week, opening the door for Simeoni to now add to the seven races he has won in ten seasons of pro racing. Their chance of success looks even better when they top the two-mile Category 4 climb out of Aubusson: They're now ten minutes ahead with only 40 miles to go.

The roads of this stage are ones that Raymond Poulidor knows intimately. He was born in Masbaraud-Marignat, a village not too far from Aubusson, before he moved to St. Léonard as a teenager. During his two decades as a racer, he took punishing training rides into these hills and gained a reputation for having the strongest legs in the peloton. Yet there was always something that stopped him from winning the Tour de France. In 1964, it was poor team support: His mechanic accidentally pushed Poulidor off his bike after changing a wheel, instead of helping him get back in the race. That cost the team leader a minute—and the Tour. In 1966, it was poor tactics: He failed to mark a chief rival on a critical stage. And in 1968, he had outrageous bad luck: A race motorcycle hit a pothole, flew into the air, and landed on Poulidor, fracturing his forehead in two places.

The race that established him as a star was the '64 Tour, when all of France was gripped by the intense battle between Poulidor, in his second Tour, and the then supreme champion, Anquetil. Over the final two weeks, it was as dynamic as a boxing match. First one, then the other delivered what seemed to be the knockout blow. Going into the last mountain stage two days from Paris, Anquetil led Poulidor by only 56 seconds on overall time. Since Poulidor was a much better climber, it looked as though the Tour was his for the taking.

That stage was 147 miles long over a rugged course through the Massif Central, and ending with a vicious climb to the summit of the Puy-de-Dôme, a conical-shaped, extinct volcano. After seven hours in the saddle on an oppressively hot day, a lead group of thirty very weary riders was still together when they reached the base of the ultra-steep road that corkscrews to the top of the Puy.

The police had a hard time controlling the estimated half-million fans lining the narrow road. In places, they were ten-deep. Many had trekked to the summit before dawn. I was there with my bike, and walked up the steep hill as far as I could before the mass of bodies made it impossible to go any farther.

The Puy-de-Dôme is only 50 miles from Aubusson, so huge numbers of Poulidor supporters were present, all of them urging their man to victory. Miraculously, it seemed, two miles from the summit, Anquetil and Poulidor were suddenly together, climbing shoulder-to-shoulder, with no other riders around. This was the ultimate duel. The cries of support for the local man—"Pou-pou!" "Pou-pou!" "Pou-pou!"—could be heard for miles as the two men struggled up the mountain.

"We were both done for," recalls Poulidor. But the defending champion was truly cooked. In an instant, a mile from the top, Anquetil was no longer alongside his rival. He was dropping back! The crowd screamed for Poulidor even more!

Describing that final mile, the incomparable French journalist Pierre Chany wrote: "Anquetil's face that until then had been crimson lost all of its color. The sweat slid in droplets down his hollow cheeks. And Poulidor, who was also at his limit, was gradually gaining meter after meter. But while he was calling on his ultimate reserves to climb as fast as he could possibly go, Anquetil, half conscious, was digging even deeper to check the hemorrhaging of time, sustained only by the instinct of preservation. At the summit, the two men collapsed. Poulidor the Limousin took forty-two seconds out of the Norman, but Anquetil had kept his yellow jersey by fourteen seconds. When he regained his spirits, Anquetil said just one thing: 'If Poulidor had taken the jersey, I'd have gone home tonight.'"

He didn't go home, and this wasn't the end of their epic battle. The Tour finished in Paris with a 17-mile time trial from Versailles. On that fearsomely hot Sunday afternoon, virtually every radio and television in France was tuned to the race. For the first time in history, the stage was covered live without interruptions, and the time gap between the two men was taken every kilometer. As the gap between them widened at one checkpoint, then narrowed at the next, the drama was reflected in the cries and sighs heard in every street around France. The public was spellbound.

Because there was a 20-second time bonus for winning this stage, with 10 seconds to the runner-up, Poulidor could still win the Tour if he beat Anquetil on this day by only five seconds. But it was Anquetil who was ahead by five seconds when he reached the top of the time trial's only climb, the graphically named Côte de l'Homme Mort ("Dead Man's Hill"). Standing on the bridge over the River Seine, a couple of miles before the finish in the Parc des Princes stadium, I couldn't believe the speed at which Anquetil blew by me. He came through like a hurricane, his yellow jersey glinting in the sunshine, followed by a flotilla of motorcycles and press cars. But the defending champion, a time-trial specialist, was not ahead by much. On the day, he was 21 seconds faster than Poulidor, and when his time bonus was reckoned in, his final margin of victory was 55 seconds. Anquetil had started the club: the first five-time Tour de France champion. Poulidor never got that close to winning the Tour again.

The Anquetil–Poulidor epic of forty years ago is one of the giant chapters in Tour history books. The battle being waged by Landaluze and Simeoni against an onrushing peloton will be one of the footnotes. Their ten-minute margin is remorselessly coming down as the sprinters' teams come to life, realizing they have a chance to catch the two breakaways. With 12 miles to go, the gap is 2:40; with 6 miles, 1:35; and with 3 miles, just 48 seconds. It's going to be breathtakingly close.

Around the final turn, 390 yards from the line, the eager Basque and the crafty Italian are still clear. They don't even see the pack behind them as they dash toward the line. Landaluze thinks he has it. "I could hear nothing," he says. "Then, when I was fifteen meters from the line, I looked to my side and saw other riders. I couldn't believe it."

Those riders are the real sprinters in the race, and in a blaze the agile McEwen captures his second stage of the Tour, ahead of the chunky Hushovd and charging O'Grady.

Back in St. Léonard-de-Noblat, where the day began, the town's medieval alleyways are again filled with people. It's 11 p.m. An enterprising restaurant has set up long wooden tables in the street to accommodate two hundred diners at a time. "We're out of the beef, out of the lamb, out of the pork," a waiter says, checking off each dish, one by one, on his fingers. "We only have the melon." Pity. From the tables near the cobbled square we could have watched an outdoor screening of the wacky, animated Tour movie *Les Triplettes de Belleville*, which is just getting under way. Instead, we're drawn to a tavern where the team buses were parked this morning, and last orders are still being taken for a "Special Menu Tour de France."

Parents holding children are out in the street, waiting for fireworks and a laser show to begin. By the time the last rocket jettisons its cargo of stars, and the *Triplettes* ends with a round of applause, the Union Musicale de St. Léonard-de-Noblat, a marching band in royal blue uniforms and peaked hats, sets off into the dark blowing bugles and banging drums. This is a night the locals will remember long after they've forgotten that an Aussie named McEwen won *their* Tour stage through *La France Profonde*.

STAGE RESULT: 1. McEwen; 2. Hushovd; 3. O'Grady; 4. Jérôme Pineau (France); 5. Zabel, all same time.

OVERALL STANDINGS: 1. Voeckler; 2. O'Grady, at 2:53; 3. Casar, at 4:06; 4. Bäckstedt, at 6:27; 5. Piil, at 7:09; 6. Armstrong, at 9:35; 11. Hamilton, at 10:11; 20. Ullrich, at 10:30; 23. Leipheimer, at 10:43; 28. Basso, at 10:52; 86. Mayo, at 15:02.

Bastille Day Emotions

JULY 14: *This 147.5-mile stage from Limoges to St. Flour is the first one to include a Category 1 climb, the Col du Pas de Peyrol, also called the Puy Mary. There are eight other official climbs, the first after 25 miles, the last 20 miles from the finish. This is the first day on which the true climbers have a chance to display their skills.*

Tyler Hamilton is just going through the motions today, the twelfth day of the Tour:

Up at 7:30. Wash face, brush teeth, tame bedhead—put on a baseball hat if hair is too unruly. Early breakfast because the stage starts at 10:30 and it takes three hours to digest a big meal. Always start the day with coffee; then omelet, rice, some fruit, cereal, yoghurt. . . . Have to eat a lot. We'll burn maybe 7,000 calories today. It's the longest stage of the Tour, almost 150 miles and nine climbs. Probably six hours in the saddle, maybe more. . . .

Pack suitcase before the osteopath has another look at my back. Hope it'll be okay on the climbs. Peel and stick numbers onto jersey . . . some cream on the seat chamois . . . short-sleeve jersey—check that it unzips all the way down. It's gonna be hot on the last climbs. . . . Put on the shorts and a T-shirt. Stuff the jersey, race shoes, eyewear, and gloves in the small daypack; energy bars, gels, and helmet are on the bus . . .

Go down for the team meeting. Remind them it's a big day. We should cover the early move if there is one. Maybe Santi Perez could go with it to-day. Tell the other guys about that big climb near the end. . . . It's time to check the bike now, got to make sure that 25-tooth sprocket is fitted for the big climb. Can check the gears and brakes on the ride down to the start. It's only a couple of miles away today.

The start is in the spacious Champ de Juillet, a park across from the Gare des Bénédictins, a towered building of white stone that looks more like a church than a train station. Limoges has hosted a dozen Tour stage starts over the years, so its city workers know how to do things right. This morning they've made sure the crowd barriers are effective so the hangers-on can't invade the area set aside for the teams and their buses.

That means that Hamilton and the other favorites don't have to fight their way through mobs of autograph hunters and glad-handers when they emerge from their buses. Some TV people still manage to trail Ullrich, though. There's a growing excitement about him this year. People are saying: "I've never seen him look so good" . . . "His attitude is different, he looks more determined" . . . "Armstrong seems to be at his usual level, but Ullrich is outstanding." Ullrich has also followed some of Armstrong's trademark techniques, like going to the Alps before the race to scout the major climbs. And today, instead of his traditional aluminum-framed bike, he wheels out a carbon-fiber machine, perhaps a pound lighter, which makes climbing a lot easier.

Hamilton seems relieved that he doesn't have to contend with crowds at this start. He doesn't even have to cope with the media. When he goes to sign in, he rides straight by all the reporters, who've been drawn like iron filings to a magnet called Lance Armstrong. The champ is speaking in his ever-improving French. He politely answers some inane questions. Are you going to attack today? "There'll be attacks . . . just like yesterday. *Comme hier.*" Are your legs good? "I don't know. I think so. *Je croix que oui.*"

Hamilton is grateful not to be bothered with questions this morning. He'll answer them, but there's something else on his mind. He calls me into the team bus, where he can sit and we can talk privately.

He's looking pale, and his easy smile is missing. I ask him about his back: How was it yesterday? "It was a little hard." The stage today is one you rode in training, right? "Yes, we scouted this stage. It's harder than a lot of people think or said." The climbs aren't that steep though, right? "Well, the Category 1 is four kilometers at 12 percent . . . I consider that steep." What about the hill at the finish in St. Flour? "We finished there in '99, I think. It's hard. Gaps could open if you're asleep."

Then I ask him if everyone on the team is in good shape. He hesitates. "Good, very good . . ." He falls silent, his thoughts elsewhere. "Hey, John . . . um . . . er . . . Tugboat's in bad shape right now." I tell him how sorry I am. We all know that his nine-year-old golden retriever fell sick just before the Tour. Hamilton left him at home in Gerona with wife, Haven. He then says gravely, his eyes starting to mist over, "We have to put him down today. Haven came up last night so I could say good-bye. For me, he was a family member. I'll miss him. . . ."

Yes, Tyler's just going through the motions today.

———————

Hamilton's grief will make this longest stage of the race seem even longer to him. Besides its length, it's the first of two stages in the Massif Central mountain region, and the first of the Tour with truly serious climbing—a total of about 11,000 feet—making it the first stage where terrain will be a factor, not just tactics and speed. It's a hard stage to face when the fatigue level in the peloton is already high. In the ten days of racing since the Tour began in Liège, the peloton has raced exactly one thousand miles, at an astonishing average speed of 27.3 miles per hour—despite foul weather, frequent head winds, and multiple crashes. Racing that fast, day in, day out, is a phenomenal athletic accomplishment and puts enormous physical stress on every rider. The stress causes fatigue, and that fatigue has led to an average of two men per stage quitting this year's race.

The Tour's flat stages never used to be this fast. Through the sixties, seventies, and eighties, the pace on flat stages held steady at around 24 miles per hour. It's only since 1990 that the speeds have whipped up. One reason is that bikes are 25-percent lighter than they were in the eighties (15 pounds compared to 20 pounds) and much more efficient. Another factor is smoother and straighter roads. Impressive improvements have also been made in sports medicine and training methods (although many say that perhaps that has been aided by more sophisticated, but banned drugs). And finally, there are 50 percent more teams in the Tour than there used to be; the cash incentives are far greater; and live television coverage has mushroomed in recent years.

When Anquetil, Merckx, Hinault, and Induráin were winning the Tour, the pace was much slower in the opening few hours of the flat stages. Serious breakaways rarely emerged until an hour or two from the finish, when live TV began. In the Armstrong era, attacks begin in the opening mile every day, and they continue until a breakaway is established. As a result, racing 30 miles or more in the first hour has become common, and the frenetic start sets the tone for the rest of the stage.

On live TV, the riders in the breakaway get far more "air time" than riders in the peloton. This extra exposure equates to increased publicity for the team sponsors, whose brand names are prominently displayed on the riders' clothing. And, of course, putting riders in the breaks increases a team's chance of winning the stage—the ultimate publicity for the sponsor.

Teams like U.S. Postal, T-Mobile, and Phonak are less concerned with winning stages and more focused on putting their leaders on the final podium in Paris. This goal impels them to chase down riders who are even a remote threat to their chances of overall victory. That's the case in the opening hour of today's stage, when Postal chases—and catches—every attack in the first 20 miles. A break of eighteen men then gains a half-minute, and even though there are no "A-list" threats in the move, Armstrong's men are on the chase again. Only two men elude Postal's grasp: Frenchman Richard Virenque and Belgian Axel Merckx, son of the famous Eddy. This duo reaches the day's first categorized climb with a lead of just 10 seconds, and Postal lets them go. Armstrong knows that neither man is an overall threat because of their poor time-trialing skills and lack of superior climbing strength. But each of them has lots of stamina. They'll need it today: For their break to succeed, they'll need to stay out front for the next 123 miles. If they do, their sponsors' publicity is guaranteed!

———————

Today, July Fourteenth, is Bastille Day. It commemorates the fall of the royalist Bastille prison in 1789, and marks the beginning of the French Revolution and a new, democratic form of government. When news of Virenque's successful attack reaches the festive French fans on this national holiday, they explode with excitement. They're gathered on every hill and in every village along this scenic wonderland of a course, which heads through the wooded gorges of the Dordogne and over the bare volcanic peaks of the Auvergne.

Virenque may have the son of Eddy Merckx riding alongside him, as they move five minutes, then ten minutes clear of the pack, but the Frenchman is the one getting all the applause and attention. At least 80 percent of the hundreds of posters and banners being waved today are for the 34-year-old Virenque. Why so much passion for an athlete involved in the 1998 Festina team doping scandal? Why so much adoration for a rider who was fingered by his Festina teammates as a ringleader in the affair, yet didn't admit until two years later that he, too, used EPO, human growth hormone, and other banned substances?

This is something that many can't understand, including Armstrong, who also happens to be a controversial figure in France because of the bad press he sometimes gets, implying that he uses drugs. The crowds on this stage even booed a Postal team vehicle that was traveling ahead of the race. In response to this apparent hypocrisy, Armstrong observes, "Don't stand there and boo me and cheer for somebody that's been involved in the biggest doping crisis in the history of sport. That doesn't make any sense."

It's somewhat ironic that the man involved in that crisis, Virenque, is wearing one of the Lance Armstrong Foundation yellow "Live-Strong" wristbands today, which raises money for programs supporting young cancer patients. The irony is probably lost on Virenque's fans, who have stood by their hero throughout his career. "Richard is our idol despite his faults," says one. "He's one of us; we understand him," says another. Virenque has been popular ever since he rode his first Tour in 1992 and took the yellow jersey for a day. His name is now indelibly linked with his country's most celebrated summertime event. "My team doesn't ask anything of me until the Tour," he says. "That's great with me."

Before the 1998 drug scandal, the French racer won three mountain stages of the Tour, and took the King of the Mountains title four straight years. Since the doping affair, and his eight-month suspension from cycling, he has added three more stage wins and two more polka-dot jerseys to his collection. Today he's looking for another one of each.

With a big lead, and knowing they need to share the workload for their break to succeed, Virenque and Merckx consider a gentleman's agreement. In return for each other's help, Merckx says he'll let the French veteran win all the King of the Mountain sprints on the nine climbs (which will enable Virenque to take over the polka-dot jersey from his own teammate, Paolo Bettini), while Virenque promises he won't sprint at the finish line if they arrive together in St. Flour, allowing Merckx to take the stage win. The deal is made. . . .

———————

The climax of this stage is the crossing of four mountain passes in the last 50 miles. The toughest pass by far is the Puy Mary, which tops out at 5,213 feet above sea level, 40 miles from the finish in St. Flour. It's not a long climb, but those final 12-percent gradients, heading from a dark coniferous forest to a grassy mountainside, are the steepest challenges of this entire Tour. These are the sorts of slopes where Iban Mayo can show his climbing strength. And he might have, had he not run into a mechanical problem right at the bottom of Puy Mary. Then, after changing bikes with a teammate, he bangs his knee on the handlebar as he mounts it. His knee is okay, but Mayo now has to work hard, weaving between scores of struggling riders, to reach the summit at the back instead of the front of the first group.

The tens of thousands of fans who've replaced the sheep on the mountaintops today are having a treat. First, they see Virenque ride away from Merckx. And then, nine minutes later, another Frenchman, yellow jersey Voeckler, is riding in the first group to follow, just ahead of Ullrich and Armstrong. Also safe in this group are Basso, Leipheimer, and most of the other team leaders. Missing is Hamilton. "I don't know if anyone noticed, but I was gapped a little on that climb." Perhaps it's the heat—he *does* have his zipper pulled down to the waist; perhaps it's the loss of his deeply loved dog; or perhaps his back is giving him more trouble than he wants to admit.

Meanwhile, Virenque seems to have broken his agreement with Merckx. The Frenchman says that after topping Puy Mary half a minute ahead of the Belgian, he doesn't quicken his pace on the steep descent, expecting that Merckx will catch him. But Merckx sees it differently, saying that Virenque attacked him on the climb and didn't wait. As a result, the gap between the two men doubles in the next 10 miles and Merckx, who is caught by the peloton on the last climb, later accuses Virenque of being a traitor.

The French fans are oblivious to all this as they cheer Virenque louder than ever, all the way to St. Flour. Their roars of support are deafening as he climbs the final half-mile past the fifteenth-century city walls to cross the finish line in victory. "I thought this would be a good stage for me," Virenque says, "that's why I came to see it before the Tour with four of my teammates."

It's five long minutes before the main pack of seventy riders can be seen climbing up the steep hillside. And just when it looks as if Erik Zabel will take the sprint for second place, the German veteran allows his 29-year-old T-Mobile teammate Andreas Klöden to cross the line ahead of him and claim the runner-up's 12-second time bonus. This moves Klöden up to 13th place in the overall standings, four spots ahead of his team leader Ullrich.

Zabel's act signified the respect the team has for Klöden. That respect seems well-founded: At the end of a long, hot day, the still-strong Klöden proved that he has the endurance and speed to help his team leader Ullrich in the days ahead, or maybe even take his place should big Jan turn out to be less strong than people expect. That's okay with Ullrich, who says he'll get behind any one of his teammates who turns out to be stronger than him. Ullrich himself crosses the line in 15th place, behind Voeckler, Armstrong, Basso, and a caught-up Mayo, all with the same time.

Hamilton is seven seconds back, in 26th place. It hasn't been a good day for the New Englander, who looks almost despondent. "I probably wasn't as concentrated as I normally would be. When you have emotions, you have to follow them," he says, betraying just how deeply the loss of his dog has affected his effort.

It has been a muted Bastille Day, even though Virenque is the four-teenth Frenchman since World War II to win a Tour stage on the Fourteenth of July. I learn from an assistant at the St. Flour tourist of-fice that later, in the main square of this walled, hilltop city, there will be an outdoor celebration: pop music from the sixties and seventies, but not the traditional holiday fireworks. "We had them last night," she explains. "We didn't want to disturb the riders sleeping here tonight."

For Hamilton, even so, sleep will not come easily.

STAGE RESULT: 1. Richard Virenque (France); 2. Andreas Klöden (Germany), at 5:19; 3. Zabel; 4. Mancebo; 5. Voeckler; 6. Armstrong; 11. Mayo; 13. Basso; 15. Ullrich, all same time; 17. Leipheimer, at 5:26; 26. Hamilton, same time.

OVERALL STANDINGS: 1. Voeckler; 2. O'Grady, at 3:00; 3. Casar, at 4:13; 4. Virenque, at 6:52; 5. Piil, at 7:31; 6. Armstrong, at 9:35; 11. Hamilton, at 10:18; 13. Klöden, at 10:20; 17. Ullrich, at 10:30; 19. Leipheimer, at 10:50; 20. Basso, at 10:52; 50. Mayo, at 15:02.

Heating Up

JULY 15: *This 102-mile stage from St. Flour to Figéac is not a long one, but the course is constantly climbing and descending, mostly on winding back roads. The climbs to Montsalvy (with 40 miles to go) and Bagnac (10 miles from the finish) should instigate the outcome.*

Nothing tastes better than cool, fresh water from a village fountain in France on a hot day. And this is the first hot day of the 2004 Tour: The mercury will touch 90 degrees before the end of the stage in Figéac. I see the sign, *"Eau Potable,"* before cupping water into my hands from a deep, ancient stone fountain, and letting it flow softly down my throat.

I'm in the tiny village of Junhac, whose artistic fountain with its wrought-iron framework played a starring role in the Tour when the race first passed through here in 1959, on the thirteenth stage. "That stage was terribly tough," remembers Robert Sergent, who today runs a bar in Junhac. He was a wide-eyed 13-year-old back then. "It was the first time they came through this region, and they were surprised by the terrain . . . didn't have the right equipment, the right gears."

Sergent is pouring draft beer for his customers at his neat little *bar-tabac*, just across the street from the Café de la Place, where some touring cyclists are snacking under sun umbrellas at tables set up in the little square beside the fountain. "I still remember what happened in fifty-nine," the *patron* continues. "The weather was much hotter then than today. The roads were melting in the sun. The race climbed up to Montsalvy, not on the road they're taking today, but on another, much steeper hill, that starts in the Lot valley at Vieillevie. That was the climb that caught them all out.

"When they came through here, after descending from Montsalvy, the race was split apart. There were only half a dozen men in the front group . . . Anquetil, who won the Tour in fifty-seven . . . Anglade, the regional rider . . . Bahamontes, the Spanish climber . . . a few others.

"Two or three minutes later, a rider on his own came around the corner, and suddenly stopped at the fountain. It was Charly Gaul, the Luxembourg champion who won the Tour the year before. He propped his bike against the fountain and dipped his head in and out of the water. His team car stopped, and the driver filled up Gaul's aluminum water bottles. When he'd finished drinking, he got back on his bike, and I pushed him off."

"You pushed his bike?"

"*Mais, oui.*"

Sergent has probably told his story over and over throughout the years at Tour time, although he says this is only the third time the race has passed through here since 1959. To remind everyone of the fountain incident, he has set up a framed display outside his bar: photos of Gaul dipping his head in the water, along with copies of newspaper and magazine clippings from that July day forty-five years ago.

An old iron bucket that now sits on the side of the fountain is the same as the one that's in the photos.

I walk across to the Café de la Place. It's cool and shady inside the thick-walled building with its well-washed flagstone floor. I talk to a small, older woman who's wearing an apron. She's too shy to give me her name. You were here in fifty-nine, and saw the race? *"Oui, oui, oui . . . "* What did you see? "Exactly like you see in the photos," she says. "They arrived to refresh themselves. I was seventeen. There was a lot less commotion back then, not like today."

For sure, there wasn't such a huge and noisy publicity caravan in the late fifties. In those years, one of the caravan's biggest attractions was Yvette Horner, who sat in an open-top car and played French folk tunes on her accordion. Dislier Pasquie remembers. Just seven years old, he too watched from the roadside in 1959. "Forty-five years later and there's still the same magic, just magic," Pasquie tells me. "I love *le Tour.*"

Some of that magic came from exciting riders like Charly Gaul, an amazing climber who spun the pedals even faster than Armstrong does today. Gaul's water stop in 1959 may have saved him from dehydration, but it didn't save him the Tour. After restarting, the revived Gaul caught up with another former Tour winner, Louison Bobet, and they rode the last 30 hilly miles of the stage together. They finished in Aurillac twenty minutes behind the day's winners, who included Federico Bahamontes. Without that twenty-minute loss, Gaul would have finished the Tour in second place behind Bahamontes. He might even have beaten the Spaniard.

The towns of Montsalvy and Junhac are both on today's route. But that's where the similarity ends between this 102-mile stage from St. Flour to Figéac and that decisive day almost half a century ago.

In 1959, attacks in the early climbs resulted in a break moving two minutes ahead of the chase group that contained all the main contenders. The seventy-strong peloton behind them was already beaten. Attacks and counterattacks continued for the rest of the six-hour stage, which was won by the regional rider, Henry Anglade. The day's average speed was 22 miles per hour.

Flashing forward to this shorter stage, none of the several attacks launched in the opening hour are allowed to gain more than 10 seconds. That's because Armstrong's Postal team feels there is a dangerous rival in each of the moves, and displays its prowess by chasing them all down. Eventually, Postal doesn't chase a break by two Spaniards, Juan Antonio Flecha and Eloi Martinez, and a Frenchman, David Moncoutié. These three arrive in Junhac seven minutes ahead of the pack, after averaging an astounding 29 miles an hour for the first two hours! And none of the riders takes the time to dip their heads in the fountain's water.

_____

Charly Gaul stopped at that fountain not only to quench his thirst on a hot day, but also to avoid the serious effects of dehydration. Moderate or severe dehydration can cause loss of important blood salts, like potassium and sodium, and without a minimum amount of water and salt, vital organs like the kidneys, brain, and heart can't function. Gaul's crude method of avoiding dehydration was effective, and it saved him from quitting the Tour. Today, on road stages, water bottles can be handed up from team cars, while specially fitted motorcycles hold fresh bottles that riders can grab on the run. That's not the case in time trials. When Lance Armstrong faced *his* dehydration problem at the 2003 Tour, it almost cost him the whole race. The Texan's crisis came in a long time trial on a stiflingly hot day, when he literally ran out of water. "The first indication that something was wrong was when I got 3 or 4 K down the road," he remembers. "My mouth was completely dry, and I thought, 'Oh no.' I only had one bottle and I knew it was going to be an hour-long race, and I'm five minutes in, and I could drink the whole thing right now. I remember thinking, 'I had better space out my sips.'"

Even so, Armstrong lost power, particularly on two short climbs near the end, and he finished the race with salt deposits ringing his mouth. He lost 1 minute, 36 seconds to Ullrich, his biggest defeat in a Tour time trial since he returned from cancer. It also brought Ullrich within 34 seconds of taking Armstrong's yellow jersey, and made 2003 Armstrong's most difficult Tour victory. The defending champion was so concerned with what happened that day that he and coach Chris Carmichael analyzed the dehydration problem in detail that winter, and came up with some answers.

"What *really* happened was, I was just chronically dehydrated from the beginning of the Tour, and even before that," Armstrong tells me. "I didn't all of a sudden go from totally hydrated to this dehydrated. I would drink water all day long, and *still* not be hydrated. My bladder was hydrated, but not my cells." Armstrong thinks that his dehydration problem may be due to the platinum therapy he underwent during his cancer treatment in late 1996, but he's not absolutely sure.

Coach Carmichael offers a different explanation. He feels that his client dug himself into a corner by overstretching himself at the Dauphiné Libéré, the eight-day preparation race Armstrong won a few weeks before that Tour. "We'd been struggling with hydration since the Dauphiné," Carmichael confirms. "It was an extremely difficult race, and extremely hot. In retrospect, Lance shouldn't have tried to win that race. . . . He dug real deep to win—you could see it from a heart-rate gauge after the race. He was tapped out."

"Normally, after the Dauphiné, he'd sleep in a hypoxic tent," Carmichael says. Hypoxic tents, used by most elite athletes, simulate sleeping at elevations as high as 20,000 feet and encourage the body to produce new red blood cells—similar to what EPO does illegally. "But to sleep in an oxygen-reduced environment was the wrong thing to do," Carmichael admits. "My gut was telling me that, and hindsight is 20/20. We just needed to get back and recover, because we were looking for that two percent gain in Lance's form between the Dauphiné and the Tour. It doesn't sound like much, but on an hour-long climb it's the difference between attacking or being attacked."

In those few weeks, Armstrong continued training for the 2003 Tour and slept in the hypoxic tent. "But the reality was," Carmichael says, "nothing was gonna happen in that period. He was just catabolic. He'd broken himself down. When you apply too great a physical load on an athlete . . . the athlete breaks down. And that's what happened. He wasn't responding. The last thing you want to do is just sit around for two weeks and do nothing before the start of the Tour. But in truth, that's what he should have done."

Carmichael believes that because Armstrong's body was not recovering, his body could not rehydrate, and the problem came to a head at the Tour time trial in the south of France.

As a result, Armstrong did not push himself at the 2004 Dauphiné, which perhaps explains why Mayo and Hamilton both beat him so handily on the climb to Mont Ventoux. Now, at the Tour, the cool weather of the opening ten days has further aided the champion's ability to add that "two percent" improvement that coach Carmichael is looking for, so that Armstrong's form will be at 100 percent when the Tour reaches the mountains. They will both find out soon, when Day 14 leads the riders into the Pyrenees.

———

On this stage to Figéac—where Flecha, Martinez, and Moncoutié are still eight minutes clear heading into the final 15 miles—Armstrong has other things on his mind. He's angered by an incident that occurred after he left the team hotel in Issoire this morning. A French TV crew was caught trying to film the room he occupied, maybe looking for "evidence" of doping, like they tried to do in 1999 with the trash bags.

Later in the day comes more disturbing news. The Paris daily *Le Monde* is about to publish an interview with America's first Tour champion, Greg LeMond. The interview is already up on the paper's Web site. One question to LeMond concerns a 2001 phone conversation between him and Armstrong that is related in the book *LA Confidentiel*, as told by LeMond's wife, Kathy. LeMond asserts in the interview that, after he publicly gave lukewarm and ambivalent support to the Texan, at the time when drug questions were most heatedly raised, Armstrong's phone call was a shock. "It was aggressive and very threatening," says LeMond. "Lance said that I wouldn't have won the Tour without EPO. That's completely false as EPO wasn't even around back then [1986]." LeMond adds, "Lance says that I'm the only Tour winner not to support him. I was a big fan of Lance's the year he won his first Tour. But with all these stories circulating, it's difficult to remain a supporter." A couple of day later, when asked to comment on LeMond's words, Armstrong says, "It's best that I say . . . nothing. It's not good what he has said."

For now, Armstrong and his team are riding comfortably in the peloton on the hilly run-in to Figéac. Still minutes ahead of them, Flecha tries to get away from his two breakaway companions with a surprise attack on a short climb six miles from the finish. Moncoutié immediately counterattacks—and rides away alone. The 29-year-old Parisian, who now lives about an hour north of Figéac, has scouted these roads many times, and he puts two minutes between him and the two Spaniards by the stage's end. It's a splendid win. The second for France in two days.

Meanwhile, Armstrong has ordered his team to the head of the peloton. They are riding like demons down the long hill into town before crossing the fast-flowing River Celé on an old stone bridge and then tackling a short uphill to the finish. This strong team effort is good practice for the day to come, when Armstrong's eight team-mates will need to be strong and disciplined as they enter the Pyrenees for the first major mountain stage. Those mountains are on the minds of all the contenders. Hamilton is hoping that his back will be strong enough, Ullrich that he'll climb stronger than he did at his last race in Switzerland, and Armstrong that it's not too hot and dehydration is not a problem.

The peloton arrives in Figéac six minutes behind Moncoutié, whose first-ever stage win at the Tour is something special. He's over-joyed, not only for himself, but especially for his scandal-scarred team, Cofidis. Moncoutié is an athlete of modest means. He trains hard, races hard, and lives clean. His victory is one that all of cycling can celebrate, especially the local old-timers, for whom a regional hero has once more emerged. No doubt, back in Junhac, there's a party going on, and Robert Sergent is pouring something stronger than *eau potable* for his happy customers, as he tells them, "I still re-member what happened in fifty-nine."

STAGE RESULT: 1. David Moncoutié (France); 2. Juan Antonio Flecha (Spain), at 2:15; 3. Eloi Martinez (Spain), at 2:17; 4. Hushovd, at 5:58; 5. Zabel, same time.

OVERALL STANDINGS: 1. Voeckler; 2. O'Grady, at 3:00; 3. Casar, at 4:13; 4. Virenque, at 6:52; 5. Piil, at 7:43; 6. Armstrong, at 9:35; 11. Hamilton, at 10:18; 13. Klöden, at 10:20; 17. Ullrich, at 10:30; 19. Leipheimer, at 10:50; 20. Basso, at 10:52; 51. Mayo, at 15:02.

DAY 14
_____

Where Eagles Soar

JULY 16: *The first stage with a mountaintop finish starts in Castelsarrasin and covers 122.5 miles. It opens with a long flat stretch through the farmland of Gascony before reaching the Pyrenees for two climbs: the Col d'Aspin after 107 miles, and the steeper one to the finish at La Mongie.*

Suddenly, after 60 miles of racing, the peloton crests a low hill, looks across a field of harvested wheat, and sees the famed and distant outline for the first time: the Pyrenees! A noble wilderness still inhabited by bear, ibex, and eagles, this fabled range of mountains stretches from the Mediterranean to the Atlantic in an unbroken chain. Today, the still-distant 10,000-foot, white-tipped peaks are dwarfed by colossal dark clouds that billow menacingly upward. We can already discern thin forks of lightning and sheets of black rain. A stage that has started in rural Gascony in a heat wave looks certain to have a stormy conclusion in the high Pyrenees.

Until 1910, Tour de France pioneers saw these mountains only from afar. Then, Alphonse Steinès, a sportswriter with *L'Auto*, suggested to his editor, Tour organizer Henri Desgrange, that a stage over the highest passes in the Pyrenees would do wonders for the race's popularity. "Have you gone mad?" said Desgrange. "You want to make the racers go over roads that don't even exist?"

Desgrange was partly right: The goat tracks that did exist were covered in snow for most of the year; and the "roads" that *were* useable were just dirt paths with grass growing along the center. But Steinès was stubborn. One midwinter's day, he took the overnight train from Paris, hired a chauffeur, and headed into the hills. He went as far as the car would take him up the Tourmalet, the highest of the Pyrenean passes, and then walked through fifteen-foot snowdrifts in the dark to prove that a road really did exist. When Steinès returned to Paris even more enthused than before, Desgrange reluctantly agreed to his assistant's crazy plan. He announced to a skeptical world that the 1910 Tour would include the Tourmalet and other high passes in the Pyrenees.

The plan seemed just as crazy six months later when sixty-three riders set out before dawn from Luchon on a stage of 215 miles. They began climbing right away, first over the manageable climbs of the Peyresourde and Aspin. But most of the field had to push their bikes up the monsters that followed, the Tourmalet and Aubisque; and they still had 100 miles to ride before reaching the stage finish in Bayonne. Thirty-nine brave men completed the punishing course, and stage winner Octave Lapize, incensed by what he called an inhuman course, said: "Desgrange is a murderer!" Murderer or not, Desgrange and Steinès had hit upon the formula that transformed their race from being merely heroic to being truly mythical.

Just over three hours into today's stage, with the first mountain climb, the Aspin, only 14 miles distant, the sunshine finally gives way to the threatened rain. At first, it's plump, isolated drops; then a steady downpour; and by the time the teams of Armstrong and overall race leader Voeckler bring the compact peloton to the very foot of the Col d'Aspin, it's a raging storm. The road becomes a river. The huge crowds lining the early slopes morph into a multihued wall of parkas, capes, and umbrellas. And a race that has been fitful immediately becomes fierce.

Ignoring the deluge, the Postal team is on fire. Armstrong orders his men to the front, to set the elevated tempo they practice at training camps and perfect in team time trials. They're going so fast that their rivals are grimly hanging on rather than eagerly breaking out. The Americans George Hincapie and Floyd Landis set the pace, followed by their Spanish teammate Chechu Rubiera, who's ready to take over if and when the first two fade. Armstrong is in line behind them, happy to finally be revving his legs on a true mountain ascent, while his Portuguese "ace" José Azevedo rides shotgun, guarding his leader's rear wheel from the riffraff as if he's secret service riding the presidential limo. And what about the other four Postal riders? The Russian veteran Ekimov and Czech powerhouse Padrnos did their work earlier in the day, racing at the front on 90 miles of flat roads that preceded the climb. The other two, Spaniards Beltran and Noval, also contributed to the early pace, only to drop back when Hincapie put his foot on the accelerator.

But there's no disgrace in not being able to follow the best on this particular climb. Besides the two Postal riders, the "already dropped" list includes yesterday's stage winner Moncoutié and his Aussie teammate O'Grady, as well as the early polka-dot leader Bettini and the Basque Landaluze, the man who almost won the stage into Guéret.

When Octave Lapize first climbed the Aspin in 1910, he probably took an hour or so to slog his single-gear, thirty-pound machine up the winding eight-mile climb—whose steepest pitch is 10 percent and ascends through 2,575 vertical feet. Until this day, the fastest recorded climb of the Aspin was made by Virenque. He rode it in thirty-two and a half minutes during a winning breakaway in 1995. But today, Hincapie and the fifty men on his shirttails are about to complete the task in 30:10! Which explains why the only man who manages to break clear of the Postal-led machine, the skinny Dane Michael Rasmussen, is a mere five seconds ahead at the top. In any other race, his enormous effort would have netted him an advance of at least one or two minutes. But all that for five seconds? No wonder it's virtually pointless—and ill-advised—for any of Armstrong's adversaries to try to attack him just yet.

———————

The rain redoubles its intensity after Rasmussen heads into the descent, which opens with a series of tight turns, down through a thick forest of pines. Racing downhill in a storm like this can be perilous. Not only is the risk of crashing increased on the slick roads, but the conditions can expose the body to other, just as threatening dangers. Rasmussen's Rabobank team leader remembers a "rain experience" he suffered at the Catalonia Week race in Spain. One moment he was riding over a hill in sunshine, the next a storm blew in. "Coming down the descent, the driving rain was hurting so much that I was putting my hand over my helmet, cupping the air vents," says Levi Leipheimer, who is bald. "When I got to the bottom my legs just would not work. I've never been so cold on the bike. My body was shaking so much I couldn't stop. My jaw was locked shut. I couldn't open my mouth. My teeth weren't just *chattering*, they were *grinding*. I couldn't stop it. And my legs were just frozen, pretty close to hypothermic."

The conditions descending from the Aspin are not *that* cold, but the air temperature *has* dropped thirty degrees. It was ninety before the race reached the Aspin, and it's now sixty. Such a drop in temperature affects some more than others—Armstrong always does well in the cold and rain, while Ullrich does not. Riders also react differently to the combination of wet roads and a fast downhill. Most just take it in stride, like all the other challenges they face every day; but it's downright scary for some, and an opportunity to attack for others.

Rasmussen, alone at the front, is in a good position to see through the rain and pick the best lines through the downhill turns. While he moves 25 seconds clear, Armstrong and his four teammates decide to ease back. They don't want to even *risk* crashing. That's not the case with Mayo, who has always been an adroit and fearless descender. The Euskaltel leader is hoping to win today's stage in front of an estimated 60,000 fellow Basques who have traveled here by bus and car to root for their man, and so he quickly slips away from the Armstrong group with a half-dozen others. Those men, surprisingly, include Ullrich and his T-Mobile teammate Klöden, along with a daring Voeckler. Why are they taking such a risk? If you can't beat Armstrong's team on the uphill, is downhill the only place to try?

On roads awash with sand and small rocks, the Mayo group is soon 300 yards ahead of Armstrong's. This potential threat to the American diminishes when the T-Mobile team realizes that their gap is small and not growing, and the effort made now will hurt them on the final climb. First Klöden, then Ullrich sits up and waits for the Postal riders. Mayo and the others follow suit. As for Hamilton, who was farther back than he should have been at the Aspin summit, he has been quietly moving forward in the Armstrong group. Perhaps he's hoping that if he starts the final climb closer to the front of the group he'll be able to finish in better position.

In the valley, just before the riders reach the village of Ste. Marie-de-Campan, Rasmussen is still ahead, while the other groups all reassemble into a fifty-strong pack. The finish line is only eight miles away, partway up the mighty Tourmalet, at the ski town of La Mongie.

As the final climb begins, the main contenders—Armstrong, Ullrich, Hamilton, Basso, and Mayo—are all together. For each of them, a year of planning, months of training, weeks of racing, and days of anxiety will all come to a head in this next half-hour.

The climb to La Mongie is not particularly long (after an easy stretch on the valley floor, the climb covers five miles), nor particularly technical (much of it is on wide, straight roads), but it *is* steep, averaging nine percent for those final five miles. This is the second time in three years that a Tour stage has finished here. The other time, it was also the first mountaintop finish, and the team that led the pack up this approach road was Postal. Now, just as then, it is an inspired Hincapie setting the pace. "I find it really exciting leading Lance like this," he tells me. "I'm very proud to be the only team member that's been with Lance for all the Tours he's won. It's been a great honor."

To prepare himself for sustained efforts on steep climbs like this, Hincapie takes long training rides in the mountains near his two homes: Greensboro, North Carolina, and Gerona, Spain. Then there are the specific training camps, like the one that Hincapie did in the Pyrenees in May with Armstrong and a few other teammates. "When we're going up these climbs in training before the Tour," he says, "you're going, 'Why do I do this?' Then you get to the Tour de France and all the hard work really pays off when you feel good on a climb."

Right now, the long, lean Hincapie is feeling good, despite the heavy rain. He and Landis are doing just what they did on the Aspin, setting a fast pace while Armstrong rides more easily in their slipstream. The pace is too demanding for the others to even contemplate attacking. And what's Armstrong's plan? "We started with the intention to win the stage," he says.

Hamilton's goal for the day is less lofty. He's simply focused on surviving. "I wasn't feeling good on the first col. I was feeling empty, just lacking power. I'm not sure exactly why." Those bad feelings are returning on this final climb to La Mongie. As the grade gets steeper, Hamilton starts slipping back in the group. Over his transmitter, he tells his director, Alvaro Pino, that he's not feeling so good, and to tell his stronger teammates to hang with the group as long as they can. And with that, more than four miles from the finish, Hamilton falls off the pace.

Hamilton is dropped! The dramatic news is met with astonishment. His fans are in shock; pressroom reporters jump out of their seats; and TV commentators go wild.

"I'm not getting any power out of my lower back," the New Englander later explains. "And when you're climbing you use a lot of your lower back. Standing on the pedals, I don't really gain any power. I don't feel myself, that's for sure. I felt ten times better in the Dauphiné. It's sad to feel this way. . . . It may have looked like I wasn't trying, but I was going 100 percent. My teammates know that."

Hamilton, who's wearing a black armband in memory of Tugboat, then adds, "I think about him a lot. Losing him definitely tore up my insides. But that's not my excuse . . . it's the legs, the legs won't turn."

Heading to the summit, he turns his legs as fast as he can, but he knows that his dream of winning this Tour has suddenly ended. His Spanish teammate Perez remains with the wounded team leader. He'll help pace Hamilton to the finish, to limit his losses, and hope that tomorrow he'll feel better.

———

After Hamilton, two other "names" fall back: yellow jersey Voeckler and polka-dot leader Virenque. Hincapie's pace is too much for the two French riders, who will both be passed by the flagging Hamilton before the top. Meanwhile, the sun has returned, and Hincapie and Landis sit up, their work completed. To conserve their strength to do the same work tomorrow, they shift into touring pace, chatting, not bothered that they'll be ten minutes back by the finish. It's now Rubiera's turn to set the tempo.

As the Postal teammates switch duties, Ivan Basso's CSC teammate Carlos Sastre sees that the gallant Rasmussen, who has been on his break now for almost 15 miles, is about to be caught. Sastre knows that this is a perfect time to try a counterattack. Those chasing a breakaway psychologically ease up when they have their goal in sight, and they're not ready to start another chase right after.

Sastre's tactic makes sense. But he hadn't counted on an acceleration by Rubiera that keeps Sastre in check and has an unexpected consequence: Ullrich is dropped!

The big German is gasping for air. His steady pedal cadence looks more labored than ever. Now, Tour commentators are truly going wild. First Hamilton, now Ullrich, and Armstrong hasn't even hit the front yet! But the German doesn't have an injured back; he hasn't even crashed in this Tour. No one can explain it.

"I already knew that I was having a bad day on the Aspin," Ullrich tells reporters later. "It was very hot at the foot of the climb, then the temperature dropped up there. I got very cold and my legs were heavy from the rain. But I wasn't the only one to suffer, so that's not an explanation, let alone an excuse."

When he sensed how bad he was feeling, Ullrich told his friend Klöden to stay with the leaders as long as he could. His teammate was up to the task. At three miles still left to climb, and with Rasmussen now passed and dropped, Azevedo is setting the pace for Armstrong—and Klöden, along with Basso and Sastre, are right behind the champion. The others still hanging are the Russian Denis Menchov and four Spaniards—Mancebo, the Phonak pair Gonzales and Pereiro, and Mayo. Instead of making one of his darting attacks, Mayo is just hanging in. "As soon as U.S. Postal accelerated, I soon understood. . . . I didn't have the legs." And when Sastre tries another attack, Mayo stays at the back of the group, unable to respond to the *"Aupa!"* cries of his masses of Basque fans in their orange T-shirts.

As Sastre accelerates with two and a half miles to go, Azevedo drops back, leaving Armstrong to finally fend for himself. Mancebo, the Spanish champion, is feeling strong and chases Sastre. Armstrong is quickly on his wheel, even though, he says, "I'm never great at La Mongie." He remembers 2002, when his then teammate Roberto Heras was doing what Azevedo has done today. "I was at my limit for the whole climb. Today, the same thing." The difference between the Texan and his challengers, though, is that even on a bad day Armstrong's "limit" is higher than theirs. That soon becomes evident.

With Sastre still 10 seconds ahead, Mancebo makes a surge and is followed by Basso and then Klöden. Armstrong watches them, gets out of the saddle, and then cranks past all three. Only Basso is able to take Armstrong's wheel as the defending champion bridges the gap to Sastre. It's now Armstrong against two CSC riders. It's hard to say who will win.

The tactics of CSC manager Bjarne Riis appear to be brilliant. Armstrong has never had to contend with two strong riders from the same opposing team this close to a mountaintop finish. Basso says that Riis has taught him how to remain calm in a situation like this, and how to "feel" the race. "Our pre-Tour training camp in Tuscany was great," the Italian racer adds. "We worked out of Bjarne's house there. That gave me a lot of confidence. I was ready for the Tour."

Riis explains that his method is to work with *all* of his riders, to give them not only confidence, but also the morale to do well. "Every single rider you have in the team is different," he says. "And if you don't take the time it takes to coach them, to motivate them in the right way they need, you can't do the best for them. I spend a little more time on that than other team directors. Every single rider."

With a mile and a half left, as the leaders race beneath one of the avalanche shelters, where thousands of screaming Basques are still hoping Mayo can return, Sastre drops back. Basso now goes to the front, showing Armstrong that he's still strong. Maybe the Texan really *is* at his limit.

Basso and Armstrong, who have been friends for a few years, share the pace to gain as much time as they can over their lagging rivals. Basso hasn't won a race of any description for two years, and he's eager to win this one. It would be the biggest of his career. He takes his turn at the front with 250 yards to go, the wide road still climbing at almost 10 percent. When Armstrong won here in 2002, he didn't have to sprint; his last rival was seven seconds behind him. Perhaps he can raise a sprint now—but he doesn't. He stays twenty feet back and watches Ivan Basso throw his arms above his head in triumph as he crosses the line in bright sunshine. Across the front of Basso's jersey is the stylized winged symbol of his boss, Riis, whose race name was "The Eagle."

———

Armstrong has moved up to second on General Classification, now only 5:24 behind the spirited Voeckler. Basso has moved up to sixth place, while Klöden edged to fifth. The two men share the same overall time, a little more than a minute behind Armstrong.

"Ivan was super today, he was very strong," says the Texan, who reveals that he and his foundation are trying to help Basso's mother fight cancer. "It was pretty special for me to be out there with Ivan. Off the bike we've been working to do what we can for his mom. That's what we've been talking about for ten days, not about the race."

An exhilarated Basso attends the post-race ceremonies, goes to the podium for his stage winner's trophy, talks into the TV and radio microphones, and finally faces the press in the interview room. "I think that Lance gave me the win," he says, "because my mother is in the hospital with cancer. But Lance is still the strongest rider in the race." As he speaks, Armstrong is slowly riding up the hill through the ski village, continuing on the road toward the Tourmalet. His team car is waiting for him a couple of miles from the summit, so he can make a quick getaway. He and team director Bruyneel will go over the pass and continue on down through Lourdes on their way to the team's hotel, close to tomorrow's stage start.

I spot Armstrong as he rides up the steep slope. When I start running after him, in the thin air at 6,000 feet elevation, I'm reminded why he and most of the other riders sleep in oxygen-reduced hypoxic tents, even during the Tour. The increased oxygenation of their blood comes in handy at this altitude.

Armstrong is already talking to some TV people when, out of breath, I reach his team car. The day's effort still marks him. There are smears of mud on his face, kicked up by bike tires from the flooded roads on the Aspin. His cheeks seem more hollowed than ever. He gasps a little, catching his breath, as he says, "It was a hard day, especially with the weather—the heat wave, then the storm, now the sun again. But for the GC, it's superb.

"For me, the biggest surprises are Ullrich and Hamilton. I didn't expect a result like that. But Jan always has trouble in the first mountain stages. He might have taken one on the chin today, but he always comes back, and he'll be strong in the last week. We'll see how he is tomorrow."

Down at the T-Mobile camper, Ullrich is trying to explain to the German media what happened, why he lost two and a half minutes on this first mountain stage. As he talks, Klöden arrives. No one goes to talk to him. He parks his bike and gets into the van. He may have finished third today, two minutes ahead of his boss, but he still says he's the worker not the leader.

Outside the Hotel La Crête Blanche, Phonak director Pino answers our questions. "The team rode well, but the problem is Tyler—and Sevilla too, our two leaders both lost time. Tyler said to me yesterday that his back is a little better, but not super."

Inside the wood-floored hotel, the Phonak and Euskaltel riders are using a couple of hotel rooms to shower and change. After twenty minutes or so, Hamilton walks down the stairs with a white visor turned backward on his head, his black day bag slung over his shoulder, and that familiar well-scrubbed look on his now dejected face. He puts down the bag and talks in a monotone voice: "I'm disappointed that I let my team down, but they understand, and they know I gave everything. But to win a race like the Tour de France you can't have a bad day. So after a day like this it makes it very difficult, as well as for Jan Ullrich. . . ." Hamilton pauses, looking resigned and expressionless. His spirit picks up a bit when he adds, "But I couldn't ask for a better team. For the first half of the Tour they did exactly what they needed to do, and this is exactly what I wanted. Today it really came down to me. It's unfortunate, but I didn't have it."

STAGE RESULT: 1. Ivan Basso (Italy); 2. Armstrong, same time; 3. Klöden, at 0:20; 4. Mancebo, at 0:24; 5. Carlos Sastre (Spain), at 0:33; 9. Mayo, at 1:03; 16.Leipheimer, at 1:59; 20. Ullrich, at 2:30; 34. Hamilton, at 3:27; 41. Voeckler, at 3:59.

OVERALL STANDINGS: 1. Voeckler; 2. Armstrong, at 5:24; 3. Casar, at 5:50; 4. Virenque, at 6:20; 5. Klöden, at 6:33; 6. Basso, same time; 12. Leipheimer, at 8:50; 16. Ullrich, at 9:01; 20. Hamilton, at 9:46; 32. Mayo, at 12:06.

The Toughest Day

JULY 17: *With seven mountain passes and 16,000 feet of total climbing, this 127.5-mile stage from Lannemezan to Plateau de Beille is the hardest stage so far. Only the strongest men will contest the victory on the 10-mile climb to the finish.*

Touched by warm sunshine and a soft breeze, the 165 riders waiting on the start line in the friendly little town of Lannemezan could be fooled into thinking this is going to be a pleasant day. Not so. In the next six to seven hours they will face what is likely to be their toughest challenge in the 2004 Tour de France. While media fanfare is focused on the final week's Alpe d'Huez time trial as the big shoot-out, Armstrong and the other contenders know that *this* is the stage, crossing seven mountain passes in the Pyrenees, where they have to stand strong. Any sign of weakness will put a team leader out of contention, or even out of the race.

Statistically, this isn't the longest stage, at 20 miles shorter than Limoges–St. Flour. It doesn't have the most climbing—"only" 16,000 vertical feet, compared with the 17,000 feet of next week's Bourg d'Oisans–Le Grand Bornand. Nor does it have the most climbs, just seven, compared with the nine they climbed on the way to St. Flour. But beyond those statistics come other significant factors: near heat-wave conditions, back roads that never cease to twist and turn, some of the steepest gradients of the race, and the climax, Plateau de Beille, which is the longest mountaintop finish in this Tour.

"It's a different type of stage," says Armstrong. "Although yester-day's Col d'Aspin was hard, it's really not very hard. But when you do five or six mountains like today, and you do some steep ones, like Portet d'Aspet and Latrape and crazy things like that, then a 10-mile climb at eight or nine percent at the finish is tough. Very tough."

For some, the Plateau is the last thing they want to think about. Ullrich, Hamilton, Mayo, and the other leaders who faltered at La Mongie have to be concerned that this stage will make their situations worse, not better. Ullrich is still not sure why his legs wouldn't re-spond to his ambitions yesterday, and he's hoping that the sunshine will transform his fortunes, as it generally does. Hamilton would also like to turn things around and reclaim his power, but he isn't sure if and how he can. And Mayo, whose injuries have healed from the crash on the cobblestones on Day 4, is still angry at Armstrong's team for riding so hard that day after his fall, causing him to lose time he has not yet regained. The Basque is also aware that his "orange army" is again hoping that he can pull off a stage win, at Plateau de Beille, where thousands of his fans have already gathered.

———

Just over two hours and two climbs into this savage day of racing we've already seen a breakaway, a crash, and three men quit the race. The stage's first break is now five minutes clear of the peloton. Up there are CSC's Jens Voigt, Rabobank's Rasmussen, and Boulangère's Sylvain Chavanel, who will need much more than five minutes if they hope to succeed. The day's first crash came when AG2R's Jean-Patrick Nazon overshot a downhill turn and hit a gatepost, and fellow sprinter Robbie McEwen fell over his bike. The three men who have abandoned the race are Mayo's co-leader Haimar Zubeldia, who finished fifth in the 2003 Tour and now has an inflamed knee and can't pedal without pain; the Russian Menchov, who looked so strong at La Mongie in seventh place, but has been stopped by a recurrence of an Achilles injury; and the Austrian Gerrit Glomser, who was dropped on the first climb.

The race has passed the white marble monument to Fabio Casartelli, where Armstrong's former teammate died in a crash on the Portet d'Aspet descent in 1995. Going up the Aspet, yellow jersey Voeckler is dropped by the pack on the 15-percent grade; but he rejoins coming down.

Now, at the foot of the day's third climb, the Col de la Core, Tyler Hamilton is about to do something he has never done in eight years of competing at the Tour de France: quit the race. "It's something I never considered before," he tells me later. "In the bus on the way to the start this morning, Alvaro Pino, my team director, suggested it. He said if I didn't think I can stay with the leaders, there's no point in continuing, just to finish in Paris. I said I would see how I felt over the first couple climbs, and then make a decision. But it was no different from yesterday. I had no power."

And so, the man who successfully built his own excellent team, trained harder than anyone, and motivated his teammates to ride a remarkable Tour, is out. The Angers crash he suffered nine days earlier has finally brought about his downfall. In other years and races, he's been in much worse pain than he is now, but when, as he says, "I can't climb to my ability," there is no choice.

When Armstrong's teammate Hincapie is asked why Lance rarely gets injured in falls, but others do, he replies, "That's just the luck of the draw. That's just how you fall off your bike. When Tyler crashed he didn't want to land on his back and mess his back up but that's just the way he landed. It's just bad luck."

Bad luck or not, Hamilton feels like a failure, a quitter. But no one forgets the pain he bravely battled through to finish fourth at the 2003 Tour. Ironically, it wasn't pain from his broken collarbone that almost sent Hamilton home from that Tour, but a mysterious back pain that began the night before the long road stage to Marseille. "I'd slept bad, and by the time we got to the start after an hour down this twisty mountain road, my back was really inflamed," Hamilton remembers. "I didn't know what was going on . . . I was breathing like with one lung. I was really, really scared. There was just pain. Luckily it was a flat stage and I survived. We then sat in the bus for about three hours to get to our hotel, and I could barely walk to my room after dinner.

"On the rest day the next day, I rode the trainer for a half-hour, but it was just too painful. My spine was twisted, and that was putting a lot of pressure on the sciatic nerve. It was murder. Ole, the osteopath, worked on it that morning, and he was able to help. But after that I didn't feel that good. Without that back pain, I think I could have been on the podium."

Perhaps Ole Kaere Føli, his former osteopath at CSC, could also have helped him get through this 2004 Tour. I ask the Danish practitioner why he thinks Hamilton could get no power from his lower back. "Tyler has a very weak neck and spine," Føli explains. "And he really needs a person around him if he has a crash, as it's very difficult to open up his neck. He has very little room for the nerves up there, because some years ago he had a very bad crash directly on his head."

Føli goes on to say that "if you're not open in the head or the neck, then the energy to the rest of the body slows down. Also, when you crash and get nervous—'Oh, what's wrong with my body?'—then your kidney slows down a little, and I think that's what happened.

"Of course, I'm a little upset that he had to abandon. I've been so close to him . . . but he went to another team, and I couldn't help him. I think I could have helped him with that problem."

Phonak has its own physical therapist, but he doesn't know Hamilton's body the way Føli does. It takes time to build a team from scratch. Phonak is in only its first Tour, and it was bound to have a few problems and crises. That's not the case with Ullrich's or Armstrong's teams, both of which are well-oiled machines. Particularly U.S. Postal.

———————

"It was unbelievable. I counted twenty-two riders in the group, with seven U.S. Postals on the front. I've never seen anything like it!" Levi Leipheimer is describing what he saw on the tremendously difficult Category 1 climb, the Col d'Agnes, four hours into what *is* proving to be the toughest day of the Tour. To put seven of a team's nine riders at the head of the pack on a *flat* stage is no big deal. But for Armstrong to have six of his eight teammates leading him up one of the steepest climbs of the Tour on a day when five riders have already pulled out and another 135 riders have been left behind is phenomenal. No wonder the Texan says, "We have the best team in the race."

Leipheimer is not alone in having never seen such disciplined hegemony at the Tour. Not this year. Not this decade. Perhaps never in the Tour's 101-year history. Sure, there have been teams that have finished more riders in the top echelon of the race. Europe's first big-money team, La Vie Claire, finished Greg LeMond, Bernard Hinault, Andy Hampsten, and Niki Rütimann first, second, fourth, and seventh, respectively, in the 1986 Tour. But La Vie Claire didn't win the team time trial, and the most riders it would have in the front group on the toughest mountain stage would be those four guys listed above. Not *seven*. Perhaps the nearest equivalent to Armstrong's Postal team was Eddy Merckx's Faema squad of 1970, which defended the yellow jersey from start to finish and helped Merckx win three mountain stages.

One big reason for the similarities between these two teams is that both Merckx and Armstrong inspire confidence. Floyd Landis, who is doing his third Tour for Armstrong, says that confidence in their leader is what makes Postal stand out from the other squads. "There are plenty of good teams, but they don't all have a leader like Lance," Landis says. "It's not as easy to motivate the whole team to train the way we do when you don't have a guy you know can win."

A week before this Tour began, Postal held a training camp in the Pyrenees. The whole team attended, except for Padrnos, who's not a climber. One day was spent riding parts of this very stage, including the Col d'Agnes and the finishing climb to Plateau de Beille. Many teams from the seventies onward held pre-Tour training camps, yet they rarely rode the actual stages. This was something that was pioneered by Armstrong and Bruyneel, starting with the 1999 Tour, but usually with only one or two riders. When *everyone* on the team rides the course and knows what to expect, putting seven guys on the front on a tough mountain climb becomes easier.

Training is one thing, though. Race performance is another. A motivational leader and great camaraderie off the bike all help. Still, every team worker also needs to be totally focused during the race to ensure that the other elements come together. Landis says he just ignores any distraction, even the landscape: "There's no time to look around, nor to talk to the people beside you in the race. Maybe that's what's compelling about it, how everything else disappears and you are completely focused on what's going on around you. You have to be, because most of the time it's dangerous, too."

Today, Landis and Hincapie are the designated front men for the three climbs, including the Agnes, that immediately precede the final ascent. Their job accomplished, the two Americans drop back when they reach the foot of the last climb, the 10-mile Plateau de Beille. It's now up to Rubiera and Azevedo to set the pace for Armstrong. Rubiera—who has his own fan club despite being a domestique—does an amazing job with his opening fifteen-minute stint. With the speed of a gazelle, he not only catches the day's main breakaways, Rasmussen and Voigt, but also forces several notable riders to fall back—including Ullrich! The German fights brutally for the rest of the climb, but he's bitterly disappointed in himself, even though he finishes stronger than he did yesterday. He'll finish this stage in sixth—again behind his teammate Klöden.

Rubiera's work done, Azevedo comes up to bat. The Portuguese sets such a brutal pace for the next ten minutes that only two riders are with him at the end of his stint: Armstrong and Basso. Great teamwork has brought Armstrong to within three miles of the finish and, once again, there's only one rival to contend with, Basso.

———

The stage is almost over. Armstrong says to Basso: "Give it full gas, we need to take as many seconds as we can." They both ride hard, just as they did the day before. Once again they take a minute out of Klöden. Two and a half from Ullrich. And Mayo? His legs are stiff today. He can't climb. He's dropped on the fourth mountain, and on the fifth one, the Agnes, he tries to abandon the Tour. His teammates persuade him not to. "We've already lost Zubeldia. We don't want to lose you, too, Iban." Mayo continues, but he's going to have to face his orange army more than half an hour behind Armstrong and Basso, knowing that his Tour is now in tatters.

Right now, those frustrated Basque fans are standing in the road two miles from the finish, and, like Mayo, they're still angry at Armstrong for the cobblestone incident. They shout and scream and give the Texan the finger as he races past. Luckily, he has Basso for protection, along with motorcycles front and rear, before reaching the barriers near the end.

In the winner's circle, Sheryl Crow is already sipping champagne. "I've come to see Lance win," she tells an inquisitive Spanish TV crew. Soon, Armstrong is in the winner's circle, too. He easily beats Basso in the final sprint to take the 20-second time bonus and the seventeenth stage win of his ten-Tour career. What he doesn't get is the yellow jersey, which is still on Voeckler's back as he approaches the finish.

Thomas Voeckler is riding the stage of his young life. Dropped on all the big climbs, he chased back on each descent. Sprinting out of the saddle in these last two miles, his yellow jersey is unzipped to the waist, sweat pours down his face, the fans are cheering, the announcer says he has to finish inside five minutes to save *le maillot jaune*, and he crosses the line at 4:42 with the biggest grin. He punches the air—he's still the race leader by 22 seconds! Ti-Blan's photo will be on the front page of every French newspaper tomorrow. Lance's won't.

After a kiss from Sheryl and a face wipe from his soigneur, Armstrong changes from rigid cycling shoes to soft trainers and, like all stage winners, is presented with a small trophy. He smiles for the cameras, waves to the crowd, shakes hands with a line of local dignitaries, and then congratulates Voeckler. Armstrong is interviewed briefly for the live France 3 telecast, and then goes over to a line of radio and TV reporters who stand behind barriers hungry for a sound bite or two. Then it's time for the press. "I have the best team in the

Le Tour arrives in La Roche-en-Ardennes, Belgium on Day 2.

Australian sprinter Robbie McEwen blows them all away to win in Namur on Day 3.

Tyler Hamilton rallies his Phonak troops in Day 5's team time trial across Picardy.

Postal's winning Day 5 lineup (left to right): Beltran, Padrnos, Landis, Hincapie, Armstrong, Azevedo, Ekimov, Noval and Rubiera.

The pack races past the château in the Loire Valley town of Baugé on Day 7.

The CSC team leads the pack on a coastal roller coaster in Brittany on Day 8.

The peloton departs Carcassonne and its multi-towered Cité for Day 16.

ABOVE: *Basque fans wait for Iban Mayo on the Plateau de Beille mountain road on Day 15.* OPPOSITE: *Through the Alps past cliffs and lakes on the delightful Col du Glandon on Day 20.*

With alacrity and panache, Armstrong dusts Basso and Ullrich at Villard-de-Lans on Day 18 … and two days later he outsprints Klöden at Le Grand Bornand.

A private moment between Lance and Sheryl Crow on Day 18.

Day 23. Next stop Paris. Race director Jean-Marie Leblanc congratulates race winner Lance Armstrong.

On the Champs-Élysées. No. 6 victory fever for the No. 1 Texan.

*The Paris podium. More Sèvres porcelain for
Armstrong's trophy cabinet.*

race," he repeats. "Now, it's just a question of whether or not their leader is the best in the race."

Is there any doubt?

———

The 160 men who finished on Plateau de Beille—from Armstrong down to the final finisher, sprinter Jimmy Casper, forty-eight minutes later—have all had a tough day. "It was probably the hardest stage I've ever done," says Leipheimer, who struggled home in nineteenth place. "Little by little I ran out of gas. I had nothing left. I was completely empty."

Sitting nearby on the mountaintop is Michael Rogers, a tall Aussie who's riding his second Tour and hopes someday to be its champion. The exhausted, overwhelmed Aussie is perhaps thinking that his dreams of someday being the Tour's champion are just that—dreams. Staring into the void of the valley from where he's just ridden, he says, "There wasn't an easy climb the whole day. I was thinking it's so long and so many climbs. There's no end to it. It'll go down in history . . ." His words trail off. But he's right, this stage *is* one that history will judge as the toughest in years.

STAGE RESULT: 1. Armstrong; 2. Basso, same time; 3. Georg Totschnig (Austria), at 1:05; 4. Klöden, at 1:27; 5. Mancebo, same time; 6. Ullrich, at 2:42; 13. Voeckler, at 4:42; 19. Leipheimer, at 6:39; 115. Mayo, at 37:40.

OVERALL STANDINGS: 1. Voeckler; 2. Armstrong, at 0:22; 3. Basso, at 1:39; 4. Klöden, at 3:18; 5. Mancebo, at 3:28; 8. Ullrich, at 7:01; 14. Leipheimer, at 10:47; 49. Mayo, at 45:04.

Cicada Country

JULY 18: *This stage of 119.5 miles between the ancient cities of Carcassonne and Nîmes is one of the flattest in the Tour. There are no climbs, but the heat and the wind may pose some problems.*

When you ride along a bumpy back road in the Midi on a hot summer's afternoon, two things are inescapable: the unrelenting heat and the shrill, resonating buzz of the cicadas that permeates your mind. It's said that a million of these broad-headed, big-eyed insects inhabit every acre of this region's vineyard-covered plain. The racket they create certainly makes you believe it. You can never get away from their primeval sound. Or from the heat. They're both always there.

They were there when I first biked through the Midi in the midsixties and saw Tour riders who put cabbage leaves under their white cotton, jockeylike caps as protection from the sun, dashed into bars for drinks, or swarmed around village fountains to fill their water bottles.

They were there in 1947 when a modest French rider named Albert Bourlon attacked from the start of a Tour stage in the town of Carcassonne, where today's stage begins. No one was interested in chasing after a rider who was an hour behind the leaders on overall time, so Bourlon raced alone for eight hours, to win by 16 minutes. His solo breakaway of 157 miles is still a Tour record.

And they were there in 1951 when another stage set out from Carcassonne that could have produced a similar result, but didn't.

———

Before the innovations of Radio Tour and live TV coverage, journalists on motorcycles were the main source of "live" reports at the race. Some reporters, like the enthusiastic Pierre Chany from *L'Équipe*, often rode alongside the racers. Others in the small band of newspapermen (women weren't allowed to cover the race until the early 1980s!) drove ahead of the race until a breakaway group developed, when, if it were interesting enough, they dropped in behind it. On July 20, 1951, most of the journalists didn't think anything "interesting" would develop on the largely flat stage from Carcassonne to Montpellier, so they motored ahead to take an early lunch. The reporters knew that if anything serious happened, their young colleague, Chany, would probably come and tell them.

While they dined, something serious *did* happen. It involved the 1949 Tour champion Fausto Coppi of Italy, then the world's greatest cyclist; Abd-el-Kader Zaaf, an Algerian no-hoper who would finish that Tour in last place; and the man wearing the yellow jersey at that point, Hugo Koblet, a Swiss, whose race lead was expected to be challenged by Coppi in the final week. Chany recounted the story in his book *La Fabuleuse Histoire du Tour de France*:

The Tour moved sluggishly onward, as if in a furnace, through the heart of an arid region burnt to a cinder by the sunshine. . . . On the stroke of noon, a number of journalists sitting in the shade of a country restaurant, savoring fresh crawfish and drinking chilled wine, were interrupted by a motorcyclist bringing incredible news. The man, who just so happened to be me, said with not a little sarcasm, "Well done, guys! There's a tragedy back there and you're stuffing your faces."

"Tragedy?" repeated one of the diners, lifting his face from the plate, with no real interest.

"Zaaf has broken out, Coppi is left behind!"

A burst of laughter greeted this remark.

"Zaaf . . . Coppi? Go on! Drink a glass of wine with us instead of talking nonsense. This *rosé* is quite special."

But I persevered.

"I assure you . . . It's true . . . Fausto has taken a rabbit punch. He's certain to quit the race."

Their crawfish remained on the plates and the *Saint-Saturnin* in the *pichets!*

Chany went on to explain to his colleagues that after a very slow start to the day's racing, Zaaf took advantage of a downhill section to break away from the pack. That was of no great import until two of Coppi's big rivals, race leader Koblet and Frenchman Raphaël Geminiani, chased after and joined Zaaf. Caught out, Coppi tried to bridge to the leaders with a teammate's help. But, suffering from the heat, the famous Italian rider fell back.

The journalists had been hoping to finish their pleasant luncheon, motor on to the finish at Montpellier, and write a nice little story about "a stage when nothing happened." Instead, they were busy all afternoon, either following the charging breakaway group of five that was splitting the race apart, or dropping back to observe the great Coppi, to see if he'd even survive the day.

Six of Coppi's Italian domestiques stayed with him to encourage and pace the champion, pouring cold water over his head and giving him friendly pushes on the hills. "Flooded in sweat, his skin ashen, Coppi pedaled in a state of semi-consciousness," wrote Chany. "From time to time, he vomited. . . . Without his teammates, he would have abandoned. . . ."

At the finish in Montpellier, Koblet outsprinted the other four to win the stage and establish the lead that won him the Tour in Paris. As for Coppi, he arrived thirty-three minutes later. His hopes of winning the Tour had evaporated in that cauldron of heat called the Midi.

———

Now another Tour stage is about to get under way in Carcassonne. It's noon. Time to sit down at a shady sidewalk table, order an aperitif, listen to the cicadas, and take in the view across the river of *La Cité*, the city's ancient fortress. One mile around and fortified by double walls and fifty-four turreted towers, this hilltop marvel dates from the sixth century, when plundering tribes were a constant threat to the citizens of towns such as this. Its medieval ramparts remained impregnable until the French Revolution, and have since been restored to their full glory.

Perhaps it was fitting that the only team to stay the night in the four-star hotel at the entrance to the *Cité* was Armstrong's. After all, his is the only team that appears to have the firepower to break down the walls of this daunting Tour. People this morning are still talking about the incredible display of strength his teammates put forth on the stage to Plateau de Beille, and the apparent ease with which he sprinted past Basso for the win—though Armstrong said afterward, "That sprint was all I had left in my legs."

While the Postal team has been celebrating, other teams have been trying to regroup in the wake of a stage that decimated their forces.

Hamilton said his good-byes to his Phonak teammates after a last supper with them at a quiet family hotel in Pamiers. He's now on his way home to Gerona, where an MRI will reveal that nothing is broken in his back. But Phonak is broken, leaderless, and all it can hope for in the final week is a stage win.

In the neighboring town of Mirepoix, T-Mobile has been having a morning powwow at the modest Hotel du Commerce. In the overall standings, team leader Ullrich is 3:43 behind teammate Klöden, who in turn is almost three minutes behind Armstrong. Their decision is to keep Ullrich as the leader, because the final week has two individual time trials, Ullrich's specialty.

Basso's CSC team has been licking its wounds at the Campanile, in the industrial section of Carcassonne. Although Basso himself has enjoyed two impressive days, his teammates are somewhat battered. Jakob Piil, the breakaway hero of the opening week, has an injured right knee, probably tendinitis; Carlos Sastre still has unhealed wounds from an early crash; and Bobby Julich, who crashed in the team time trial *and* at the pileup in Angers, has been worked on this morning for a badly bruised right wrist and forearm—the result of yet another crash during yesterday's mountain stage.

"It was the craziest crash I've ever had," says the American, showing me his bandaged arm. "I normally don't go back to the team car to get water bottles, but I was the only CSC guy still there with Ivan and Carlos at the top of the Col de la Core. Bjarne had just handed me a bottle from the car and I was holding onto it when my handlebars got caught on the rearview mirror. Just then a Gerolsteiner rider bumped me from the left and I went down really hard. I had to ride the last hundred kilometers on my own. It was hard to hold the bars, and I was in excruciating pain every time I went over a bump. If Ivan didn't have a chance of winning the Tour, I'd have stopped, the pain was so bad." It turned out that his wrist was broken, but Julich didn't find this out until after he finished the Tour in 40th place.

Another rider in the wars is the man wearing the green jersey as leader of the points competition, sprinter Robbie McEwen, who also survived a frightening crash on that toughest stage. "I was coming down the descent of the Portet d'Aspet in a small group, trying to come back to the peloton. I was following Jean-Patrick Nazon, and he approached one of the corners superfast. I thought he was going too quick, because you couldn't really see what the corner was like. I gave him a bit of distance, and he kept swooping into it. I thought he must be able to see that it's an okay corner, but he suddenly locked it up, couldn't make the corner, went off the road, went over the handlebars and crashed into a big concrete gatepost. By that time, *I* was going too quick. I tried to stop, but I was going into someone's driveway and the big iron gate was shut, so there was nowhere to go. I hit Nazon's bike, went up in the air over the handlebars, and landed on top of the bike. So I got a chainring in the arm, and hit my face on something. Now I've got a fat lip and a black eye, like I've been in a fight."

———

With the Pyrenees behind them, McEwen and the other mediocre climbers have just this one stage left to shoot for a win before the race heads into another mountain range, the Alps. This is the last chance for the sprinters to grab some points in the battle for the green jersey, which is still being closely fought: McEwen leads with 210 points, followed by Zabel with 201, Hushovd with 195, and O'Grady at 186. But McEwen is not so sure that the day will end in a mass sprint. "I think it's gonna be the type of day when guys that want to get away in a break will take their chances," he says. "Maybe they'll build up a big lead that can't be brought back, because the sprinters are tired . . . *everybody's* tired."

The stage strikes east along flat country roads that parallel the tranquil Canal du Midi. Here, under the trees that border the canal, the cicadas are at their most deafening. Yet they have little impact on these twenty-first-century Tour riders. With their hard-shell helmets and earpieces—from which pours continuous chatter, generated remotely by their team directors and team leaders—it's hard for the riders to hear much else. What's more, despite the riders' fatigue and a head wind, the racing is as fast as it was in the flat stages of the opening week.

The Phonak riders are particularly anxious to have a break succeed. They put three riders in the day's opening twenty-rider move, which causes three big echelons to develop in a crosswind. But the break is caught and the peloton soon regroups. Phonak's Santos Gonzales then spearheads a new break of four that is unable to gain more than a minute. They're caught in the city streets of Béziers, after 40 miles, where the speed is so high that the pack is riding in a long, single line. Once out of the city, the line snaps and a dozen men go off the front. This time, O'Grady is one of them, and since he's a danger in the points competition, the other green-jersey contenders' teams take up the chase.

When O'Grady's group is finally brought back, everyone is totally exhausted from two hours of flat-out racing in the hottest part of the day. That's when Phonak's Nicolas Jalabert seizes the moment to start the key break. He's joined by nine others, none of them a threat to green jersey McEwen or yellow jersey Voeckler. So the ten men are allowed to gain 14 minutes before they fight out the stage in the last six miles, as first one, then another tries to get clear. Finally, Aitor Gonzales, a Spaniard who hasn't lived up to expectations since winning the 2002 Vuelta a España and moving to Fassa Bortolo with a huge salary increase, breaks the deadlock. He speeds alone into Nîmes, where he's greeted by massive crowds in the streets of the ancient city and crosses the line 25 seconds ahead of his break companions. Perhaps the win will help him get his career back on track. The sprint for second place goes to Jalabert, who's distraught that he came so close to taking his first-ever Tour stage win, a victory that would have lifted the spirits of his Phonak team.

But Julich's spirits are just fine, thanks, because "that must have been the smoothest road in the whole of France."

So yes, some things have changed: The back roads are less bumpy, and there's no time for riders to stop at fountains. But some things have stayed the same: the enervating heat and those eerily loud cicadas. Much of the race has stayed the same, too. Voeckler is still in yellow and there's been little movement in the overall standings. You could say this was "a stage when nothing happened," a day when journalists could sit, relax, eat crawfish, and drink rosé.

STAGE RESULT: 1, Aitor Gonzales (Spain); 2. Nicolas Jalabert (France), at 0:25; 3. Christophe Mengin (France); 4. Pierrick Fedrigo (France), all same time; 5. Peter Wrolich (Austria), at 0:31.

OVERALL STANDINGS: 1. Voeckler; 2. Armstrong, at 0:22; 3. Basso, at 1:39; 4. Klöden, at 3:18; 5. Mancebo, at 3:28; 8. Ullrich, at 7:01; 14. Leipheimer, at 10:47; 49. Mayo, at 45:04.

Reflections on *Le Tour*

July 19: *Rest day at Nîmes*

When Ernest Hemingway had a summer place in the hills outside of Nîmes, he'd come into town on June weekends to catch a bullfight at the Roman Amphitheatre, have dinner at a restaurant on the Avenue Victor Hugo, and then drink through the night at the Hotel Imperator. The marble-topped bar at the Imperator is a pleasant spot to choose on a warm evening like tonight's, to listen to a string quartet playing in the elegant restaurant and then sit in the cool shade of waxy-leafed trees in the charming courtyard.

It's another "rest day" at the Tour de France, a Monday, and the eponymous Bar Hemingway is closed tonight. *"Desolé, messieurs,"* says the concierge. And so, being writers and journalists who never take *desolé* for an answer, the four of us chug over to the Place de la Maison

Carré, a flagstone plaza in front of a 2,000-year-old Roman temple. There, at an outdoor café, we order some beers and a bottle of Côtes-de-Rhône. A pleasant breeze blows in from the Mediterranean, and the supercharged *mobylettes* that scream around the broad curves of the avenue aren't *too* disconcerting.

After our wine is delightfully uncorked by a stunning, dark-haired waitress who would have certainly caught Hemingway's eye, we raise our glasses to *"Le Tour."* And that's the subject at hand. What do we—Andy the American, Rupert an Australian, Jonathan a Canadian, and myself, an ex-pat Englishman—think about the Tour de France. Not just this particular Tour but the event itself, its charisma, its chauvinism, its idiosyncrasies, and, yes, its Americanization.

Where to start? Well, it *is* the last week of the Tour, and it *has* been twenty days since three of us left our wives for this annual rite of summer. So what better starting point than women? The lovely waitress wiping down the adjacent tables is a reminder of what we are missing; so are the lovers she's serving coffee to right now.

The story of women and the Tour is a complicated one. It's one that has taken a long and circuitous route that, for us, reached its high point today at the Park Hotel in Orange, when the Tour's paparazzi surrounded Ivan Basso's wife, Michaela, who was wearing a fashionable Italian dress and the most outrageously shaped Dior sunglasses that any of us had seen since those black-and-white Antonioni movies of the sixties.

Up until fairly recently in its long history, women weren't officially allowed on the Tour, not even in a professional capacity. And the only race photos you'd see were of men: sweating, struggling, mud-splattered cyclists. Now, here we have an Italian beauty posing for the Tour photographers by a swimming pool with her husband and baby daughter. At least Basso isn't being outscored in the female stakes by Lance, who's staying with his rock-star honey, Sheryl, at a swank sixteenth-century inn.

"We've come a long way from the doctrine of Tour founder Henri Desgrange," I remind the others. "He wrote in his training manual that sex and cycling don't mix. He even recommended abstention for several days—and nights—before a race."

To guarantee that happened, neither the Tour nor their teams allowed women to be anywhere near the race. The racers' wives were sometimes permitted to visit them at their hotels on rest days, but not stay the night.

Women have always watched the Tour, of course. But no women photographers, journalists, or TV reporters were allowed to officially join the Tour's media entourage until the mid 1970s. And today, while the Tour is far more open, it's still a world that's 90 percent male.

"I think the first woman who wrote about the Tour was Colette," I say, lifting my glass to toast her. "When she saw the finish of the Tour in 1912, she was amazed by all the vehicles that preceded and followed the race. She ended her piece talking about this huge 'mechanical tempest' that was stirred up by 'two miniscule untiring cranks . . . the two spindly legs of the winner.'"

"Spindly?" says Rupe. "That's a little insulting."

"Yeah. Maybe she was just reacting to an event that seemed so dominated by men and machines."

Although women were banned from the Tour for its first eight decades—other than an annual Miss Tour de France beauty contest started in 1920—some exceptions were made. As the oldest at the table, I remember Yvette Horner, "who played her accordion in the publicity caravan for a dozen years, starting in the mid-1950s. She slipped past the system because she didn't have to be accredited by the Tour organizers. She was one of its attractions."

The biggest breakthrough against sexism at the Tour was achieved about twenty years ago, Rupe says, by America's Greg LeMond and Australia's Phil Anderson. "Both raced for French teams, both were married, and they both hated the system—especially the part about no visits from your wife. So they ignored it. Kathy LeMond's family and Phil's wife then, Anne, rented RVs for July and followed the race around. Sometimes they parked outside their husbands' hotels. Those French officials finally got the message."

"That's a big contrast to the Tour today," Andy says. "Look at George Hincapie. He started dating that podium girl at the Tour last year. Now they're about to have a baby. I wonder what Henri Desgrange would have made of that?!"

"Then there was Shelley Verses," I add, "the first woman soigneur at the Tour. She came with 7-Eleven in 1986. I was reminiscing with her last month, and she told me how she was kind of *interrogated* by the team directors before they hired her, to make sure she wouldn't consort with the riders! Shelley's pretty buxom, and a blonde, so you can imagine what the traditionalists thought about her; but she won over the other soigneurs at the race with her professionalism."

"I guess that was the first Americanization of the peloton," Andy says. "Now a lot of teams have women soigneurs and PR people."

"I've even seen a woman working on the heavy-lifting gang that takes down the barriers every night after the finish."

"But let's get back to the Americanization of the Tour," Andy persists. "Or should we say the Lance-ification?"

"When Lance shows up, it's not really a race," Jon complains. "We know what's gonna happen, and if he wants to win, he's gonna win, and that's that. Is he too strong for his own good? And yet the audience plays into that. They seem to love it. . . . But there's a sense that he's depriving us of the show that we want, right?"

"That's what happened during the Induráin years," Rupe remembers.

"Thing is, Americans love winners," says Andy, going back to the Lance factor. "Jan Ullrich finished second in the Tour last year and won Germany's Sportsman of the Year award. If Lance had finished second at the '99 Tour, he wouldn't even have gotten on David Letterman that first time!"

"Truth is, Lance needs the Tour de France as much as the Tour needs Lance."

"Yeah. The Tour and Lance. It's a marriage they both benefit from. He needs the Tour, he *continually* needs it, and when he does retire from the sport he's gonna have to think carefully if he wants to keep that high profile."

"But he's not bigger than the event," Rupe says, lifting his glass to make a point, "because he's *needed* the event."

"That's the same for a lot of other people," I point out. "Look at Virenque."

"Yeah," Rupe agrees. "When he won the stage on Bastille Day, all the French journalists in the pressroom stood up and clapped, while the rest of us just groaned. How can the biggest drug cheat in the sport be so popular? He wouldn't be if it weren't for the Tour de France."

"Let's talk about this year's Tour," I suggest, pouring wine for the others. "There's a week to go. Lance still doesn't have the yellow jersey. And he's only 1:17 ahead of Basso. Does Basso have a chance of winning?"

"No," says Jon. "Basso can't time trial, so Lance will probably win by six minutes."

"But Lance still considers that Ullrich is his biggest rival, even though he's almost seven minutes ahead of him."

"There's no way Ullrich can win," Andy says.

"You're right. So Ullrich has nothing to lose. And if he attacks tomorrow, that could open up things for Basso, especially if Postal just focuses on chasing Ullrich. There are a lot of climbs tomorrow and they're not too long. That means guys like Voigt and Sastre can help Basso. Too bad that Julich is injured. He could've helped, too."

"Look, Postal is so strong, they don't have to worry," Andy says. "They can ride like they did the other day and just kill everyone off."

"They can't do that all the time, though. Those guys must be getting tired, too, even Lance."

"We'll see," says Rupe. "I'll never forget my first Tour in eighty-seven. Jean-François Bernard took the yellow jersey on the Ventoux and all the French thought he'd win the Tour. Then the next day, on a stage like tomorrow's—same start and finish, but some different climbs—Mottet, Roche, and Delgado all attacked in the feed zone, and Bernard finished four minutes back."

"The Tour has changed since then," I reflect. "It's much harder to do things like that now. But I still think guys like Ullrich should try something. They're not gonna beat Lance in the time trials or the mountaintop finishes, so they have to try on stages like tomorrow. It's hard to understand why none of the challengers made a move in the Massif Central, on those stages to St. Flour and Figéac. That was perfect terrain to attack on. If you don't try something on stages like those, there's no way to beat Lance."

"Yeah," Andy agrees, finishing off his Cointreau. "But it's a pity guys like Tyler and Mayo had crashes. *They* would've done something. I guess we'll have to wait another year to see what they can really do. Anyway, guys, I have to go and work now. Sorry to break up the party."

Pas de problème. Because even if it's a rest day here, our newspapers and Web sites still need stories from us. We pay the bill, and leave a nice tip for that waitress.

It's late, past one o'clock again. But it's invigorating to be in Nîmes, with its balmy air, beautiful old buildings, and cafés that stay open late into the night. "Wouldn't it be great if all the stage towns were like this?" I say to no one in particular, as we walk down the tree-lined boulevard to our hotel. "Maybe next time the race comes here, we can get to the Bar Hemingway."

Hemingway was drawn to bullfights, boxing, deep-sea fishing, and bike races. He loved his women. But he also loved the world of men.

DAY 18

Resistance Fighters

JULY 20: *This 112-mile stage from Valréas to Villard-de-Lans first heads north on the flanks of the Rhône valley before turning east into the wooded hills of the Vercors region. Five climbs in the last 60 miles make this a challenging stage.*

Tiny finches chatter among the flickering leaves of birch, chestnut, and ash trees. Humming bees feed from yellow, blue, and purple alpine flowers that cling to a crumbly limestone cliff bordering the narrow road. And warm sunshine angles through the upper branches of pines that crown this high crest, elevation 4,500 feet. Looking beyond the primitive road, whose pummeled bedrock shows through a veneer of tar, I see a meadowlike valley reaching south toward distant ridges.

Along this tortuous strip of roadway over a mountain pass called the Col de Chalimont, the Romans transported barrels of wine from

Provence to their city of Gratianopolis, today's Grenoble; the French Resistance fighters toted supplies to their secret headquarters in the hills; and, today, the cyclists of the 2004 Tour de France will speed past these cliffs and pines on their way to a stage finish in Villard-de-Lans, some 10 miles distant.

Although the highly trumpeted L'Alpe d'Huez time trial is only twenty-four hours away, the riders can't hold anything back today. There are seven climbs on this 112-mile course from Valréas, and history counsels the main contenders: Beware of unexpected dangers. The final 60 miles of the stage pass through the Vercors, a craggy range of wooded mountains split by rocky canyons and grassy vales. It was in the Vercors sixty years ago that the Resistance fighters defended their land against an army of 15,000 German troops. Over a few days in July 1944, 840 villagers and fighters were killed and two villages were burned to the ground, but the Resistance lived on. A memorial to those fallen heroes stands on a clifftop, just where the steep descent of the Col de Chalimont emerges from the pine trees on its way to Villard.

This is only the second time that the Tour has crossed the Chalimont ridge. The other time was in 1987, when a stage nearly identical to today's caused a dramatic upheaval in the overall standings. With less than a week remaining in the Tour, the young Frenchman Jean-François Bernard looked solid in the yellow jersey, with a nearly three-minute lead over his three closest challengers. These three all had the incentive to attack on the stage from Valréas to Villard—and they did.

The team of Frenchman Charly Mottet had secretly plotted some guerilla-style tactics. First, Mottet sent a couple of teammates into an early move, so they'd be at the head of the race in case he needed their help later in the day. Next, he and his teammates put enough food in their jersey pockets so they wouldn't have to slow down to collect their cotton food bags at the feed zone. That day's feed zone—

located on a narrow stretch of road through the valley town of Léoncel—is where they planned to attack. They would take Bernard by surprise.

It worked, far better than expected. The yellow jersey suffered a flat tire a few miles before descending into Léoncel, and he was only joining the tail of the fast-moving peloton as the pre-planned attack took place at its head.

But the tactic didn't catch out the other main contenders, Irishman Stephen Roche and Spaniard Pedro Delgado, who both joined in the attack. Mottet's teammates who were still in the early breakaway group waited for their leader, and they then put as much time as possible between them and Bernard. After the feed zone, the yellow jersey's teammates also regrouped around him, and for the next three hours they chased after the lead group containing all of his rivals. The gap between the breakaways and Bernard's chase group stayed at one minute for many miles, up long hills and down sharp descents through the Vercors. Eventually, Bernard's men cracked and dropped back in the hilly terrain, and by the end of the stage the man who had been first lost four minutes and the yellow jersey, and dropped to fourth place in the overall standings.

When the dozen-strong lead break reached the Col de Chalimont, Delgado, a famed climber, burst from the group. He was chased and joined by Roche, and the pair raced together on that narrow road along the ridge, and then down to the finish in Villard. Delgado won the stage, and Roche claimed the yellow jersey.

That epic day of racing excited the crowds, thrilled the media, and gave Roche the boost he needed to become the first (and still only) Irishman to win the Tour. It also proved that smart tactics in challenging terrain can be just as effective as brute strength in the high mountains.

As the peloton gathers at the start of a new day in the 2004 Tour, the race leader is still the young Frenchman, Voeckler, by those 22 seconds over Armstrong. He's not expecting to keep his yellow jersey much longer, especially as Armstrong looks stronger than ever. Meanwhile, the list of challengers grows shorter by the day. This morning, another of the original contenders, Mayo, is missing in action. The shell-shocked Basque has finally quit the race and is headed back home.

Seasoned race followers wonder if today's Valréas–Villard stage might be as destructive as that one seventeen years ago. Basso's CSC team and the T-Mobile forces of Klöden and Ullrich must be bold if they want to truly challenge Armstrong. Maybe some other teams will attack in an effort to destabilize the race. Or perhaps Armstrong and his troops will again hang tough, dispose of Voeckler, and finally deliver the yellow jersey to their boss.

Armstrong has been keeping a low profile since winning the stage at Plateau de Beille. He had his team work minimally in the flat stage to Nîmes, and after the finish he hurried off to his team bus without stopping for post-stage interviews: There was a 90-minute drive waiting to Postal's hotel in St. Paul-Trois-Châteaux, a regular team haunt when it's racing or training in this northwestern part of Provence. Armstrong didn't even give a rest-day news conference; he left it to his team director Bruyneel to deliver the usual platitudes: "Ullrich is still the biggest danger, and he always has a strong final week. So we're happy he's seven minutes back."

Ullrich, whose team stayed in the far-off town of Grignan beyond the Côtes-de-Rhône vineyards, did issue a few rest-day words. "I still don't understand what happened in the Pyrenees," the German said. "I feel that I have done the right preparation this year, and I hope to prove that's true in the Alps."

The most voluble of the contenders was Basso. Besides a photo-op with his family, he gamely sat through an hour-long press conference in a hot, stuffy meeting room at his team's hotel. Now that he is Armstrong's main challenger—less than one and a half minutes behind him—it was standing room only, with journalists hanging out the door. The young Italian smiled his way through the grilling, confidently answering all the questions in his halting English. The first questions focused on his second-place finish at Plateau de Beille. How did he find the climb? "Pain, normal. The climb is very hard. But I feel good. I hope to continue this form." Are you going for the podium? "It's too early to talk of the podium. The Tour is still very long, and I like my pedals to do the talking."

The most interesting part of his press conference came when he was asked about the team's early-winter get-together in the Canary Islands. Team manager Riis uses varied methods to build teamwork and his riders' confidence in each other. Basso described an exercise in which the riders paddled rubber dinghies out to sea in the dark, and Basso—who doesn't swim—was thrown overboard. His teammates had to figure how to get him back to the distant shore without using a dinghy. He said he was scared but happy his mates are such strong swimmers. Perhaps their strength, and the mutual confidence this exercise created, will come in handy today.

As in 1987, the stage takes in the stretch of road where Bernard was chasing to rejoin the peloton after his puncture. But instead of then turning right into Léoncel, through a feed zone, and up the aptly named Col de la Bataille ("Battle Pass"), today's course heads straight down a valley. So far, there's no sign of unexpected tactics.

A twelve-man break is three minutes ahead of the pack, but the only rider in it of possible strategic importance is Basso's German teammate, Voigt. Climbers Virenque and Rasmussen are also there, but they're just looking for King of the Mountain points. Another man in the break is the sprinter O'Grady. He now takes the lead for 10 miles, making a huge effort on a fast, twisting descent to grab a paltry four points at the day's final intermediate sprint at St. Jean-de-Royans.

Tens of thousands of excited spectators have gathered on the steep hill leaving town, as this is the start of the fourth, and toughest, climb of the day. They thickly line the first five miles up the Col de l'Echarasson, which takes the riders on a bumpy road that winds through a forest of sweet chestnuts at a steady but demanding eight-percent grade. The steep climb proves too much for most of the breakaways. Only Rasmussen and Virenque push ahead to lead the stage, with Voigt not far behind. But the crowd is about to witness some real excitement when the group being led by Armstrong's "blue train" arrives a few minutes later.

It seems that the hard-riding Postals are doing their usual damage. One by one, then two by two, riders fall behind the American team's pace. One of them is Voeckler, who has ridden courageously to keep his yellow jersey for ten stages. It looks as though his tenacity has reached its end.

The pace stays fast, and then, just over a mile into the ascent, in an obviously planned move, T-Mobile's Giuseppe Guerini, Klöden, and Ullrich take over the front positions. To prove they're up to the task, they immediately rev up the pace a few notches! The line of riders behind them stretches to the breaking point as Guerini, Ullrich's best support climber, gives it everything he's got. His effort ends halfway up this opening stretch, where the German team continues its full-out effort via the slim, spinning legs of Klöden, who is still acting as Ullrich's top domestique despite his higher placing in the overall standings. The skinny Klöden—six feet tall, 138 pounds—stays at the front for almost a mile, impressively pounding the pedals. His long surge splinters the already meager-sized group—and, for the first time in the Tour, reveals that even the Postal team has limitations. Hincapie, Rubiera, and Beltran drop back, leaving Armstrong with just Landis and Azevedo to pace him, and there are 40 miles still to go.

When Klöden is spent, and with another mile of the eight-percent grade remaining, Ullrich raises the speed even more and pushes on alone. The German superstar is back to his powerhouse best, and he's hungry to show the world all the fight that's still in him. He opens up a big gap, turns a corner, and then heads into a narrow back road that twists through open woodland toward the plateau summit. This section is much less steep so Ullrich immediately increases his speed.

Before the German disappears from Armstrong's sight, the Texan has a quick chat with Landis that shows he's not in the least bit stressed by his rival's attack. "Hey, there's your parents, Floyd." Armstrong has spotted on the roadside his teammate's father, mother, and three younger sisters. This is the first time that Landis's Amish family is watching him race at the Tour, and it's also the first time they've been to Europe. "I waved at them," Landis says, "but I didn't have much time to look, as we decided to go fast at that point."

Landis is now doing all the work to limit Ullrich's lead, which is up to almost a minute when he crosses the summit, after less than four miles of solo effort. Ullrich continues overtaking the riders who have dropped back from the original break, including Voigt. By the time he reaches the top of the next short climb, stage leaders Rasmussen and Virenque are less than 90 seconds ahead.

With Ullrich's lead over the Armstrong group still increasing, now at 66 seconds, the dynamics of the race suddenly change—to the detriment of Ullrich. CSC team manager Riis tells Voigt to wait for the Armstrong group, and then agrees with Postal's Bruyneel to share the workload. So Landis now gets Voigt's dynamic assistance in chasing Ullrich, and the gap slowly falls on the next eight miles of descending roads.

If Riis hadn't made the decision to help Postal, it's possible that Landis and teammate Azevedo would have burned themselves out in the chase, leaving Armstrong to fend for himself on the next ascent—the Chalimont. In that event, he would have been up against Basso, Sastre, and Voigt from CSC, Klöden and Ullrich from T-Mobile, and Rabobank's Leipheimer.

This would have been an intriguing tactical advantage for CSC, so I later ask Riis why he didn't make Postal do all the chasing. The wily Dane replies, "I was thinking about it, you know, but . . ." His words trail off as if he's considering that maybe that should have been the way to go. But no, he explains that he didn't want to risk Ullrich gaining time on Basso in the overall standings, and that Basso told him he was feeling good and wanted to try to win the stage.

Riis's tactic is not a bad one: Ullrich is caught at the foot of the Chalimont, with 15 miles still to go; Rasmussen and Virenque are caught soon after; Leipheimer makes a short-lived attack; and then an exhausted Landis falls back. This leaves three CSC men against two each from Postal and T-Mobile, and the solo Leipheimer. But the weary Voigt is soon dropped on the final mile-and-a-half climb in Villard, and his teammate Sastre is also left behind when Klöden accelerates. The ambitious Leipheimer is the last to drop back, which leaves just Basso, Ullrich, and Armstrong following Klöden. Basso hangs tough, and then streaks past the others. The Italian is making a great bid for the stage win, but Armstrong is not conceding. He comes from behind, swoops by Basso, and as he crosses the line pumps first one fist, then two, to celebrate another impressive victory.

The Postal camp was clearly concerned about Basso, though. Before Armstrong made his final burst, Bruyneel screamed at him through the team radio to absolutely sprint for the stage winner's time bonus of 20 seconds. Without that bonus, the champion's overall lead on Basso would have dropped to about a minute, instead of increasing to 1:25.

Armstrong is thrilled to have won the stage in a group sprint, something that he hasn't done since winning his very first Tour stage as a 21-year-old, eleven years ago. He's also energized by reclaiming the yellow jersey that was "on loan" to Voeckler for the past twelve days. The weary young Frenchman finishes the stage nine minutes back, and drops to eighth in the overall standings. He has had a great run, but the *maillot jaune* is back on the shoulders of the man who desperately wanted to be wearing it for the Alpe d'Huez time trial. "I can't think of anything better than riding up that mythical mountain in yellow," Armstrong exults.

———————

Once the stage is over, the presentations made, and the interviews completed, the teams all head down to their hotels in Grenoble. The riders are anxious to recuperate from another tough day and prepare for the big one coming up tomorrow: the fearsome Alpe d'Huez mountain time trial everyone has been talking and thinking about since the Tour course was unveiled last October.

Up on the Col de Chalimont, the crowds have dispersed after watching the tailenders pedal their weary way along the ancient road a full half-hour behind the leaders. The sun has dipped below the western horizon. And thirty miles to the east, across the blue ridges of the Vercors, a half-million fans on the flanks of a mountain called L'Alpe d'Huez are staking out their claims to the best viewing places for tomorrow's stage, as they prepare for a long night under the stars.

STAGE RESULT: 1. Armstrong; 2. Basso, same time; 3. Ullrich, at 0:03; 4. Klöden, at 0:06; 5. Leipheimer, at 0:13.

OVERALL STANDINGS: 1. Armstrong; 2. Basso, at 1:25; 3. Klöden, at 3:22; 4. Mancebo, at 5:39; 5. Ullrich, at 6:54; 8. Voeckler, at 9:28; 10. Leipheimer, at 10:58.

Pilgrims and Legends

JULY 21: *A 9.6-mile individual time trial, climbing the 21-turn mountain road from Bourg d'Oisans to the ski resort of L'Alpe d'Huez. It's a stage that could determine the outcome of the 2004 Tour.*

While the 157 athletes still left in this Tour are peacefully asleep in their beds in Grenoble, the place where they will compete later today is wide-awake and buzzing with expectation. Thousands of people are roaming the streets of Bourg d'Oisans at 1:30 a.m. when we drive into town. Shops are open, pubs are overflowing, and there are long lines at every stand that sells pizza or pomme frites. Excited fans gather on street corners, beer mugs in hand, as they talk about the upcoming race. Some are testing the bells they'll be ringing for their favorites, while others have already painted their faces in the colors of their countries or teams. Gendarmes in long blue coats direct the slow-moving traffic with flashlights as we head down main street. It's here that the start house will be erected in the morning, and here that the tense racers in the L'Alpe d'Huez time trial will hear that magic mantra: "*5–4–3–2–1–partez!*"

———————

L'Alpe d'Huez is a mountain climb that became a legend of the Tour de France in 1952, when Fausto Coppi, a legend himself, won the first-ever stage to finish at its summit. Since that auspicious beginning, seventeen others have won a stage on this spectacular ascent, some of them multiple times. But this is the first time in Tour history that any rider has been asked to race L'Alpe d'Huez in an individual time trial. Each rider will launch his bike from this glacial valley town of steep roofs and shuttered windows, follow the black serpent of tarmac lacing up the precipitous side of a verdant, rocky mountain, speed through twenty-one switchback turns, and top out at the wood chalets and concrete condos of a ski resort that's three-thousand five-hundred seventy-six feet above. A race to the top of the Tour's most mythical peak, with a flat one-mile rollout to the 8.6 miles of climbing at an average grade of 7.9 percent. An awesome challenge in an awesome setting, with the towering Alps, some snow-capped, surrounding them as far as they can see. It's a severe test for riders already wearied by two and a half weeks of toil and tribulation.

There's no hiding place in a time trial, an event that was invented in 1895 by the British and is renowned for its athletic purity. No drafting, no tactics, no skullduggery—just a man and his bike racing as fast as he can from point to point. Each man races, as the British inventors said, "alone and unassisted," vulnerable and exposed. The French call it *l'epreuve de verité* the "race of truth." Every rider must compete not only against the tick of time, but also against unseen opponents who are trying just as hard as he is.

A time trial on a flat course, like the prologue in Liège on the first day of this Tour, is a race of pure speed. The high speeds mean that aerodynamics and positioning are just as important as the power in a racer's legs and the focus and concentration in his brain. A time trial up a mountain demands some of the same qualities: power, focus, pacing, concentration. But because speeds are much lower—less than 15 miles per hour on a climb like L'Alpe d'Huez—a comfortable position on the bike is preferred to a low, stretched-out tuck. On the other hand, a sustained all-out climbing effort is much more destructive to the body. After finishing steep uphill time trials, riders have been known to vomit because of the lactic acid that their bodies release when they go anaerobic for too long.

All of these factors have to be considered when preparing for a time trial like this one. There's no point in going too hard, too soon, on a climb that's almost 10 miles long, and find yourself gasping after the first uphill mile. Nor can you go too easy, or you're likely to finish with a full tank of gas and a losing time.

———

Driving between the cars and campers that fill the flat road out of Bourg d'Oisans, we soon reach the turnoff where the racers will turn left toward the foot of the climb. It's 2 a.m. and the road has just been closed to the public because every parking space on the mountain road has already been taken. But the police flash their lights on our green *Tour de France Médias* sticker and wave us through. As we head to an apartment at the top of the shadowed mountain, we sweep from one hairpin bend to another—numbered 21 at the bottom to 1 at the top—and get a feel for the course on which Armstrong will be battling Basso, Klöden, and Ullrich later today. All of them have ridden the Alpe in training, but only Armstrong has been so obsessive in his reconnaissance work, riding up, then down . . . up, down . . . to examine in detail the angles of every turn, each change in grade. "I split the climb up into three sections," he says, "from the bottom to the first village (la Garde), then up to the next village (Huez), and from there to the finish. I look for the numbers of the turns, and I know that the steepest part [a grade of almost 12 percent] is between turn numbers nine and eight." Since each of the villages has a church steeple as its prominent landmark, Armstrong makes these his goals, a way to pace himself and know how much energy to exert on each of the three sections. He says he comes here to test the course in May because "I like climbing Alpe d'Huez on my own, when no one else is around, just a few people in the couple hotels that are open, and some guys working on the road."

On this dark night in July, there are thousands of people around. As we drive up the climb, starting with the first mile that's so steep it looks like a wall, we have to stop now and then where camper vans are still maneuvering to get into tight parking spots just off the road. We also have to creep around raucous street parties and watch out for fans on bikes struggling up the hill or bombing down—yes, at two o'clock in the morning! Besides the camper vans with their satellite dishes, bike racks, and territorial flags, there are small tents pitched on every available square inch of hillside, and even folks in sleeping bags lying in the ditch.

Seeing people sleeping rough, I remember the Tour of 1979, the summer that my newspaper, *The Sunday Times*, went on strike. With no reporting to do, I came to the Tour anyway and made a pilgrimage to the Alpe by bike. I came from the north over some mountain passes, expecting to find a favorite hotel open near the Col du Glandon. It was closed for renovations, so I continued on up the pass, stopped for some cheese and wine with a family of fans camping out near the top, and headed on over the summit on a night like this: cool, windless, and very dark. It was probably around two o'clock when I arrived at Bourg d'Oisans. Everything was shut, so I spent the rest of the night on the wooden bench of a bus shelter.

There are many more pilgrims on the Alpe tonight. The lower half of the climb is the most popular with spectators because there are no crowd barriers here. That means they'll be able to stand on the road and experience that incomparable frenzy of road cycling when the riders are just inches away from you, and you can see the sweat on their faces, their bloodshot eyes staring ahead, and their open mouths drinking in as much of the thin air as they can. The crowds get sparser where the barriers start, about four miles before the finish. Not only is it impossible to park at the roadside on this section, but the barriers are so close to the edge of the road that there's little room to stand. Besides, there's something sterile about barriers. They take away the sense of connection and interaction between racer and spectator that's so integral to the sport.

There were *no* barriers here in 1986, except at the very finish. That was the day Greg LeMond proudly wore the yellow jersey to the summit of L'Alpe d'Huez in a breakaway with his French teammate Bernard Hinault, the day after LeMond became the first American to lead the Tour. Nor were there barriers here in 1992, when Andy Hampsten of Boulder, Colorado, became the first American to win an Alpe d'Huez stage. Hampsten was so badly jostled by the close-packed crowds that he used his fist to swat the fans away like flies.

It's just after 5 p.m. when another American in the yellow jersey, Lance Armstrong, starts to race up the fabled climb, dealing with crowds even denser than those faced by Hampsten. Every inch of the road is covered with throngs of people. Police are saying it's a crowd of 500,000—all of them intoxicated by the race.

They line each side, leaving only three feet for the Texan to bike through. The advancing police motorcycles with their blaring sirens clear a temporary path. But once they drive on, the fans fall forward. Soon, they are right in Armstrong's face, leaning in to shout their encouragement, thrusting their flags or fists or signs just inches in front of him, running alongside for a few yards to urge him on, or even kneeling on the road to snap a photo before diving out of the way. "Some of the fans were a little aggressive," Armstrong says later with understatement. "But the Tour de France is a huge event, and you expect people to get excited."

The excited sounds of the cheering crowds follow each rider up the craggy, green-treed mountainside: the jarring honks of Klaxons, the beating of African drums, exuberant chanting, beer-drinking songs, blasts of a brass band, clanging cowbells, and the *"Allez, allez, allez!"* shouts from the French. As if this weren't clamor enough, there's the wail of the police motorcycles in front and the roar of the helicopters above.

Some riders are the victims of patriotic fervor. The German fans, wielding large pink plastic T-Mobile hands, jeer Voigt for having chased down fellow German Ullrich on yesterday's stage, and they catcall McEwen just because he's wearing the green jersey and beating *their* Erik Zabel on points.

As the *yellow* jersey holder, Armstrong is the final starter in the time trial, and he's glad to be under way. Before the start, his mechanic had a crisis with Lance's bike, having to present it to the race inspectors four times before it weighs in above the fifteen-pound minimum. The bike hit the scales correctly a few days before, but everything weighs less at altitude. Slightly heavier cranks and chain wheels were eventually fitted.

To achieve the same goal, Basso's mechanic has bolted on to his regular handlebars a pair of small forward-pointing aerodynamic handlebars, called clip-ons. If Basso chooses to use the clip-ons, they might help the man who is now second overall gain a few seconds on the straighter, flatter parts of the course. There are no weight problems with Ullrich's time-trial bike, but he too has the aero clip-ons, as he is planning to use them throughout his time trial.

The hot sunshine in the valley cools down as the day moves on, making it slightly easier for the last men to start. Even so, they quickly heat up from their effort, and some fans dash out to throw cooling water over their heads as they speed past.

Armstrong's only remaining challengers for the overall victory are spaced at two-minute intervals ahead of him: Basso at two minutes, Klöden at four, and Ullrich at eight. This allows Postal's manager Bruyneel—who's driving as close behind Armstrong as the rules allow—to inform the Texan by transmitter of where he stands at each checkpoint compared with the others. Already, they know that after the first mile of flat roads, Lance is three seconds *slower* than Ullrich, one second *faster* than Basso, and five seconds ahead of Klöden.

There's another legend about L'Alpe d'Huez. They say that the rider who's in yellow at the end of the Alpe stage will still be in yellow on the Champs-Élysées. And more often than not, it's true. Armstrong is well aware of this legend, and so are the other major contenders. They know that this will be the decisive day, and they all have big dreams—particularly Ullrich. "I'm upset that I couldn't do well in the Pyrenees," he says, "but I have great condition now, and I want to win the time trial."

To make that happen, the powerful, courageous German is putting everything he's got into his ride. He knows that the only way he can beat Armstrong is to maximize his superior power by pounding a massive gear, far bigger than the one used by Armstrong. To do this Ullrich needs to remain seated, so that his strong back and quadriceps come into play, while he turns his pedals at a metronomic 80 revolutions per minute. Also, by gripping the outstretched aerobars, Ullrich keeps his body low and more aerodynamic, perhaps gaining a second or two on the faster sections. He even has his skinsuit zipped to the neck to give him slightly smoother penetration through the air. The big German may look slow to his fans because of his lower pedal cadence, but they need only look at the grimace on his face and the tensing of his arm muscles to sense his true and unbelievable climbing speed.

In contrast, Ullrich's teammate Klöden unzips his top and keeps rising from the saddle to generate more power on the steeper pitches. Basso, too, has to overcome his relative lack of power with short bursts standing on the pedals. Once again, the popular, dark-haired Italian is surpassing everyone's expectations. His early pedal cadence of 87 revs keeps him virtually level with Klöden, one of the top time-trial specialists in the Tour.

But all of their efforts pale in comparison to Armstrong's. With the help of coaches Carmichael and Ferrari, he has perfected a dynamic pedaling style using a smaller gear than the others use, which he pedals with amazing speed. This enables him to use less power for each pedal stroke and maintain a higher speed for a longer time. Halfway up the climb, when he first sights Basso, his cadence is as high as 96 revs per minute. But it's not just technique he's winning with; it's also his power and aerobic capacity—the efficiency of his body to use available oxygen—both of which he has progressively built up through the spring and summer with a rigorous training program. The program runs him through mind-numbing interval training on both long and short climbs, over and over. No wonder Armstrong says his success is based on his dedication and preparation, and that a race like today's is just "a term paper."

The evidence of the yellow jersey's A-grade performance comes with the time-split print-outs. After six miles, in the middle part of his village-to-village section, he's already 40 seconds ahead of Ullrich, 67 seconds up on Klöden, and 75 seconds faster than Basso. And the gaps keep growing as he sweeps around hairpin turns and fast approaches the man who started two minutes before him.

"When I got Ivan in my sights," Armstrong says, "that really motivated me." Poor Basso doesn't see the Texan behind him, but he hears the screams for Armstrong growing louder and louder, and he knows that he will soon be passed and soundly beaten.

With two miles to go, the Texan mercilessly catches Basso—his last remaining rival—and surges past his Italian friend without even a glance in his direction.

At the same moment, Ullrich is finishing his climb out of the saddle, riding as hard as he can, shaking side to side, his wide-open mouth gulping in air, his muscles screaming with pain. He crosses the line with the fastest time yet posted: 40:42.

Klöden is next to arrive, out of the saddle, covered in sweat, on the verge of collapse. His time is impressive, too, though 40 seconds behind Ullrich, who showed today why he's still T-Mobile's team leader, even though he's behind his teammate on overall time.

Ullrich stands at the finish, watching Armstrong on TV. The German has a look of both envy and anger on his face, knowing he's going to be beaten once more. The fans lining the barriers now turn to see Armstrong speeding through the final corner. The hundreds of Americans here scream him on. As if carried forward by their shouts, the champion is flying up the last 220 yards like a track sprinter, knowing that he has won but wanting to eke out every possible second over his adversaries. Till the very end he's pumping like a madman, his energy and power as inspiring as the mountain itself. Armstrong's time flashes up: 39:41. Another one minute gain on Ullrich; 1:40 on Klöden; and 2:10 on Basso.

Armstrong's performance is one that only he and past champions like Coppi, Merckx, Hinault, and Induráin could achieve. "They have a capacity to go beyond human tolerances," says Shelley Verses, the massage therapist who has an intrinsic knowledge of an athlete's physiological limits. "They have a capacity to go beyond anger, beyond heat, beyond cold, beyond pain. They are gifted human beings."

Reflecting that assessment, Phil Liggett, the Tour's best-known British announcer, proclaims to his TV audience: "Lance now has no rivals except the race itself!"

It's true. If there was one point where Armstrong clinched his sixth Tour de France victory, it was here on the top of L'Alpe d'Huez. On this legendary mountain, Lance made the climb of his life to become a legend himself.

STAGE RESULT: 1. Armstrong, 39:41; 2. Ullrich, 40:42; 3. Klöden, 41:22; 4. José Azevedo (Portugal), 41:26; 5. Santos Gonzales (Spain), 41:51.

OVERALL STANDINGS: 1. Armstrong; 2. Basso, at 3:48; 3. Klöden, at 5:03; 4. Ullrich, at 7:55; 5. Azevedo, at 9:19; 10. Leipheimer, at 15:04; 13. Voeckler, at 16:04.

No More Gifts

JULY 22: *This road stage from Bourg d'Oisans to Le Grand Bornand is statistically the hardest of the Tour: 127 miles and 17,000 feet of climbing over five mountain passes. It guarantees a long and exhausting day.*

Everyone is hurting. Almost six hours have passed since the 152-strong peloton set out from Bourg d'Oisans this morning to face 127 miles and 17,000 feet of mountain climbing. It's been a day of attrition. Only six men are left in the lead group—three Americans, two Germans, and an Italian. They are all at their limit as they head toward the summit of the day's final mountain pass. In the front is a young American, Floyd Landis, who has set a phenomenal pace all the way up this steep, seven-mile climb. There were more than twenty riders on Landis's wheel at the bottom. All but five of them have been dropped.

Right behind Landis comes his team leader, Lance Armstrong, in the yellow jersey. Next in line is a dogged Jan Ullrich, followed by Ivan Basso, Levi Leipheimer, and Andreas Klöden. After three weeks of brutal racing, they are proving to be the strongest riders in the Tour.

Landis, the 28-year-old domestique from rural Pennsylvania, has been a surprise and revelation. On this final major climb of the Tour, he's simply soaring. "I was on my limit just trying to stay there," says Leipheimer, a keen observer of his fellow racers. "Everyone was hurting. Klöden was yo-yoing, so I went around him. I could see that Ullrich was low . . . that Lance was getting lower . . . and that Floyd was still strong. It was obvious he was riding too fast for anyone to attack."

Too fast for Leipheimer, who is simply trying to hang on. He knows that if he can endure and keep up with this torrid pace for only one more mile, the six leaders will reach the summit. And from there it's all downhill to the finish line in the mountain chalet-town of Le Grand Bornand. If he can just hang on, he'll even have a chance at winning the stage. That would make up for all the disappointments he has suffered in this race. It would also save the Tour for his team, Rabobank, which so far is winless.

It's a nice dream. But this brutally hot day is turning out to be a killer, and Leipheimer is its latest victim. "I just cracked," he says.

As the American drops back, Klöden hopes that he won't be the next to go. The German desperately digs in. He's fully aware that if he drops off he'll almost certainly lose his chance of finishing second in Paris. As Klöden battles, and Ullrich and Basso envision getting to the summit, Landis and Armstrong talk.

"Floyd," says Armstrong to his protégé, "how bad do you want to win a stage in the Tour de France?"

"Real bad."

"How fast can you go downhill?"

"I can go downhill real fast. But can I do it?"

"Sure you can do it. Run like you stole something, Floyd."

This is a chance that Landis had never expected. After all, in six years, not one Postal team rider, other than Armstrong, has won a Tour stage. Now Landis's boss is giving him the green light to go. But *can* he do it?

———

Every year at the Tour, there is always a day when the riders know that if you can just get through it, you are sure to finish the race in Paris. That day is today, and it's not an easy one. Besides the temperatures being in the nineties, there are five high mountain passes to climb: one Category 2, three Category 1's, and an Hors-Category. It's such a daunting task that three men decide to not even start. One of them is Roberto Heras, the Liberty team leader. The Spanish climber started the Tour with high ambitions to challenge Armstrong in the mountains, but he failed completely. Heras was hoping at least to put in a good performance on L'Alpe d'Huez. His 61st place, almost six minutes behind Armstrong, was not what he had in mind. "Under the circumstances," he says, "there's no point in continuing."

Heras's poor form, and now his withdrawal, are a big disappointment for his U.S. teammate Christian Vande Velde. Before the Tour, the American was looking forward to helping the Spaniard seek a top placing in the Tour. Now, his only goal is to simply finish the race. And Vande Velde knows that's not a given when you have a stage like today's, especially if he ends up in the *gruppetto*, the big group of riders that gets dropped on the climbs and has to race hard simply to make the finish inside the time limit.

"I know I'm not assured of finishing in Paris," says Vande Velde, who then remembers how he struggled to get through his first Tour in 1999. "I was only 22 and had tendinitis in my knee going into the second mountain stage. I bonked at the bottom of Alpe d'Huez, and I barely made it to the finish. There were guys that were worse than me though. I looked around in the *gruppetto* and there were spectators pushing big Magnus Bäckstedt up those last few kilometers of the climb. And another guy was throwing up right next to me. It was an ugly scene."

This year, Vande Velde is nearing the Tour's finish in much better shape. But he knows he can't relax, not on this stage. Just in the opening miles, the Estonian Janek Tombak has a freak accident: He is leaning over on the fly to fix his transponder—a small computer chip that's on every rider's bike to determine finish positions—when his hand slips into the spokes of the rear wheel and they almost rip off the fourth finger of his right hand. He's rushed to the hospital in Grenoble to get stitched together. Then, on the day's second climb, the giant hors-category Col de la Madeleine, French veteran Didier Rous is dropped. Rous worked tirelessly for the Boulangère team in defense of Voeckler's yellow jersey. But now, with his morale low, he coasts to a stop and quits. The Italian Massimo Giunti, who's totally exhausted, also abandons the Tour. And coming down the Madeleine's dangerous descent, a young German on the Balears team, Daniel Becke, crashes hard. Covered with cuts and bruises, he is forced to quit, too.

Others plow on. There are fifty riders at the back end of the field in the *gruppetto*, which includes most of the sprint stage winners from the opening week: Cancellara, McEwen, Nazon, Boonen, Pozzato, and Hushovd. They will finish today's Day 45 minutes behind the leaders—but they *will* finish, and they will all be in Paris on Sunday trying to win the final stage.

———

Up at the head of the race, on the narrow, twisting descent of the Col de la Croix-Fry, Landis is running "like he stole something." It looks like he might succeed in getting clear away . . . but after a great three miles of fast downhill work on a narrow back road, he emerges onto a much wider, less steep highway, where he's easier to spot and catch. The pursuing Ullrich is the first to reach him. Armstrong then chases up to them, while Basso and Klöden look beaten. Ullrich urges the two Postal teammates to work with him, as the German is hoping to gain time on Basso and perhaps overtake the CSC leader before the finish in Paris. When they refuse to help, Ullrich makes a face at the two Americans. Despite the speed they're descending at, Armstrong has time for a little fun with a race photographer, who's riding beside him on a motorcycle. He first mimics Ullrich's grim face and then smiles for the camera.

As the pace momentarily slows, Basso and a grateful Klöden catch back up. The five now head toward the finish, with Armstrong still trying to set up Landis for the win. The younger American again makes an attack, but he doesn't get far. Then, with a half-mile left, it's Klöden who takes a flyer. The other four look at each other. And just when it seems as if they will allow him to win his first stage in this Tour, Armstrong goes charging after him. The yellow jersey is riding like a kid in his first race, exuberant and ambitious. He's still annoyed that Ullrich chased down Landis, so he's doing the same to the German's teammate. Armstrong is going all out, sprinting as fast as he can. He's closing fast, pulling nearer and nearer . . . and passes Klöden just a few feet before the line. The Texan races by the German and bags yet another stage win. It's his third victory in three days—and his fourth mountain stage win in a row! No racer has ever done that—not Coppi, not Merckx, not Hinault. No one.

———

When Armstrong goes to the podium to be presented with his stage prize and another yellow jersey, he's met at the top of the stairs with a handshake from Bernard Hinault, the five-time Tour champion of the 1980s. Hinault says to the Texan, "Well done, Lance. Perfect. No gifts in the Tour de France. No gifts. This is the Tour. No gifts."

After later revealing what the Frenchman said to him, Armstrong comments, "I've given gifts in the Tour de France in the past, and very rarely have they come back to me. This is the biggest bike race in the world, and I want to win. No gifts."

French TV asks the American if he considers himself to be the new "Cannibal," which was the nickname given to Eddy Merckx during his heyday, when he "devoured" the opposition. "Me, the new cannibal? The answer is no," says Armstrong, who has only reverence for the man he considers "the greatest bike racer in history." "I feel more like the son of Eddy. And his son Axel feels like my brother. But I'm not the new Eddy Merckx."

Not everyone is pleased with Armstrong's sweep of the four mountain stages (and it might have been five had he not "gifted" the first one to Basso at La Mongie). The two-time Giro champion Gilberto Simoni, who made a massive effort today—getting into the early break and riding at the front of the race for 112 of the 127 miles—is very upset. He feels that a race leader like Armstrong should leave a few crumbs for the other riders. Deeply disappointed and frustrated, Simoni is asked whether he judges Armstrong's fourth stage win to be the act of a "Cannibal." The Italian climber replies, "That's not a cannibal, that's a piranha."

STAGE RESULT: 1. Armstrong; 2. Klöden, same time; 3. Ullrich, at 0:01; 4. Basso, same time; 5. Floyd Landis (USA), at 0:13; 7. Leipheimer, at 1:01.

OVERALL STANDINGS: 1. Armstrong; 2. Basso, at 4:09; 3. Klöden, at 5:11; 4. Ullrich, at 8:08; 5. Azevedo, at 10:41; 9. Leipheimer, at 16:25.

Le Patron

JULY 23: *There are no truly difficult climbs on this 103.5-mile stage from Annemasse to Lons-le-Saunier, but it's hilly enough to inspire breakaways. The main contenders will be looking for an easy day before the final time trial.*

During his reign as champion of the Tour de France, Lance Armstrong has been asked many times if he is the new *patron* of cycling. And every time he has said no. *Patron*, a French word, literally translates to "boss" or "director." But in cycling parlance it means much more. Perhaps the "godfather" best describes this person. He is the rider who controls the peloton by the strength of his character, personality, *and* his performances. The previous five-time Tour winner, Miguel Induráin, was respected for his tremendous athletic ability and repeated victories, but this gentle man was never considered *le patron.* Then you have Bernard Hinault, who established himself as the leader of the peloton in his very first Tour, 1978, and exercised his authority for the remainder of his cycling career.

Race followers who were around in 1985, the year of Hinault's fifth Tour victory, will never forget an incident on the Col de la Colombière, the first climb of an enormously long alpine stage. A cocky young French rider, Joël Pelier, decided to make a breakaway and went tearing up the climb. This did not please Hinault, who was wearing the yellow jersey. He knew that an early attack on a mountain stage 167 miles long could trigger other attacks, and this would disrupt the slow, steady pace that Hinault and his team had decided to set in the early going. Pelier's break could raise the speed, split up the peloton, and maybe cause all of the weaker domestiques to be dropped. And riders left behind this early in an eight-hour day would almost certainly finish outside the time limit and be eliminated.

So Hinault, *le patron*, took charge. In his prominent yellow jersey, the Tour leader raced away from the pack, caught Pelier, and began shouting and gesticulating at him. Pelier, humiliated in front of the whole peloton, stopped his attack and drifted back to the peloton behind *le patron*. Hinault had shown the young rider—and the cycling world—that he was in charge, and no one questioned his authority.

———

Twenty miles into this transitional road stage between the challenges of the Alps and the 2004 Tour's final time trial, the peloton has just crossed the River Rhône and is headed up a short winding hill. As on that stage in 1985 when Hinault disciplined Pelier, the majority of the riders are looking for a quiet day of racing after three difficult stages in the Alps. A breakaway group of six riders is leading by 45 seconds, and it looks likely to continue moving away from the pack. No one is concerned, though, since not one of the six is remotely dangerous to the race leaders—the best placed in the overall standings is the young Spaniard Juan Mercado, in 44th place, an hour and twelve minutes behind Armstrong.

Suddenly, Filippo Simeoni, who has been in a number of break-aways in the past ten days, breaks clear of the pack, hoping to catch the six leaders before they get too far ahead. The Italian rider wants one last chance at winning a stage. He came the closest to his goal at Guéret on Day 11, when he and breakaway companion Iñigo Landaluze were caught by the pack in the final fifty yards.

The peloton continues to roll up the hill out of the Rhône valley. Heavy morning rain showers have given way to a pleasantly warm afternoon, and Armstrong's Postal team has settled into an easy rhythm, quite happy to see the six-man break succeed. But Lance Armstrong isn't pleased. He suddenly shoots away from the pack, catches Simeoni, and rides in his draft for several miles. A mile after cresting the hill, the six breakaway riders look over their shoulders and get quite a shock to see the man in the yellow jersey joining them with Simeoni, a rider of modest skills.

Most of them later say they were unaware that Armstrong and Simeoni have been engaged in an on-and-off battle of words in the media over the past two years. But aware or not, they don't complain when Armstrong and Simeoni share the workload for a few miles and push their lead up to more than two minutes over the peloton. Still, they all know that the presence of the yellow jersey in their midst is bound to backfire: The pack will feel compelled to chase and their break will be finished. After a brief discussion between Armstrong, a Dutch rider, Marc Lotz, and a Spanish rider, Vicente Garcia Acosta, Simeoni is asked to leave. So he and Armstrong drop back and wait for the peloton, while the break goes quietly on its way.

Armstrong later tells the media, "I don't want to make this a bigger story than it is. The problem with you guys and journalists is you don't research the story. You don't tell both sides. With Simeoni, there's a long story there."

In particular, Armstrong takes issue with an extensive interview with Simeoni that L'Équipe published in the first week of the Tour. The interview gave Simeoni's side—and only his side—of how and why he changed his testimony in the Italian court doping case against Dr. Michele Ferrari, one of Armstrong's advisors. In the article, Simeoni said that he didn't change his testimony, he only went into more detail. When he first gave evidence as a witness, he said, he did not tell the full truth, whereas he did in subsequent court appearances. The Italian cyclist, who is the same age as Armstrong, said in his final testimony in 2001 that with Ferrari's advice, he had used EPO between 1996 and 1998. Simeoni was subsequently suspended from cycling for six months.

When Armstrong was asked by Italian TV in March 2002 to comment on Simeoni's testimony against Dr. Ferrari—whom Lance deeply respects—he said that the Italian cyclist was a liar to blame his drug use on Ferrari, and he accused Simeoni of bringing his sport into disrepute. Simeoni later sued the American for defamation of character, a case that remains unresolved.

The L'Équipe interview also asked Simeoni if he had had any exchanges with Armstrong during the first week of this Tour. Simeoni replied, "He acts as if I do not exist. . . . That doesn't bother me. But he is the *patron*, the champion of the moment. So all the riders respect him and get out of his way when he comes through in the peloton. They fight to get behind him, not to be in front."

The original six-man break stays together until the last climb, where Mercado and Garcia Acosta break clear. After the stage finishes in Lons-le-Saunier, with Mercado outsprinting his fellow Spaniard for the victory, Simeoni crosses the line 12 minutes later, at the back of the peloton, alongside two of his Domina Vacanze teammates. He talks briefly to the media and says that many riders in the pack verbally abused him and said he is a disgrace to professional cycling. But he doesn't want to publicly state what Armstrong said to him during the race. Simeoni does say, however, "When a champion stops a small rider like me in a race as big as the Tour, it says something about that person." With that, he leaves the finish area accompanied by one of the race organization's burly security people.

Armstrong says, "I was protecting the interests of the peloton, and the other riders were very grateful. . . . When I finally came back to the peloton, I had a lot of people tapping me on the back and saying thank you."

That's how the riders reacted when Hinault returned to the peloton with Pelier in 1985—although for very different reasons.

Three years after Hinault retired from cycling, Pelier won a stage of the 1989 Tour de France in unusual circumstances. Pelier reportedly asked the race leaders for permission to sprint up the road so that he could pull over for a bathroom stop. Trouble was, Pelier didn't stop, he carried on riding—and won the Rennes to Futuroscope stage in a solo break a minute and a half ahead of the peloton. The Tour didn't have a *patron* at the time.

STAGE RESULT: 1. Juan Mercado (Spain); 2. Vicente Garcia Acosta (Spain), same time; 3. Dmitry Fofonov (Kazakhstan), at 0:11; 4. Sébastien Joly (France); 5. Marc Lotz (Netherlands), all same time.

OVERALL STANDINGS: 1. Armstrong; 2. Basso, at 4:09; 3. Klöden, at 5:11; 4. Ullrich, at 8:08; 5. Azevedo, at 10:41.

Inspiration and Motivation

JULY 24: *This individual time trial of 34.2 miles, starting and finishing in Besançon, is particularly challenging, with several hills in the countryside south of the city.*

The year is 1983. I'm in Bagnères-de-Luchon, a Victorian spa town that's in need of a little sprucing up. The defining stage of the Tour de France ended here about an hour ago, in spectacular fashion. A grueling six-hour mountain stage through the Pyrenees turned the standings upside down. The day's winner is a lithe Scottish climber, Robert Millar, while his French teammate Pascal Simon comes in third and takes over the yellow jersey. It's going to be an evening of celebration for the Peugeot–Shell–Michelin team, the U.S. Postal of its day. Besides Millar and Simon, the squad boasts star riders Phil Anderson of Australia and Stephen Roche of Ireland, a future Tour champion. I go to interview the team in their accommodations, to hear their stories of this momentous day.

The Peugeot riders are not staying at a hotel. Instead, they are billeted with a dozen other teams in an unattractive institutional building that once housed patients who came to Luchon for treatment at the town's famed sulphur springs. I walk up a wide, creaky, wooden staircase to a huge room filled with hospital cots and bunk beds. Riders are walking around, some with towels around their waists, after using square cakes of lye soap to shower in the communal bathroom. There are probably fifty riders changing in this one room alone. I sit down on a small stool next to Millar's bed. Clothing spills from his large suitcase that's opened on the dusty wooden floor. Across the aisle, Simon is arranging his things, his brand new yellow jersey lying on a coarse woolen army blanket, under which he'll sleep tonight.

———

The year is 2004. I'm in Besançon, an old watch-making city whose fortunes have recently revived thanks to its precision-engineering industries. The penultimate stage of the Tour de France ended here about an hour ago. It has been a defining day for the Tour, a challenging individual time trial that put the finishing touches on the overall standings. The day's winner is Lance Armstrong, who has just been awarded the sixty-fifth yellow jersey of his Tour career. It's going to be an evening of celebration for his U.S. Postal Service team. Besides stage winner Armstrong, the team placed five others in the top twenty today. Floyd Landis of the United States was fourth, Chechu Rubiera of Spain ninth, and José Azevedo of Portugal tenth.

I walk over to the spacious pressroom in a glittering, modern expo building called Micropolis. Armstrong is about to give a news conference, before being driven to his team's accommodations, 25 miles away in the green countryside of the hilly Franche-Comté region.

Awaiting Armstrong is an elegant suite in a white-painted, eighteenth-century château that has its own spacious gardens set behind a wrought-iron gateway. Once there, he can toss his brand new yellow jersey on a finely upholstered armchair in a bedroom with luxuriant rugs on a cedar floor. The American's private bathroom has white-velour robes and designer toiletries. And tonight he'll sleep under soft linen sheets in a canopied bed.

———————

"Tonight, at the château, we're going to have a great meal, maybe a little wine, in one big dining room for the riders and the staff. And we're going to reflect on six Tours. If you come to this race and you don't prepare and you're not motivated and you don't win the Tour, you don't get to have these highlights in your life. And we're going to have one tonight. That's what motivates me. When it's pouring rain and you have to go out and ride six hours in the mountains, there's no fun in that. There's nobody on the side of the road cheering you on, or even booing you. But days like that make the difference, and allow for nights like tonight."

With these words, the soon-to-be-crowned six-time Tour champion walks with his team director Johan Bruyneel through a glass door into the evening sunshine where their blue-and-red team car is waiting.

Before leaving for the château, Armstrong says he has thoroughly enjoyed this Tour. "For some reason, and I can't really explain it, I'm enjoying the competition more than ever. Not to make history, not to make money . . . but just for the thrill of getting on a bike and racing against two hundred other guys. This year, that was really, really special for me, and a big motivation. If you look at the stages here, to win in sprints or to win in little intense situations, that was something that I'd never done before in the Tour. I can't explain it, but to do these things at almost thirty-three years of age, after having been here for twelve or thirteen years, I'm having more fun racing a bike than ever."

————————

A long, flat time trial demands utter concentration, thorough preparation, peak power performance, superb bike-handling skills, and the strength of muscle to maintain the extremely uncomfortable aerodynamic tuck for well over an hour. Today's 34.2-mile loop course at Besançon is particularly challenging because of its varied terrain: several climbs of a mile or longer, razor-sharp turns through village streets, and fast downhills, mostly on narrow back roads. This forces the rider to constantly shift gears, to brake at the exact moment needed to slow down before a turn, and to remain constantly alert for each subtle change in the wind. That's why Armstrong was here in March, to ride the course and to examine its many idiosyncrasies.

Three hours before it's Armstrong's turn to climb into the start house of this stage, our press car pulls out from the center of ancient Besançon behind Armstrong's Czech teammate Pavel Padrnos, the seventieth man to start. Rolling mist covers the stone battlements on the wooded bluffs above the river; temperatures are in the mid-sixties; and the thousands of parka-clad spectators hold umbrellas besides their flags and banners. The 33-year-old Padrnos, at six-three and 178 pounds, is big for a cyclist. He's the ultimate domestique: a man who hasn't won a bike race in eight years and yet commands the respect of the whole peloton. He will ride around today's time-trial course with no specific goal except to finish safely and inside the time limit.

After an initial short climb and tricky descent, the course exits from town around a curve of the high-flowing Doubs River. The Czech colossus makes nothing of the ensuing long climb, riding at a steady 25 miles an hour on a hill that rises through 575 vertical feet in two miles. Without really trying, he's going to record a respectable final time of 1:15:18, averaging more than 27 miles an hour, to take 67th place, ahead of eighty other riders.

On our trip around the course, we also follow the former world time-trial champion, Santiago Botero of Colombia, a teammate of Ullrich's. He dashes through the middle part of the course that includes tricky turns through half a dozen old villages on low hillsides and in deep valleys. Thick crowds line every foot of several climbs that barely register on the day's official profile map, but are a severe challenge when you're trying to average 30 miles an hour. It's an extremely tough course, demanding every skill that a pro bike rider possesses. Botero, who is riding to maintain T-Mobile's overall lead in the Tour's team race, comes through with a solid time of 1:13:34, which will place him 38th by the end of the day. It will be good enough to make him the team's third counter (the team race is based on a squad's top three finishers each day), which ultimately will help T-Mobile clinch this year's overall team title by a couple of minutes over Postal.

We end our lap around the course by following a Spaniard, Isidro Nozal. He seems bogged down on the last plateau section, as do many other riders. American Bobby Julich describes it, saying, "It felt like I was pushing through quicksand." Once Nozal has tackled this section, he drops down a winding four-mile hill back to the Doubs, before racing over the flat two-mile run to the finish outside the Micropolis.

One hour later, Julich speeds home with the fastest time at that point: 1:09:37. "After I put on my skinsuit before the start I said this race is between me and the Tour, no one can help me. I just want to go, ride to 100 percent of my ability, and let it be that. My goal was to finish top five." He meets his goal, finishing fifth when all the times are collated.

Half an hour after CSC's Julich finishes, Postal's Landis moves to the top of the leader board with a time that's 23 seconds faster than

Julich's. To achieve such a performance at the end of a Tour in which he has ridden at the front of the peloton day in and day out for Armstrong is remarkable. "It's muggy and hot out there," he says, "but I have my wife in the car for inspiration." Did you have any hard moments? "In the middle, I was getting a little worried that I went a little too hard at the beginning . . . but I started feeling better at the end." That was a great ride. "Thank you, man." Do you feel that next year or the year after you could be the guy in the yellow jersey? "Huh. I don't like to make predictions, but it's fun to dream." Well, you're headed in the right direction. "Thank you. I appreciate it, man. It feels good to have support like that."

———

Landis is asked what advice he would pass on to his team leader, Armstrong, who is just starting his own race against the clock. "Huh!" Landis grunts. "He doesn't need any help." And does the course suit the Texan? "What course *doesn't* suit him. He's won every kind of stage in the last five days, so I think he's all right."

Armstrong is more than all right. He is sensational. The man who has already won four stages in a week—two on mountaintops and two in sprints—is about to put an exclamation point on this Tour by winning the final time trial. To have done what he did in the Pyrenees, and again in the Alps, has been an exceptional athletic accomplishment. And now he is attempting to complete this Tour's "week from hell" with another outstanding performance in one of his sport's most difficult disciplines. There is no need for Armstrong to win, since he already has a comfortable lead over all his rivals. But he *wants* to win. He wants to prove he is the best. The best climber . . . the best sprinter . . . the best leader . . . the best time trialist.

The sun has come out, the roads have dried, and he's soon churning along the top part of the course at 108 revs per minute. After 11 miles, the Texan is already 43 seconds faster than Ullrich. Basso and Klöden are tied, a further four seconds behind. After 25 miles, the gap to Ullrich is 51 seconds, while Klöden has pulled 52 seconds ahead of Basso—and is headed for second place on the Paris podium. At the line, Armstrong has won by one minute, one second over Ullrich. Klöden takes third, 26 seconds behind his German leader. Give the man the yellow jersey! And when five of his Postal teammates placed so highly on this stage, the squad took home the day's team award, too.

There will be private celebrations in the château tonight . . . and a public consecration in Paris tomorrow.

STAGE RESULT: 1. Armstrong, 1:06:49; 2. Ullrich, 1:07:50; 3. Klöden, 1:08:16; 4. Landis, 1:09:14; 5. Bobby Julich (USA), 1:09:37; 6. Basso, 1:09:39; 12. Leipheimer, 1:10:55.

OVERALL STANDINGS: 1. Armstrong; 2. Klöden, at 6:38; 3. Basso, at 6:59; 4. Ullrich, at 9:09; 5. Azevedo, at 14:30.

On the Elysian Fields

JULY 25: *After the riders take a three-hour train journey in the morning, this largely ceremonial stage of 101.5 miles starts from Montereau, in the suburbs of Paris, and finishes with eight laps of 3.8 miles each around the Place de la Concorde and Champs-Élysées. Those laps, as always, will be completed at breakneck speeds, with a probable mass sprint at the end.*

Paris is looking magnificent. Her golden domes and eagles and gilded gates are all glowing in the late-afternoon sunshine. The dark-green plane trees along the Champs-Élysées have been newly trimmed. Rainbows shimmer in the spray from the crystal fountains of the Place de la Concorde. And across the Seine River, the thousand-foot-high Eiffel Tower stands starkly regal against an opaque blue sky.

Another Tour de France has just ended, this one culminating in a historical sixth consecutive victory for a long-jawed young man from the lone star state of Texas. He stands now on the top step of the podium, at the finish line on the Champs-Élysées. Dressed in a golden tunic, Lance Armstrong holds a yellow LiveStrong cap over his heart as a full-blooded rendition of the "Star Spangled Banner" rings out, resounding proudly over the russet-brown cobblestones of these Elysian Fields.

Other competitors stride up the yellow carpet to the final podium to receive the acclaim of the crowd and the admiration of their colleagues. A young Belgian named Tom Boonen, the winner of this ultimate stage, wears the smile of a young sprinter who knows he'll stand here again. An Aussie named Robbie McEwen, clothed in green as this Tour's best sprinter, holds his son Ewen high above his head for the whole world to see. A Frenchman named Richard Virenque, in polka-dot red, is crowned King of the Mountains for a record seventh time. And Jan Ullrich—for the first time finishing outside the top three places—still gets to stand on the stage when he and his T-Mobile teammates take overall honors as best team in the race.

Then it's time for the traditional podium shot. Armstrong is on top, flanked by two slim, black-haired men in their twenties: a former East German, runner-up Andreas Klöden, and a northern Italian named Ivan Basso. They smile with accomplishment, excitement, and pride. Their thoughts must reflect the joys and the agonies of the long three weeks just ended.

At the foot of the yellow steps of the canopied, most prestigious viewing stand, Armstrong's coach Chris Carmichael reminds me: "I told you back in March, it wasn't even going to be close. You gotta know the intensity of this guy. Nobody has got his intensity. Nobody. It's just phenomenal."

The six-time winner said on the eve of this day, "Winning in '99 was a complete shock and surprise for me. Not that I've gotten used to winning the Tour de France, but I do know what it means and I know what it feels like to ride into the Champs-Élysées. . . . This one is very, very special for me. They're all special, but this one is something that in '99 I never believed possible. I never thought I'd win a second one, or a third, or however many. This one is incredibly special. I'm humbled by it. A lot of people just one month ago thought it wouldn't be possible for me to do it. We tried to stay calm, the team tried to stay calm . . . and we were confident that we had a good chance."

I think back to December, and remember something Armstrong told me in Austin: "I'm doing three or four hours of exercise every day right now. Yesterday I was in DC, so I got up early—I'd just come back from Europe and had jetlag—and I went down to the gym for an hour and a half . . . yes, lifting weights. It was pouring with freezing rain outside, so I went back to the room, and rode my bike for an hour on the rollers. It's not easy to ride rollers. I hate that."

But he doesn't hate this: homage from a half-million people lining the most glorious boulevard in the world. When he and his U.S. Postal team are introduced by race announcer Daniel Mangeas, as the last team to start their lap of honor around the Champs-Élysées, the modern "anthem" of the British rock group Queen thumps into the balmy Paris air: *"We are the champions, my friend. . . . We are the champions. We are the champions. We are the champions . . . of the world."*

Girlfriends perch on boyfriends' shoulders to get a better view. Banners unfurl, one saying, "The eyes of Texas are upon you." Thousands of fans from all over the United States line the barriers, most dressed in yellow. Two guys from Texas in the crowd say, "We did it. And next year we'll come again!"

As the T-Mobile team rides by, German fans greet them with cries of support for Ullrich and his close friend Klöden. The Italians cheer for Basso as he pedals past with his CSC colleagues, including manager Bjarne Riis, "The Eagle," who's also on a bike. French fans give a rousing reception to eighteenth-placed Thomas Voeckler, grateful for his ten days in yellow. And there's Tyler Hamilton, riding with his team but not in uniform. He's come up from Spain to congratulate his Phonak teammate Oscar Pereiro for his top-ten finish, and to again thank his other mates for their powerful riding that, as fate would have it, he couldn't use in the end. But nothing can compare with the rush the fans get from the Postals, all in their yellow caps, as the champion rides up the Champs-Élysées for a victory lap with his teammates. The flags of Texas and the United States billow in the wind.

"It hasn't sunk in yet, it just hasn't," says Lance's coach Carmichael. "People keep asking me what it feels like to have won six of these, and I keep going, 'I don't know what to say.' It just hasn't hit. I think it's going to hit a week from now when I'm sitting with my wife and having a glass of wine and just going, 'Oh my God.'"

Now they're playing another song over the loudspeakers. Its words float down the boulevard backed by the thumping guitar chords of the champion's gal: "All I want to *do* . . . is have some fun . . ." And Lance *is* having fun. The celebrations will continue all night, maybe for the rest of his life. A life that almost ended in 1996. Six Tour de France wins have come along since then, since his chemo nurse La-Trice gave him that silver cross.

"I really love this event," Armstrong says. "I think it's an epic sport. It's something I will sit around the TV and watch in ten years, and in twenty years." He will always be a fan of the Tour, but right now he's the champion. *Le patron.*

It's after 7 p.m. and the crowds are starting to leave. One of the last to go is a friendly, middle-aged American. He rolls up his Texas flag, grabs his wife's hand, and, before he walks down the stone steps into the Metro, proclaims to the world, "He's the man!"

STAGE RESULT: 1. Boonen; 2. Nazon; 3. Hondo; 4. McEwen; 5. Zabel, all same time.

FINAL OVERALL STANDINGS: 1. Armstrong, 2,107 miles in 83 hours, 36 minutes, 2 seconds (average speed 25.199 miles per hour); 2. Andreas Klöden, at 6:19; 3. Ivan Basso, at 6:40; 4. Jan Ullrich, at 9:50; 5. José Azevedo, at 14:30; 6. Francisco Mancebo, at 18:01; 7. Georg Totschnig, at 18:27; 8. Carlos Sastre, at 19:51; 9. Levi Leipheimer, at 20:12; 10. Oscar Pereiro, at 22:54.

Meeting Destiny

April 21, 2005

Almost nine months have passed. Lance Armstrong is back in America, preparing to tackle the Tour de France for one last time. It will be the last race of his career. Many expect him to leave cycling on a high note by claiming a seventh yellow jersey to hang alongside the others at his downtown Austin home. But adding yet another jersey to his collection doesn't have the same cachet for Armstrong. "To win a seventh Tour is my objective," he replies to questions about the upcoming race. "But seven, that will be just one more, while six, that was magic!"

That magic didn't happen with the wave of a wand. It resulted from Armstrong's compulsive ambition. "Lance was obsessed with being ready for the Tour last year," his coach Chris Carmichael tells me. "He realized there was this one opportunity to become the first six-time winner, to go down in history."

When Armstrong achieved his breathtaking goal, and with such panache, he was elevated to the status of all-time American sports legend, right up there with Babe Ruth, Jesse Owens, and Muhammad Ali.

His epic feat merited epic celebrations. They began the night the Tour ended, with a banquet in Paris. In the chandeliered beaux arts ballroom of the Musée d'Orsay, hundreds of invited guests stood and cheered when the American entered with Sheryl Crow at his side. Then, in the days following his triumph, tens of thousands honored him in a series of exhibition races around Europe. Yet Armstrong didn't fully realize the significance of his accomplishment until he attended a big-as-Texas homecoming in August. Standing with his three children and Crow on a stage next to the golden-lit Texas State Capitol, the champion said to his fellow Austinites, "To think that I'm standing here—a few blocks from where I announced to the world I had cancer—as someone who has made cycling history . . . it's something that, in 1996, I never could have thought possible."

But little in the "Lance Armstrong Story" seems possible—from the time he became a champion triathlete at age 16, to being the youngest man in more than 50 years to win a stage of the Tour de France, to recovering from a life-threatening cancer and going on to win Tour, after Tour, after Tour. And now this, a record-breaking sixth Tour victory.

But what toll has this six-year streak taken on the man? "Nobody can keep up that intensity year after year," says coach Carmichael. "Not even Lance."

When the celebrations are over, Armstrong doesn't even want to think about another Tour. He is aware that in the two-year contract he signed to race for his team's new title sponsor, the Discovery Channel, there's a clause that commits him to racing the Tour one more time. But, then, contracts have been broken.

"After the 2004 Tour, he was noncommittal about planning another," Carmichael confirms. "I didn't even put together a training schedule for him until January, although he was riding the bike in November, December. But he's such a celebrity now, I saw that his life . . . is such that he can't say he's going to do something and not do it."

That's why Armstrong delayed a decision on defending his Tour title until mid-February, and then quietly announced on his Web site that he will ride the 2005 Tour. It's not unexpected, because one of Armstrong's finest qualities is honoring a commitment. But can he refocus his energy after a winter filled with so much glitter and glare? His multiple television appearances with Crow, especially the Academy Awards, the Grammys, and the *Oprah Winfrey Show*, have greatly enhanced his celebrity status, while a succession of doping-related allegations have dented his image and added untold stress to his life.

The book *LA Confidentiel*, published in France just before the 2004 Tour, cast doubt on Armstrong's integrity and spawned a series of court actions. His response to the various allegations was summed up in a brief submitted by Armstrong's lawyers to a Dallas court on April 1: "[This is] an egregious character assassination founded upon a demonstrably false string of sensational, untrue and fabricated allegations."

Amid all these distractions, and with the 2005 Tour only months away, Armstrong resolutely followed Carmichael's schedule before returning to Europe in March. "He made a mistake in doing Paris–Nice as his first race," observes Carmichael. "That's a tough race even if you've already been competing." Armstrong did just four snow-truncated stages of the eight-day race before dropping out. He overcame that setback by heading to the Canary Isles for long days of climbing in warm sunshine, and then showed good form in three single-day races in France and Belgium. His pre-

Tour program is similar to the one he followed in 2004: attempting to win the Tour of Georgia in late April, Tour scouting trips in May, and the Dauphiné Libéré race in June.

While Armstrong's name has been constantly in the news, his archrival Jan Ullrich has kept out of the public gaze, rebuilding his health and confidence. Repeated colds and stomach problems prevented him from racing until April. Then, after a winter spent training in the warmer climes of Tuscany, South Africa, and Majorca, the German arrived at a low-key French race, the Circuit de la Sarthe, in a mood that is uncharacteristically upbeat. "I'm getting lots of pleasure out of cycling right now," Ullrich says. "I feel wonderful and the form and condition are good." He proved his readiness by finishing tenth in the four-day race.

His friend and teammate Andreas Klöden, who was walking on the heady air of unexpected accomplishment after taking second to Armstrong at the Tour, is back on harder ground. In the winter, he had some enticing offers to race for rival teams, but decided to stay with T-Mobile. He's having a difficult time with the new season, and he unexpectedly pulled out of April's five-day Tour of the Basque Country. "It's not going the way I imagined it would," says Klöden, who underwent some performance testing with his team doctor and trainers. They are refocusing his training in the hope that he'll be ready to ride for Ullrich at the Tour.

As for Ivan Basso, the tragic loss of his 49-year-old mother to stomach and liver cancer followed the excitement of his third-place finish at the Tour. Now, Basso is taking on the difficult task of racing the three-week Giro d'Italia in May, counting on its tough mountain stages to harden him for the 2005 Tour. "I'm coming to the Giro thinking of the Tour," he says, "starting it at 100 percent and with even bigger hopes."

Hope is what Tyler Hamilton is clinging to, while his career is in limbo. After winning the time trial gold medal at the Athens Olympics, the Tour contender whose race was cut short by severe back pain said, "The month of July was terrible for me. But if you can't live through the tough times it's best not to continue in this sport." He didn't know how prescient his words would become.

Blood samples taken from him in Athens and after he won a time trial at September's Vuelta a España both came up positive in a just-introduced test for homologous blood transfusions (blood injected from another person). Hamilton was stunned, and has continued to claim his innocence. Testing anomalies allowed him to retain the Olympic gold medal, but the Vuelta "positive" was confirmed. The bad news became worse when he was handed down a two-year suspension from racing by the U.S. Anti-Doping Agency on April 18. He's now making a last-chance appeal to the Court of Arbitration for Sport. "This is far from over," he insists. "An innocent athlete was suspended."

If Hamilton is cleared, and in time to do enough preparatory races, he might well line up at the 2005 Tour, to face the same strong contenders: Ullrich, Basso, and Armstrong. And given his innate strength and talent, Hamilton could even be the one to finally topple Armstrong. Or perhaps that role will go to Spain's Iban Mayo, who is keeping a lower profile this spring, or Italy's rising star Damiano Cunego, who sped to victory at the 2004 Giro at age 22. Then again, Armstrong could be headed for his seventh. But right now, in April, nothing is certain.

What is certain for Lance Armstrong is that no experience can compare with the one he lived through in July 2004, when he set out with unnerving determination to win a record sixth Tour de France.

Some say it was a miracle that any man could overcome life-threatening cancer, return to his sport, and win its most prestigious event six years in a row.

Some say there are no miracles, just miracle drugs, and cast aspersions on a man who has always tested clean.

Some say it was his genes, or his rage, or his obsessive training and intense preparation . . . or maybe that he's simply a superb and unbeatable athlete.

Some say he did it for all cancer survivors, to show them and the world that anything is possible.

But in the end, all that matters is he did it. On July 25, 2004, Lance made his mark as the only six-time winner of the Tour de France in its 101-year history.

He did it less than eight years after doctors said he had only a 50 percent chance of living.

He did it after racing 2,107 miles at an average speed of 25.2 miles per hour, and defeating 187 other riders.

He did it in 23 days in July.

ACKNOWLEDGMENTS

First, I want to thank all my colleagues at Inside Communications, especially the publishers and editors at VeloPress books and *VeloNews* magazine, for their help, understanding and cooperation while I was working on this project. The book couldn't have been completed without the skillful writing and editing input, and strong support of my wife Rivvy Neshama. Also integral to the evolution and execution of the book have been my New York friend and literary agent, Jim Levine, and my editor at Da Capo Press, Kevin Hanover. I want to thank all the athletes, especially Lance Armstrong, Tyler Hamilton, Jan Ullrich, and Ivan Basso, for their patience and sincerity in answering even the most routine questions. Similarly, I much appreciated the time and insightful responses of Chris Carmichael, Eddy Merckx, Jean-Marie Leblanc, and Jim Ochowicz.

Thanks also for the enjoyable times and stimulating conversations with Tour de France *compadres* past and present, including Graham Watson, Rupert Guinness, Andy Hood, Louis Viggio, David Walsh, Steve Wood, Charles Pelkey, Lennard Zinn, Kip Mikler, Bryan Jew, Felix Magowan, Sam Abt, Susan Bickelhaupt, Robin Magowan, Chico Perez, Julia Dean, Jonathan Fowlie, and Noël Truyers. The support of my Boulder friends has been invaluable. Paul Hansen helped finalize the book's title; and Willie Wilson provided a different viewpoint in critiquing the manuscript. Thanks also to Chas Chamberlin for his cartography, Darcy Kiefel for her photography; Anne Becher for Spanish translation; Luuc Eisenga for German translation; Jenny Wrenn and Andy Kayner for a perfect place to write; and Coleen Cannon for the coffee, phone line, and encouragement just when I needed it.

Finally, I want to remember three men who spawned my interest in the Tour de France. My father, Arthur Wilcockson, from whom I inherited a racing bike and a passion for cycling; John B. Wadley, who passed on his love for the Tour through his wonderful storytelling; and Pierre Chany, whose prose brought to life the drama, history and excitement of the greatest sports event in the world. *Merci à tous!*

How is the Tour structured, and who gets to win?

The Tour de France lasts for 23 days: 17 road stages, four time trials, and two rest days. In a road stage, all the riders start together and the one who crosses the line first is that day's winner. In a time trial, each rider (or team in the team time trial) races the entire stage alone, and the one who completes the course in the least time is the winner.

At the end of each day, every rider's accumulated time from all the stages to that point is calculated, and the one with the lowest overall time is now the race leader, and gets to wear the yellow jersey. Think of a golf tournament, where scores are added together after each round, and the lowest score leads. At the end of the 23 days, the overall winner and champion will be the one whose accumulated time is the lowest. Because the race is scored on overall time, the final overall winner doesn't have to win *any* of the stages, as long as he gains enough time over his chief rivals in both the time trials and the tougher road stages.

What are the different kinds of stages?

Each of the two types of races, road stages and time trials, has its own sub-categories.

ROAD STAGES

- *Flat stage* (also called a sprinters' stage): A stage contested on flat or rolling terrain that generally has few, if any, categorized climbs. It frequently ends in a mass-sprint finish and is often won by a sprint specialist.
- *Mountain stage* (also called a climbers' stage): A stage contested in mountain terrain that includes several severe climbs and often finishes at the summit of a mountain climb. It usually ends with a rider finishing alone, or sprinting it out with one or two others.
- *Medium-mountain stage:* A stage that has more challenging terrain than a flat stage, but is not as severe as a mountain stage. It often ends in a sprint between several riders (who may even be sprint specialists).

TIME TRIALS

- *Individual time trials:* Starting at one- or two-minute intervals, the riders race entirely alone against the clock on a point-to-point course. The one who records the fastest time wins the stage.
- *Team time trials:* Starting at five-minute intervals, the nine riders on each team race together in a tight formation, taking turns to set the pace. The team recording the fastest time (which is taken when the fifth rider of the team crosses the line) is the winner of the stage.
- *Prologue:* An individual time trial of less than five miles that opens the Tour on the eve of the first road stage.

Why do riders like to race in a pack?

The simple answer is: It's easier to ride in a pack and you go faster. By riding in the slipstream of other riders on a flat road you use roughly 30 percent less energy than when riding alone. And at most speeds, the momentum of a big group can mean that you work up to 60 percent less. However, when the speed is extremely high (when the pack is chasing a breakaway or several teams deliberately increase the pace toward the finish), the pack can stretch into a single line. This forces each rider to race very hard to remain in the slipstream of the rider ahead of him.

On flatter stages, team leaders generally ride in the pack to conserve energy for the tougher climbing stages and time trials to come.

Why are there so many crashes?

Because the riders are so close together in the pack, there is always the danger that two wheels can touch and cause a rider to fall. This can have a domino effect in bringing down dozens of riders at the same time. Crashes are also likely on fast downhills when a rider misjudges the angle of a turn and falls, or when the roads are slick and a rider is more likely to skid or slide out on a turn.

How does a team help its best rider?

Although an individual wins the Tour de France, he could not do so without the help of his eight teammates. The duties of a team rider (or "domestique") include:

- riding hard at the front of the pack to control the pace of the peloton, in an effort to prevent attacks by rival team leaders;
- riding in front or to the side of his leader to protect him from the wind or possible crashes;
- slowing down to fetch fresh water bottles from the team car and taking them up to his leader;
- stopping when a leader has a puncture, crash, or mechanical problem, and helping pace him back to the peloton;
- giving his leader one of his wheels (or his entire bike!) if the team car doesn't arrive quickly enough to help;
- pacing his leader up to a threatening breakaway;
- riding fast up a mountain climb as long as he can, to protect his leader from the wind for the longest possible time, and to discourage attacks by his rivals.

When and why do riders from different teams help each other?
There are two main situations when riders from opposing teams will help each other:

- A breakaway will only succeed if all (or most) of the riders work together, taking turns to set the pace. Only toward the end of the stage will they race against each other in an effort to win.
- When the pack is chasing a breakaway, the teams that have the fastest sprinters (and they're *not* in the break) will combine forces to catch the breakaway. That's because the break has to be caught if any of their sprinters is to get a chance of going for the stage win.

What are the strategies in a mass-sprint finish?
Each team has one or more lead-out men, whose job is twofold:

- to ride so fast at the head of the pack that a rider from another team will find it very difficult (or impossible) to make a successful late attack;
- to ride fast just ahead of their sprinter to protect him from the wind until he's ready to unleash his final sprint.

It's also important for a sprinter to have a teammate riding immediately behind him to discourage rival sprinters from taking advantage of his lead-out men.

When might a team work to *slow* the pace?
When a breakaway has, say, six riders representing six different teams, their teammates in the group behind will deliberately try to slow down that chase pack. They do that by getting into the line of riders at the head of the group and then slowing the pace when it's their turn at the front. This gives the breakaway group a better chance of succeeding, and improves the chances of their man getting the stage win.

How fast do Tour racers ride?
A Tour racer can attain speeds of up to 70 miles per hour on the straighter

sections of mountain descents. The record *average* speed for a road stage longer than 100 miles is almost 32 miles per hour. The fastest *average* speed for an individual time trial is more than 34 miles per hour.

How much do their bikes weigh?

The legal minimum weight for a Tour bike is 14.9 pounds, so most Tour bikes weigh slightly above that limit. Using carbon-fiber technology, it is now possible to build a bike that weighs as little as 13 pounds.

How do riders get enough water to quench their thirst during a long stage?

One rider can go through as many as twenty water bottles on a hot stage (usually drinking the water, but sometimes squirting it over his head for added cooling). There are usually two bottle cages mounted to the bicycle frame to carry the bottles. New bottles are handed up to the riders in feed zones, while domestiques go to the back of the peloton to pick up replenished bottles from the team car, or from a special race motorcycle that carries a dozen or so bottles in a rack

What qualifies a team to be in the Tour?

Every January, from fifteen to eighteen teams automatically qualify for the Tour de France (based on world team rankings and performances in the previous year's three grand tours). The remaining teams (perhaps as many as seven) are selected by the race organization on the basis of performance, but also on the organizers' perceived need to have a minimum number of French riders starting their race. These last selections are called "wild cards." In 2004, fifteen teams automatically qualified for the race, while the other six teams were selected by the organizers.

Aerodynamics

Technology and techniques used to make a rider and his bike more streamlined, and so reduce the effects of air resistance. The faster a rider goes, the more important this becomes. Air resistance at 30 miles per hour is four times what it is at 15 miles per hour. The thinner the bike and the lower the rider's position, the more aerodynamic he is.

Attack

When one or more riders sprints away from the pack. This can be done accelerating on a climb or making a flyer from the back of a small group to take the others by surprise.

Best young rider

The Tour's highest-placed rider on overall time who's age 25 or younger. The leader of this competition wears a white jersey.

Break (or breakaway)

A rider or group of riders that escapes from the main field after making a successful attack.

Chase group

A group that chases a break.

Counterattack

An attack made by one or more riders immediately after a breakaway is caught by the group.

Domestique (team worker)

A rider whose main task is to help his team leader. (See FAQ: "How does a team help its best rider?")

Doping (banned drugs)

Using performance-enhancing drugs or methods that are banned by the International Cycling Union (UCI), International Olympic Committee (IOC), and World Anti-Doping Agency (WADA).

Drafting

To gain the maximum shelter (or draft) from the wind or to counter air resistance, it is best to ride directly behind or slightly to the side of the rider in front. Riding in a draft saves approximately 30 percent in expended energy compared with riding alone.

Echelon

When a strong wind is blowing from the side on flat roads and the racing is fast, the riders form an echelon—an angled line of single riders—to gain the maximum amount of draft from each other. The echelon (sometimes called the pace line) rotates as the riders on the leeward side move forward and those on the windy side move back (like flying geese). The echelon can only be as wide as the road, so a field of 180 racers may split into five or six echelons, angled into the wind.

Feed zone

Midway on every stage, the Tour organizers designate a feed zone. A vehicle from each team drives ahead of the race and parks in the feed zone, where team personnel fill canvas bags (also called *musettes*) with food and drinks (including nutrition bars and instant-energy gels) to hand up to their riders as they pass through the feed zone.

General Classification (or GC)

(See "Overall standings.")

Grades (gradients)

A measure of the steepness of a hill or mountain climb, expressed as a percentage. For example, a 10-percent grade (or gradient) is a grade on which a rider climbs through 10 vertical feet for every 100 feet of horizontal distance covered.

Grand tours

The collective name for the world's only three-week stage races: the Tour de France, the Giro d'Italia (Tour of Italy), and the Vuelta a España (Tour of Spain).

Green jersey (points leader)

The green jersey is worn by the leader of the points competition, who is almost always a skilled sprinter. Points are awarded at intermediate sprints (see below) and at the finish of each stage. For so-called flat stages, each of the first twenty-five finishers scores points (35 points for first place, down to one point for 25th). For mountain stages, only the top fifteen riders score points (20 points for first, down to one for 15th). And just the top ten riders score points in individual time trials (15 points for first, down to one for 10th).

Gruppetto

The group of lagging riders that forms at the rear of the field on mountain stages, and that moves at a pace just fast enough to finish within the day's time limit (see below). The *gruppetto* (Italian for "a small group") is sometimes called the autobus, the bus, or laughing group—but this is no laughing matter, since riders in this group are often sick or injured and struggling just to finish the stage.

Handlebars (aero, clip-ons, drop bars)
In time trials, the bikes have forward-pointing aero handlebars that allow the rider to have a lower, more aerodynamic "tuck" position, as opposed to the normal hand position on drop bars when the rider is more upright and his body catches the wind. Aerobars that are fitted in the center of regular drop bars are called clip-ons.

Helmets (and removing them)
Hard-shell helmets are compulsory in all stages of the Tour. However, on a summit or mountaintop finish that is longer than five kilometers (three miles) the riders are allowed to remove their helmets at the bottom of that finishing climb.

Individual time trials
Each rider races alone against the clock, and the one with the fastest time wins. At the Tour, riders start at one- or two-minute intervals. The starting position of riders is in the reverse order of their overall standings, so whoever is the race leader at that time goes last.

Intermediate sprints
On every road stage of the Tour de France, the organizers designate two or three points along the course called intermediate sprints. The first three riders to pass this point are awarded time bonuses (6, 4, and 2 seconds) to deduct from their overall time, along with points for the sprinters' competition.

International Cycling Union (UCI)
This is the world governing body for cycling—often referred to by its French name, the Union Cycliste Internationale (UCI)—and is based in Switzerland. The Tour is basically run using the rules and regulations of the UCI.

Leaders (of race competitions)

Each day, distinct jerseys (yellow, green, polka-dot, white) are awarded to the leaders of the various competitions. There are small daily prizes for these leaders, and a much larger prize for the ones who win the overall competitions at the end of the Tour.

Leaders (team)

Each team usually has a designated leader (like Lance Armstrong on U.S. Postal). This rider is the one who has the best chance of winning or placing high in the Tour's overall standings, usually because he is both strong on climbs and fast in time trials.

Lead-out (for sprint finishes)

Heading into a mass-rider finish, you will often see the teammates of a sprinter racing flat out at the head of the field. These are the lead-out men. (See Appendix: "What are the strategies in a mass sprint finish?")

Mountain climb categories

There are no set rules on how an organizer can categorize a hill or mountain climb. For the Tour de France climbers' competition (the King of the Mountains), five categories are used:

- the easiest is a Category 4, which is typically less than a mile long and about 5-percent grade, or up to three miles at a 2- to 3-percent grade.
- a Category 3 can be as short as one mile with a very steep grade, perhaps 10 percent; or as long as six miles with a grade less than 5 percent.
- a Category 2 can be as short as three miles at 8 percent, or as long as 10 miles at 4 percent
- a Category 1, once the highest category, can be anything from five miles at 8 percent to 15 miles at 5 percent.
- an *hors-categorie* (or above-category) rating is given to exceptionally tough climbs. This could be either a Category 1 whose summit is also the finish of the stage, or one that is more than six miles long with an

average grade of at least 7.5 percent, or up to 15 miles long at 6 percent or steeper.

Overall standings (General Classification or GC)

Overall standings show the order of the riders on overall time, computed by adding together each rider's stage times less any time bonuses they have earned. The race leader is first in the overall standings or General Classification (GC). At the Tour de France, the leader in the overall standings after any stage is given the yellow jersey to wear on the next.

Pace Line

(See "Echelon.")

Pack

(See "Peloton.")

Peloton (pack, bunch)

A French word meaning "platoon" that's used to describe the largest group of men riding together at any point in the race. This group is also called the pack or main bunch. In addition, all the riders in a race are loosely called the peloton, since at the start of any day's race they are all together.

Podium

In Tour jargon, this specifically refers to the podium in Paris for the riders who finish the Tour in first, second, or third place.

Polka-dot jersey (King of the Mountains)

The white-and-red polka-dot jersey (*maillot à pois* in French) is worn by the leader of the climbers' (or King of the Mountains) competition. Points are awarded on every categorized climb, ranging from three points for being first across a Category 4 climb, four points on a Category 3, 10 points on a Category 2, 15 points on a Category 1, and up to 20 points for taking first on an *hors-categorie* climb. Double points are awarded for the last climb of each stage (assuming that climb is Category 2 or higher).

Prologue

The Tour opens with an individual time trial held in the afternoon and evening before the first road stage of the Tour. The distance of a prologue is limited to five miles or less.

Race director

The person who is in overall charge of the Tour. (See "Tour organization.")

Race leader

This is the man who is first in the Overall Standings, and wears the yellow jersey at the start of each new stage. Sometimes, a rider who temporarily leads a stage is mistakenly referred to as the race leader.

Radio Tour

A race information service provided by the organizers and broadcast to every vehicle on the race. The information given includes the numbers and names of every rider in every break, results of every sprint and mountain climb, and the time gaps between groups. Radio Tour also relays information on upcoming road hazards (narrow bridges, roundabouts, speed bumps, etc.), and the race director's daily welcome and introduction of guests and VIPs who are riding in race and team vehicles each day.

Road rash

Rider slang for the cuts and grazes they get from falling on the road.

Road stage

A stage that starts with all the contestants in one mass group, with the stage winner being the one who crosses the line first.

Skinsuit

The one-piece shorts and top designed to give a rider a more aerodynamic performance in time trials. Unlike regular race jerseys, a skinsuit has no pockets in which to place food or drinking bottles.

Soigneur

A rider's masseur/masseuse who also performs other tasks such as preparing food bags and handing them up at feed zones, carrying riders' suitcases at hotels, and meeting riders at the finish line with a sponge, towel and dry clothes.

Sprinters

The specialist fast finishers who contest mass sprints (see "Sprints").

Sprints (group or mass sprints)

Most road stages end in a sprint between two or more riders. When a large group, perhaps the entire peloton, arrives at the finish together, the resulting dash for the line is referred to as a mass sprint. All the riders who finish in a mass sprint are given the same time, unless the group splits, and there is a gap of more than one second between the last rider in the leading group and the first rider in the next group. In that case the time given the second group is that of their first rider to cross the line.

Stage (stage town)

Each day's race is called a stage, whether it's a time trial or road stage. The towns where the stage starts and finishes are called stage towns.

Tactics (and strategies)

Cycling tactics are varied and often complicated. Generally, every team director and his riders meet before a stage to discuss that day's tactics. This could mean delegating certain riders to instigate or follow breakaways, or deciding to chase every breakaway to give their sprinter a chance of winning in a sprint finish.

Teams

Top professional teams are named after their major sponsor and usually have between twelve and twenty-five riders on their season's roster. Nine of these riders are chosen to start the Tour de France.

Team time trial
Similar to the individual time trial, in a team time trial each team races separately against the clock, with the fastest team winning the stage. For the Tour, with its nine-man teams, the time of a team's fifth rider across the finish line counts as that team's time. Every rider on the team who finishes together is given that time as their time for the stage. Teams start at five-minute intervals.

Time bonuses
Besides the small time bonuses earned at intermediate sprints, the first three racers across the finish line of each road stage are awarded time bonuses of, respectively, 20 seconds, 12 seconds, and 8 seconds—which are deducted from their overall race times.

Time gap (in road stages)
The interval of time between the various groups when they pass any specific point on the course. Time gaps usually measure the interval between a breakaway group and the peloton.

Time limits (or time cuts)
On every stage of the Tour de France, each rider has to finish within a certain percentage of the winner's time to remain in the race. Riders not making this time limit (or time cut) are eliminated from the Tour. Time-cut percentages vary considerably, with more leeway given for time trials.

Time split (in time trials)
This is the time recorded by each rider (or team) in a time trial to get from the start to various checkpoints along the course. (The places where the time checks are taken are sometimes referred to as "splits.")

Tour de France organization
The Paris-based group Amaury Sports Organisation (ASO) organizes the Tour. The race director is employed by ASO, which is part of the Amaury newspaper group that publishes various magazines and newspapers, includ-

ing the only French sports daily, *L'Équipe*. This paper was originally called *L'Auto*, whose first editor-in-chief was also the first Tour de France race director.

Transmitters (team radio, earpieces)

Every team has its own short-range radio communication system on separate wavelengths, used by the team director (who has a transmitter) to talk to his riders (who have earpieces). Some of the riders on the team also have a transmitter to talk back to the director (or to the other riders).

World Championships

Most riders who compete in the Tour also race in the annual world road championships. These are contested by national teams (not the "trade teams" that contest the Tour). The principal world championship is a one-day road race, usually held on a circuit of between 8 and 15 miles that is lapped multiple times for a race distance longer than 160 miles. The world champion is awarded a white jersey with rainbow-colored stripes around the chest, which he wears throughout the year at other races.

Yellow jersey

The yellow jersey (or *maillot jaune* in French) is worn by the leader in the overall standings. It's usually worn by several different men in the course of the Tour, but only the final leader *wins* the yellow jersey. The racer wearing it is often referred to as "the yellow jersey."